SNATCHED!

Also by the Author

Steinway — from Glory to Controversy: The Family, the Business, the Piano
Troubled Skies: Crisis, Competition and Control in Canada's Airline Industry
Global Pursuit: Canadian Business Strategies for Winning in the Borderless World
Hands across the Ocean: Managing Joint Ventures (With a Spotlight on China and Japan)
Trading: Inside the World's Leading Stock Exchanges
The Thomson Empire
Canadian Pacific: Portrait of Power
Men of Property: The Canadian Developers Who Are Buying America

SNATCHED!

The Peculiar Kidnapping of Beer Tycoon John Labatt

BY SUSAN GOLDENBERG

THE DUNDURN GROUP
TORONTO

Copy-Editor: Lloyd Davis
Design: Andrew Roberts
Printer: Transcontinental

Library and Archives Canada Cataloguing in Publication

Goldenberg, Susan, 1944-
Snatched! : the peculiar kidnapping of beer tycoon John
Labatt / Susan Goldenberg.

Includes bibliographical references.
ISBN 1-55002-539-2

    1. Labatt, John Sackville, 1880-1952--Kidnapping, 1934.
2. Kidnapping--Canada--History. 3. Kidnapping victims--Canada--Biography. I. Title.

HV6604.C32G64 2004   364.15'4'092   C2004-904890-2

1   2   3   4   5   08   07   06   05   04

 Conseil des Arts
du Canada Canada Council
for the Arts

ONTARIO ARTS COUNCIL
CONSEIL DES ARTS DE L'ONTARIO

We acknowledge the support of the **Canada Council for the Arts** and the **Ontario Arts Council** for our publishing program. We also acknowledge the financial support of the **Government of Canada** through the **Book Publishing Industry Development Program** and **The Association for the Export of Canadian Books**, and the **Government of Ontario** through the **Ontario Book Publishers Tax Credit** program, and the **Ontario Media Development Corporation's Ontario Book Initiative**.

Care has been taken to trace the ownership of copyright material used in this book. The author and the publisher welcome any information enabling them to rectify any references or credit in subsequent editions.

J. Kirk Howard, President

Printed and bound in Canada
Printed on recycled paper

www.dundurn.com

Dundurn Press   Gazelle Book Services Limited   Dundurn Press
8 Market Street   White Cross Mills   2250 Military Road
Suite 200   Hightown, Lancaster, England   Tonawanda NY
Toronto, Ontario, Canada   LA1 4X5   U.S.A. 14150
M5E 1M6

To My Parents

CONTENTS

Chapter 1
THE SNATCH

On the morning of Tuesday, August 14, 1934, John Sackville Labatt, the millionaire president of John Labatt Ltd., one of Canada's biggest companies, took a little-used shortcut on his way to the office, a choice that was highly unusual for him. What resulted was a very peculiar kidnapping.

The police had warned him as far back as 1930 to beware of potential kidnappers, and just the previous summer he had narrowly escaped being abducted, daringly outwitting would-be kidnappers while vacationing at Corunna, on the St. Clair River south of Sarnia, Ontario. As he and his children, five-year-old Jack and three-year-old Mary, enjoyed their customary evening boat ride on the river, a high-powered boat of the type used by rum-runners darted out from the Michigan shoreline on the American side of the river and headed straight for his launch.

There were conflicting reports as to what happened next. The *London Free Press* reported that "the manoeuvre was so suggestive of trouble that Labatt raced for the Canadian side and by a narrow margin reached a place where there were too many people for the [apparent] kidnappers' nerve." The *Toronto Daily Star* wrote that "to evade his pursuers he was compelled to run to the United States instead of the Canadian shore. After a time he obtained protection and returned to his summer home." Whether these would-be kidnappers were the same gang as those who snatched him a year later was never determined, although the second group insisted that "the first mob went cold on the idea of snatching Labatt and dropped out" after their attempt failed.

The scare caused Labatt to rent a summer house at a different location in 1934. He still wanted a place near enough for him to commute easily to and from his office in London, Ontario, and decided upon Brights Grove, on the shores of Lake Huron about ten miles east of Sarnia. There he rented the Holland property, a beautiful brick mansion. Labatt believed Brights Grove a safer location than the previous year's because it was not as near the border. He was particularly concerned for his children's safety because of the 1932 kidnap-murder of Charles Lindbergh's baby son, and he had hired guards to protect them.

Why, after all these precautions, did he then take a chance on an isolated route on the morning of August 14, 1934? He had been late leaving Brights Grove, and his pressing concern became making up the lost time in order to be punctual for a 10:30 a.m. appointment at John Labatt's London headquarters. There he was to meet his brother Hugh, who was three years his junior and served as vice-president and secretary-treasurer of John Labatt Ltd., and Major General Sidney Chilton Mewburn of Hamilton, Ontario, an uncle by marriage and a director of the company. Mewburn had phoned Hugh early that morning, requesting a meeting with him and John to discuss, among other matters, John's trip to Detroit the preceding Saturday. Hugh had called John to ask if he could arrive in time, and John had said yes.

As the drive from Brights Grove to London took a little over an hour, John should have left around 9:15, but he was slightly delayed. He never explained why publicly. Perhaps he was concerned about his wife Bessie, still recuperating from the birth of their third child, Arthur, born just over three months earlier on May 11.

Despite his frightening escape from the would-be abductors in 1933, Labatt was, as usual, travelling alone, even though he could easily have afforded to be chauffeured and/or been accompanied by a body-guard. His mother-in-law had frequently implored him and her daughter to "be careful, because you are very well off." But they always laughed at her fears. Labatt had also ignored threatening letters he had received, dismissing them as the work of cranks.

Labatt foolhardily placed punctuality before safety. Instead of taking his usual route along the heavily travelled county road that ran directly south from Brights Grove to join the main Sarnia–London route, Provincial Highway 22, he chose to save a few miles by taking the isolated shortcut. After driving east along the beach resort road that skirts Lake

Huron for about twelve miles, he branched off at the village of Camlachie onto Egremont Road, a little-used, heavily forested, narrow dirt road, as a diagonal shortcut to the highway. Egremont joined Highway 22 at Warwick, a distance of about twelve miles from Camlachie. Since there was never much traffic on Egremont, Labatt calculated that he could travel at a high speed and make up for his delayed departure.

Labatt's car, a black Reo Sedan A — a luxury car that bore the initials of its manufacturer, Ransom Eli Olds, the founder of the Oldsmobile company — had a six-cylinder engine capable of seventy-five miles per hour, placing it far ahead of the maximum speed of fifty to sixty miles per hour typical of cars of that era.

Shortly after he started along Egremont Road, throwing up clouds of dust as he sped along at fifty miles per hour, Labatt noticed in his rear-view mirror a car following him rapidly. "While I was in a hurry, they seemed to be in a bigger hurry," he would later testify. He slowed down to let the car, a Hudson — a good car, but not as good as the Reo — pass, observing that it had American licence plates. When the other car raced past and disappeared out of sight, a relieved Labatt concluded that he had been wrong in suspecting it had been following him. Thus, he was surprised to see, after driving a few more miles, that the other car had halted. When he got within about thirty yards of it, Labatt also stopped, this time seeing there were three men in the car, one in the front seat and two in the back. Although he thought the stopping and starting "strange," Labatt was "not alarmed" because the other car resumed its journey. He waited until it was out of sight before he, too, continued.

While Labatt was pondering the "strange" behaviour of the other car, its occupants — ex-rum-runners and fledgling kidnappers Michael McCardell, Albert Pegram and Russell Knowles — were equally bewildered by Labatt's actions. When he kept stopping to match their abrupt halts, McCardell, the gang's leader, feared that Labatt "has tumbled to us" and told Pegram to drive on, "continuing to pretend we're not interested in him." As Labatt again followed, McCardell couldn't "believe that he's dangling right along behind us."

The location was approximately fifteen miles from his summer home at Brights Grove. "This bastard wants to be taken," McCardell smilingly told Knowles and Pegram. "Head around at the next crossroad and go straight back at him," he directed Pegram. Pegram did so, and a short distance further Labatt was startled to see their car racing towards him. Fearing a collision on the narrow road, he stopped between one and a half and two car lengths away. Suddenly, the three men leaped out of their car and ran towards Labatt's. They had made no attempt to conceal their faces by wearing masks. They surrounded Labatt's Reo, with McCardell at the driver's door. Pulling out a revolver, he shouted, "Stick them up quick! This is a kidnapping!"

McCardell then ordered Labatt out of the car and angrily cursed him when he did not comply quickly. An injury to Labatt's left leg, sustained while playing football as a boy, had resulted in his walking with a limp, and he had to use a cane. Before getting out of a car, he needed to flex his knee to get rid of the stiffness from having kept it bent. Thinking Labatt was poising himself to attack him, McCardell snapped, "None of that," yanked Labatt from his car and propped him against the car door.

With Labatt leaning against the door, McCardell pulled out a lead pencil and a writing pad with a loose piece of paper on top. Holding the pad, McCardell demanded, "Write what I say." He then dictated: "August 14, 1934. Dear Hugh: Do as these men have instructed you to and don't go to the police. They promise not to harm me if you negotiate with them. Your affectionate brother, John S. Labatt." Most people in such a terrifying predicament would be trembling, and their handwriting would be shaky. But Labatt carried out the demand in firm, clear handwriting. On the other side of the piece of paper, these words were printed in crude block letters: "We are holding your brother John for $150,000 ransom. Go to Toronto immediately and register in the Royal York Hotel. We will negotiate with you from that point. Be prepared when I get in touch with you there to furnish me with the names of two or three reliable parties who you can trust to deliver the money. We advise you to keep this matter away from the police and newspapers so as we can return your brother safely. You will know me as 'Three-fingered Abe.'" The name was Pegram's invention. Knowles, a college graduate, had come up with the wording, and McCardell did the lettering.

The $150,000 ransom demand was one of the largest in history, the equivalent of $2 million today according to the Bank of Canada's inflation calculator. In 1934, four men's shirts could be purchased on sale for $5, three neckties for $1.50, and a man's suit for $21.50. Millions of unemployed people were strapped for cash because of the Great Depression.

Grabbing the ransom note, Knowles leaped into Labatt's car and sped off towards London. En route, he placed the note under the driver's seat. Arriving at London, he headed for Grosvenor Street, on the north side, and parked at St. Joseph's Hospital in the very spot Labatt had used when he visited Bessie after Arthur's birth. McCardell had selected this location because it was a busy, public place where Knowles could park the car without drawing undue attention. As Knowles raced off, McCardell sealed Labatt's eyes with pink court plaster, a type of adhesive tape. As a double precaution, he made Labatt put on a pair of goggles, to which round pieces of black court plaster had been stuck to the inner sides of the lenses. McCardell would later boast, "We paid eight bucks for them. We fixed old John up in style."

McCardell then shoved Labatt into the rear seat of the Hudson and sat beside him, jamming his gun threateningly against Labatt's side. But Labatt's hands were not bound, nor was he gagged.

The kidnappers sped along Egremont to Highway 22, then brazenly travelled in full view of other traffic as far as the Lambeth turnoff. Unbeknownst to them, whether because of a slit in the tape or because the tape had been attached to his eyebrow rather than his eyelid, Labatt was able to make out place names on the road signs. When he saw the Lambeth sign, he must have felt great frustration at being so near to his London home and business. At this point, the car left the main road and began travelling north over deserted roads. As they headed northeast, Labatt saw signs for Orangeville, Tottenham and other communities before night fell and he could no longer make out the letters.

The kidnappers' destination was Bracebridge, in the heart of Ontario's picturesque Muskoka Lakes vacation region. It was a lengthy drive of about two hundred and fifty miles from where they had abducted Labatt. Because they were on unpaved roads, following a circuitous route, the journey took far longer than normal, and lasted into the evening. Pegram was silent as he concentrated on his driving. McCardell was chatty. He began by informing Labatt that "we have demanded $150,000 for you and hope to get the deal done in twenty-four hours or so. If it should fall through, what will you do on your own to get released?" He did not tell Labatt about the death threat in the ransom note.

"What have you got against me?" Labatt asked.

"Nothing. Hasn't the brewery as much money as three years ago?" McCardell responded, referring to the time when he had first thought of kidnapping Labatt.

"There's been a depression, but I suppose it has."

Even though Labatt had signed the ransom note "John Labatt," McCardell asked if he was indeed the president of John Labatt Ltd., perhaps because John and his brother Hugh looked so much alike. The greatest difference between the two was that, despite being three years older, John had dark hair while Hugh's was turning grey.

"Yes, I am."

"You're the man we want, because you're smaller — although it would have been all right to have got your brother, or both of you." Thereafter, McCardell chummily addressed Labatt by his first name.

"Have you any money with you, John?" he asked.

"Yes."

"Hand it over."

Labatt counted $99 in bills from his trouser pocket. "Do you want the silver, too?" he asked.

"No, keep that," McCardell said.

During the long drive, the kidnappers stopped three times: to buy gas, then groceries, and finally meat. At one of the stores, Pegram overheard that a county constable had been seen on the road. He dashed out of the store, scurried into the car, and speedily drove off. Not once did Labatt call out for help, nor did he when their car was momentarily blocked by other cars on the road. He later explained, "The kidnappers were armed but the gasoline attendant, shop owners and myself were not and we could have suffered physical harm if I'd cried out for help."

The kidnappers were triumphant. The snatch had gone off perfectly. Great wealth was about to be theirs, they thought.

Who were these ecstatic hoodlums who had just pulled off the first-ever kidnapping of a prominent, wealthy Canadian? All told, there were four members in the kidnap gang: McCardell, Knowles, Pegram, and a Windsor man named John (Jack) Basil Bannon, who helped plan the kidnapping but was not one of the abductors. Although they were first-time kidnappers, all were in their forties and had been part of the underworld for some time.

Michael McCardell, the forty-two-year-old garrulous, wisecracking ringleader, was born in a small village near Stratford, Ontario, although whether it was Seaforth or Dublin is not certain. He had lived in the United States since the age of sixteen. Drifting from Detroit to Pittsburgh, Baltimore and Texas, he worked on railroads for many years as a switchman. Later, he ran a gambling house in Alabama. In 1930, he went to Chicago and became part of that city's violent gangland of rum-runners, armed robbers and racketeers.

Forty-year-old Russell Knowles, a friend of McCardell's, was dapper, debonair, and a smooth talker. He lived in Detroit. He liked to claim that, before turning to crime, he had been in advertising, had invested in natural gas and oil leases in West Virginia, and owned an interest in two saloons. He also had been in what he euphemistically called "the liquor business" — in reality, bootlegging. His only run-in with the law had been a pair of shoplifting charges. He was never caught in his illegal rum-running.

Jack Bannon, a forty-eight-year-old father of three children, claimed that his wealth had been made in real estate. In fact he was a rum-runner who made extra money as a police informant, betraying his associates so adroitly that none had yet suspected him of being a double-crosser. He and Knowles were acquaintances. Bannon had stored the kidnappers' revolvers at his home at 343 Campbell Avenue in Windsor while they prepared for the abduction. His house was across the street from a church, but this proximity did not stir his conscience, nor that of his fellow conspirators. He hid their guns in a hollow post on the verandah. The top lifted off the post, leaving a three-foot-deep space into which the guns fit easily.

Knowles was responsible for bringing Albert Pegram into the plot. He and Pegram had known each other from their days as rum-runners operating between Detroit and Chicago. Knowles recommended Pegram because he was an experienced getaway driver and because his burly physique — he weighed two hundred pounds — suited him well to the task of guarding Labatt in captivity. Pegram's aliases were "Albert

Leon" and "Jack Snead," but McCardell's favourite term for him would come to be "that rat" after Pegram deserted them at a crucial time.

McCardell, Knowles and Bannon had waited three years to kidnap Labatt, generating ideas, then quickly dropping them. The main reason for their hesitation was that they learned that Labatt had had several heart attacks. They were afraid that he might die from the shock of being kidnapped. In 1931, McCardell switched his attention to the Montreal distiller Samuel Bronfman, head of the Seagram Company. He joined forces with six other hoodlums from Detroit and Chicago and, armed with submachine guns and revolvers, they set out for Montreal.

En route, they stopped in Toronto and parked one of their cars, leaving their guns in it. Three of them were picked up on suspicion by the Toronto police. One of the three had in his pocket the parking ticket for the car containing all the guns. He slipped the ticket into his mouth and swallowed it while the police were busy fingerprinting and searching his two companions. Had it been discovered, the Bronfman kidnap plot would have been nipped right then.

Unable to find any incriminating evidence on the men, the police let them go. They joined their accomplices and continued to Montreal. For two days they trailed Bronfman and studied his habits closely enough to schedule the kidnapping for the next day. They were so confident that they held a pre-victory party that night in their hotel. They got drunk and, in his alcoholic haze, one of the gangsters decided that he wanted a woman. Posing as a policeman, he talked his way into the room of a female guest. She called the police and he was arrested for impersonating a police officer. The rest of the gang fled, fearing their pal might disclose their plans to kidnap Bronfman. As it turned out, he didn't talk, but the group disbanded. The $1,200 they had invested had gone down the drain.

After that debacle, McCardell revived his idea of kidnapping Labatt. In June 1934, he convened a planning session with Knowles, Bannon and David Meisner, a Kentucky bookmaker and gambler whom he thought "might be interested in a little dealing," at the Hotel Lexington in Detroit. All McCardell wrote to Meisner was that he "had a little business proposition."

"How about it, Ted?" McCardell asked Meisner, using Meisner's nickname, after outlining his scheme to kidnap Labatt.

Appalled that they were discussing an extremely serious crime, and not a "little business proposition," Meisner firmly declared: "I don't like it. I don't want anything to do with it and you shouldn't either!" Rejecting McCardell's suggestion that they meet again the next day, Meisner packed his bag and returned home, thinking that that was the end of the matter and he would never hear of it again. Time would prove him very wrong.

In selecting Labatt as their victim, the kidnappers had chosen not only a very rich man, but a member of Canada's business aristocracy for whom all of London, and indeed the country, would feel deep concern. John Sackville Labatt was widely respected and admired for handling wealth and privilege responsibly as well as for his diffident charm and generous philanthropy. John Labatt Ltd. was London's largest firm and one of Canada's biggest. Its name was well known from coast to coast and in the United States.

Under John Sackville and Hugh, the almost ninety-year-old brewery was in its third generation of family ownership and management. In 1833, their grandfather, John Kinder Labatt, emigrated at the age of thirty with his wife Eliza from Ireland to Upper Canada and settled on a farm south of London. In 1847, he sold his farm and invested in a small London, Ontario, brewery, near the forks of the Thames River, called The London Brewery. In 1855, he became the sole owner. His third son, John — the father of John Sackville — was born in 1838. His parents were so impressed by his aptitude for business that, in 1859, the twenty-one-year-old was apprenticed to George Weatherall Smith, an English brewer of ales in West Virginia. In 1863, Smith, his business ruined by the Civil War, bought a brewery in Prescott, Upper Canada, and took John with him. A year later, John returned to London and two years after that his father John Kinder died. Although he was his father's designated successor to run the business, nonetheless it was bequeathed to his mother, and John acquired it with a mortgage that provided her with a steady income.

Renaming the brewery Labatt and Company, John directly supervised marketing and sales and developed new products so as to become competitive with larger companies. He advertised heavily in newspapers, magazines and calendars and participated in contests at trade fairs in the United States that drew thousands of visitors. Pictures of awards were incorporated into Labatt's labels, which were deliberately designed to resemble the red triangle on England's highly-regarded Bass Ale in an effort to convince consumers that Labatt's beer was as good. The brewery prospered, but when John Labatt ventured into other businesses, the results were disastrous. A farm machinery firm that he backed to compete against the Massey Manufacturing Company defaulted, saddling him with substantial debts. An attempt at banking also failed, and thereafter he concentrated on brewing. Choosing to remain independent, in 1889 he rejected a bid from an English syndicate to merge with the Carling brewery, and nine years later he rejected a merger offer from O'Keefe's. In 1911, he incorporated the firm as John Labatt Limited, keeping almost 100 percent of the shares in his own name. That year, he also drew up a will that would ensure the continuity of the company as a family business, bequeathing an equal number of shares to each of his nine children. His sons, John Sackville and Hugh Francis, who would manage the company in succession to their father, could make no decisions without the consent of their seven sisters.

Through the marriage of John Sackville's second-oldest sister, Frances Amelia, to Hume Blake Cronyn, the Labatts were linked to another powerful London family. In 1857, Benjamin Cronyn Sr., who had immigrated to London in 1832, was named the first bishop of the new Anglican diocese of Huron. He organized Huron College in 1863. Benjamin's daughter Margaret married Edward Blake, who was a founder of Blake, Cassels & Graydon, one of Canada's oldest and biggest law firms, and the second premier of Ontario. Benjamin's son Verschoyle was a leading figure in Huron & Erie, a financial institution now known as Canada Trust, and was an incorporator of the London Street Railway in 1873 and its president until 1893. Hume Cronyn, the second-oldest son of Hume Blake Cronyn and Frances Amelia Labatt, who became one of Canada's most acclaimed actors, was twenty-three and just beginning his lengthy stage and film career at the time of his uncle's kidnapping.

John Sackville Labatt was born on March 10, 1880, in London. He attended Trinity College School, an exclusive, expensive, private boys' school in Port Hope, Ontario, then earned a bachelor of science degree at McGill University before studying at the National Brewers' Academy in New York City. He joined the family business at the age of twenty as a clerk, was appointed vice-president in 1911, and as the eldest son became president in 1915, at the age of thirty-five, following the death of his father.

John and Hugh, who was three years younger, were very close. Like John, Hugh attended Trinity College School, but he did not go on to university. When John joined the family firm in 1900 in a junior position, the seventeen-year-old Hugh also did. In 1911, when John was named vice-president, Hugh became secretary-treasurer. Four years later, when John became president, Hugh assumed the vice-presidency, at the same time continuing to act as secretary-treasurer. In 1917, he enlisted as a gunner in the Royal Canadian Artillery. He refused a commission, but did accept the rank of sergeant when he was demobilized in 1919. He later held several posts as honorary colonel in artillery units. Both John and Hugh waited until their forties to marry. John was forty-six when he married, Hugh forty-eight.

At the time of his kidnapping Labatt's height was variously described as between five feet, six inches and five feet, eight inches, and his weight between 165 and 180 pounds. He was good-looking, with dark eyes and dark hair. An unruly lock usually escaped onto his forehead below the brim of his hat. Because of his heart condition, his doctor had advised him to always carry a box of amyl nitrite pills with him in case of emergency.

In June 1926, he married Elizabeth ("Bessie") Lynch of Ottawa, the tenth of eleven children in a family that was fiercely proud of its Irish Catholic heritage. Her father, William, was the retired chief of the federal patent bureau. Bessie grew up in a life of comfort. She excelled at figure skating, attended receptions and balls at Government House, and spent holidays at her parents' Bermuda home. Upon graduating from the McGill Library School in Montreal, she became a librarian aboard the *Empress of Britain*. She was in her early thirties when she married.

As the wife of one of London's wealthiest citizens, she possessed the time, financial wherewithal and spousal encouragement to pursue her interest in helping the sick and needy. "John was so generous," she said of her husband. "I became generous, too. My love for sick people is so great." She was a volunteer for four decades with the St. John Ambulance Association and Brigade and the St. Joseph Hospital Auxiliary. She regularly visited the sick in their homes and at the hospital, and often would take one of her children along for the experience. "She was forever sending over chicken soup, forever feeding people more than they could possibly eat and covering them with extra blankets, giving away favourite mohairs by the dozen," her daughter Mary later recalled. Her son Arthur described another of her many kindnesses. "She came home with a young Ecuadorian who she had heard was about to have his wisdom teeth removed and felt he needed to be cared for. He stayed with the family for three months."

Bessie also assisted the poor and the unemployed. Both the Canadian National and Canadian Pacific railways ran through London, and during the Depression of the 1930s, unemployed men who rode the rails in search of work would find their way to the Labatt home at 256 Central Avenue, which was located halfway between London's two railway stations. At first, one or two at a time would be given supper in the kitchen, but before long there were so many that Bessie would buy rolls of 25-cent tickets from the Salvation Army. A ticket entitled the recipient to dinner and a bed for the night at the Salvation Army hostel.

Within a couple of years of John Labatt becoming president of the family business, all of Canada's provinces had passed legislation prohibiting the sale of alcohol except for medicinal or scientific reasons or for export. And in the United States, the Eighteenth Amendment to the Constitution, ratified in 1919, prohibited the manufacture, sale or transportation of intoxicating beverages. Prohibition in both countries pushed John Labatt Ltd. to the brink of extinction. Several competitors made takeover offers, but like his father before him, John Sackville rejected them, determined to ride out the downturn and keep in family hands the firm that his grandfather and father had worked so hard to build.

In Ontario, the temperance movement was so powerful that John's wife, Bessie, preferred to be discreet when she identified the source of the family's income. Instead of saying beer or ale, she used the euphemism "the product." Bessie once welcomed two female canvassers into her home, served them lemonade and gave them a $15 donation. When her husband looked at her receipt, he saw the words *Women's Christian Temperance Union.* "If the newspapers learn about this, we'll be the laughingstock of the year," he said. The press didn't find out.

Prohibition had mixed results. Drunkenness did decline, but boot-legging (the illegal sale of beverage alcohol), illicit stills, home-brewed moonshine and unlawful drinking places known as "speakeasies" or "blind pigs" proliferated. People craving a drink took advantage of the medicinal exemption; feigning illness, they persuaded obliging doctors to write prescriptions for alcohol that could be filled at drugstores. Many doctors did landslide business from doing this, particularly during the Christmas season.

By 1930, all the provinces except Prince Edward Island had abandoned Prohibition and introduced the sale of liquor under government control, a move that provided a substantial boost to provincial treasuries. Although Prohibition remained in effect in the United States, outlawing the consumption and sale of liquor, there was no law preventing spirits produced legally in — or imported into — Canada from being exported south of the border. Smuggling was rampant. Nor was the traffic all one-way. To dodge Canadian excise and sales taxes, large quantities of liquor ostensibly designated for export wound up being smuggled back into Canada and were sold illegally.

While the bootleggers, rum-runners and other racketeers prospered from the underground cross-border liquor trade, legitimate distillers and brewers, like Labatt's, also thrived. It was commonplace for Londoners to see trucks and freight cars, loaded with what Bessie Labatt liked to call "the product," leaving Labatt's brewery, bound for the United States via nearby Windsor. Labatt's was far from unique in this regard; similar shipments were being made from distillers and breweries across the country. The Canadian government proved unable — or unwilling — to stop the practice, which brought in welcome revenue and created jobs during the worst of the Depression. During Jack Bannon's trial in August 1935, his lawyer would ask Labatt "about the old rum-running days when Canadian beer used to be taken across the border to the United States." Noting that it was not contrary to Canadian laws, Labatt admitted that beer from his breweries was sold to rum-runners.

In 1934, John Labatt Ltd. was estimated to be worth about $5 million, the equivalent of $68 million today. But the end of Prohibition in the

United States the year before had deprived bootleggers, rum-runners and smugglers of their lucrative incomes. Desperate for money, some resorted to kidnapping, and given their familiarity with the liquor and brewing industries, they naturally targeted executives from those businesses. Early in 1934, Edward Bremer, a brewer in St. Paul, Minnesota, was kidnapped for a ransom of $200,000, believed to be the highest amount paid to kidnappers to that date. His capture inspired McCardell and his gang to revive their plan to kidnap Labatt.

"We don't like kidnapping," McCardell told Labatt. "It requires too much planning, takes too long and is very dangerous. We like holdups better. The boys don't care for kidnapping unless they're all broke."

McCardell and his accomplices had done considerable planning for their snatch of Labatt. They had selected Muskoka as the best place to hold him captive, calculating — correctly, as it would turn out — that the police would concentrate their search on London and its vicinity, as well as areas near the U.S. border where they would have been expected to make their getaway. Also, since Muskoka was popular in the summer with American vacationers, their American accents would not seem unusual.

On August 1, McCardell, Bannon and Pegram drove to the Bracebridge area to search for an ideal hideaway in which to hold Labatt captive. Their choice was peculiar for people whose priority was not to be seen. They settled on a cottage about fifteen miles from Bracebridge, in a densely wooded area at Lake Muskoka that was accessible only by a winding, rutted road surrounded by trees and concealed from the lake by an almost seventy-foot-high ridge. But although the cottage was isolated from highway traffic, it was not at all remote from other people, in that it was part of a large holiday camp of cottages available for rental during the summer. There were other cottages only a short distance from theirs.

For $25 a week, McCardell rented one of the Prowse Cottages, named after the campsite's owner, Horace Prowse. The clapboard cottage measured just fourteen feet by thirty and had two small bedrooms. One bedroom contained a double bed, and the other, intended for Labatt, held a white enamel cot, a bureau and a washbasin. There was a tiny kitchen with a wood-burning stove and a combined living and dining room furnished with a round table, chairs and a couch. There was no electric wiring, but there was an oil lamp. The windows were heavily shaded so that, even in daylight, the interior was quite dark. There was a small porch, and behind the cottage there was an outhouse.

Their hideaway procured, McCardell, Pegram and Knowles went to London to trail Labatt. They stayed at three different hotels so that their faces would not become too familiar at any one place. For two weeks, they studied their target's habits. Then, believing they were ready, they picked Monday, August 13 as the day for the snatch. But when they arrived at Labatt's summer home at Brights Grove and McCardell approached the house for a final look at the millionaire's car, Labatt's dog ran towards him. It took some time for McCardell to persuade the dog to go back to the house, then he quickly rejoined Pegram and Knowles, who were waiting for him in their car.

When a man seeming to be the brewer got into Labatt's car and drove off, McCardell instructed Pegram to follow. It was indeed Labatt. He drove to his home in London, where he handed a basket of laundry to a maid. Then he went to the brewery. McCardell brazenly got out of his car and walked near Labatt, memorizing his features so that there wouldn't be any mistake as to his identity the next day, when he and his crew intended to try again. That night, the trio moved to the third of the three hotels.

On the morning of Tuesday, August 14, Labatt emerged from the Brights Grove house five minutes after McCardell and his accomplices arrived. They pursued him and captured him. McCardell obviously believed in the adage, "If at first you don't succeed, try, try again." He had failed in 1931 and again the day before, but today seemed to be his lucky day.

When John Labatt did not arrive for the 10:30 appointment with his brother Hugh and Major General Mewburn, they didn't think he had been delayed by anything unusual and so they proceeded with the business that Mewburn had wanted to discuss. Around noon, Hugh received a call from his home, asking if he and Mewburn would be coming for lunch. Leaving a message at the switchboard for John as to where they would be, Hugh and his uncle left the office.

At about 12:35 p.m., the phone rang in Hugh's apartment at 860 Waterloo Street, near John's home. Hugh was washing his hands before lunch and called to the maid, "Is that for me?" When she said yes, he went to the phone, expecting the caller to be his brother. Instead, he received the shock of his life.

"Your brother's car is at St. Joseph's Hospital with a note under the front seat that should be acted upon immediately," the voice at the other end of the line — that of Knowles — said. Knowles had obtained Hugh's telephone number — Metcalf 8567 — simply by looking it up in London's telephone directory. Both Hugh and John Labatt were listed.

Hugh reacted furiously. "I'll hang up on you! I'll call the police!" he yelled.

"You cool down," Knowles firmly ordered. "After all, we have your brother kidnapped. You better listen to what I'm telling you to do."

"Who are you?" Hugh demanded.

"Three-fingered Abe," Knowles answered, then hung up.

Anxiety and anger consumed Hugh. He dashed from the hallway telephone to the living room, where Mewburn was waiting for him. "John has been kidnapped," Hugh gasped.

Mewburn stared in disbelief.

"John has been kidnapped," repeated Hugh, "and the message I just got over the telephone says to go to St. Joseph's Hospital and look in his car there."

While Hugh stood rooted to the spot in shock, Mewburn, the military man of action, immediately dialled the police. By both background and demeanour, Mewburn was a take-charge individual who commanded immediate attention and respect. A former cabinet minister, he was a prominent lawyer and a director of many major corporations besides Labatt's. In 1881, he had enlisted as a private in the army in the Thirteenth Regiment (later the Royal Hamilton Infantry) and became its commander in 1910. At the outset of World War I, he was appointed commander of an infantry brigade, and in 1917 he was made director-general of the Canadian Defence Force. Five months later, he became acting adjutant general of the Canadian Militia. In November of that year, he was named minister of militia and defence by the prime minister, Sir Robert Borden. One of Mewburn's two sons had been killed in action the year before. Newspaper articles hailed his appointment, praising him as a skilled administrator and describing him as "modest, kind and unobtrusive — unless something goes wrong because of some foolish unfortunate who does not attend to duty, and then he can give vent to his wrath in stentorian tones."

Over the years, as they searched for the right words to describe an irate Mewburn, the newspapers resorted to comparing him to the fiercest animals. "When he gets mad, he is a bear," *The Globe* wrote. Others compared his shouted commands on the parade ground to an "almost elephantine roar." One anecdote about his powerful voice involved an occasion when he was bellowing orders in a Toronto barracks. "Which squad are you drilling, Mewburn," a veteran soldier inquired as he passed by the square, "this one here or the one on the island?" (There are a number of islands across the harbour from Toronto.) But Mewburn's troops knew that he was only gruff on the exterior. One day at Camp Borden, he was bawling out an officer. The wooden building they were in veritably quaked. "What's all that noise?" asked a visiting staff officer from Ottawa, who, along with the rest of the soldiers in the vicinity, was getting a very good idea of what Mewburn thought of the man. "Oh, that's Colonel Mewburn when he thinks he's mad," replied a clerk. His troops knew that Mewburn was actually kindhearted, never a bully to his subordinates, and always ready with an appreciative word.

A lawyer by profession, Mewburn returned to the law after World War I. He was regarded as exceptionally well organized with a "mind always at work," but never too busy to help others. At seventy-one years of age in 1934, seventeen years older than Labatt and twenty years Hugh's senior, Mewburn was still strong, resolute and used to being obeyed. Thus, when he telephoned the police, he was treated deferentially and was instantly connected with Inspector of Detectives Thomas Bolton, who agreed to meet Mewburn and Hugh right away at St. Joseph's Hospital.

They found Labatt's dust-coated car quickly, commenting that it was in the very spot where Labatt had parked when visiting Bessie at the hospital recently. Bolton searched the car and found the ransom note. Seeing handwriting on the reverse side of the paper, he turned it over and read aloud the "Dear Hugh" note the kidnappers had dictated to Labatt, instructing Hugh to comply.

Bolton immediately contacted his office and ordered that Ontario Provincial Police headquarters in Toronto, as well as the Royal Canadian

Mounted Police, be notified and a general alarm issued throughout the province. He also ordered that fingerprint experts examine the car for any telltale fingerprints.

While Hugh, Mewburn and Bolton read the ransom note, Knowles was boarding an afternoon bus for Hamilton, where he transferred to one headed for Toronto. He had timed his phone call to Hugh to be close to his departure time. Although the note threatened that Labatt would be killed if Hugh called the police, somehow the kidnapping became public knowledge within minutes of Mewburn's call to the police. The news spread so quickly that, when a man got on the same bus as Knowles, he asked the bus driver, "Did you hear that John Labatt has been kidnapped?" Knowles, sitting a few seats back, squirmed nervously. The kidnappers had figured they would get the ransom within twenty-four to forty-eight hours without the police being notified.

Upon arriving in Toronto, Knowles checked in under the name "Mr. Tracey" at the King Edward Hotel, a deluxe hotel a few blocks north of the Royal York, within easy walking distance. Knowles was able to afford to stay there because of money he and other members of the kidnap gang had amassed in holdups.

During the afternoon, Labatt's wife, Bessie, was informed of her husband's kidnapping, and she and their children were placed under police protection. Accompanied by her brother, William Lynch of New York City (where he was formerly the manager of Bermuda Railways), who had been vacationing at the Labatts' Brights Grove summer place, she and the children left for Hugh's apartment to await developments. A husky police officer was placed on guard near Hugh's apartment. Although naturally worried and sad, in a telephone call Bessie assured her mother, who lived in Ottawa, "I am keeping up for the sake of the children."

The kidnapping was the second misfortune the Labatt family had suffered in 1934. In January, Labatt's cousin, Henry Labatt of Hamilton, Ontario, who was accustomed to sailing only on a lake, had disappeared along with two friends on a sailing expedition by way of the Atlantic Ocean to the West Indies and Bermuda. They had little or no knowledge of navigation, and when weeks passed without word from them or any sighting of the group, it was surmised that their small schooner had been submerged by heavy waves and, weighed down with ice, had foundered. By June, when no trace of the schooner had been found, it was presumed that Henry and his friends had drowned.

As Knowles travelled by bus to Toronto, Hugh Labatt — who was too distraught to drive himself — was rushing there in a car driven by Louis McCaughey, the sales manager at Labatt Ltd. and a former policeman. So intent was Hugh on getting to Toronto that he left London with only $10 in his wallet. He planned to arrange for the ransom with a cousin who was chief accountant at the Bank of Nova Scotia in Toronto.

Arriving in Toronto at about 9:00 p.m., Hugh held a quick strategy session with General Victor Williams, head of the Ontario Provincial Police, and D.C. Draper, Toronto's chief constable, as the chief of police was then called. Next, Hugh moved into a three-room suite on the fifth floor of the Royal York Hotel. At the request of the police, hotel management closed off the wing in which the suite was located and police guards were posted along the corridor. Nevertheless, some persistent reporters managed to circumvent the guards and knock on Hugh's door in search of interviews. "I'm sorry I can't say anything," Hugh replied politely. "I wish the papers would say nothing. You know you are making it very difficult for me. I don't want to say a word."

Deeply concerned that, as a result of the shock of the kidnapping, his brother might suffer a fatal heart attack — he had already had a number of attacks — Hugh paced restlessly back and forth in his hotel suite awaiting the kidnappers' phone call.

Meanwhile, the kidnappers and Labatt arrived at Wyldewood Tote Road, the rutted, mile-and-a-quarter-long track winding through the dense woodland about fifteen miles from Bracebridge towards the Prowse Cottages. The brush was so thick that it was impossible to drive the car all the way to the cottage the kidnappers had rented. McCardell and Pegram helped Labatt out of the car, and, holding him between them, took him the last hundred yards to the front door. Since several vacationers used the same parking area, they felt confident that nobody would take any particular notice of their car. Nonetheless, they had timed their arrival for after dark so as not to attract the attention of nearby cottagers.

Guiding Labatt up the steps, McCardell and Pegram led him inside, then took away his clothes except for his underwear. They left his blindfold on and used a dog leash to chain his right wrist to the cot in the bed-room they had designated for him. Right afterward, McCardell ordered Pegram to patrol around the cottage overnight. Contrary to what might be expected of kidnappers, he fed Labatt generously, serving him pork chops and beans. Exhausted from the day's events, Labatt then fell asleep. McCardell tidily washed and dried the dishes, after which he, too, went to sleep. Both men were awakened in the morning by the sound of chil-dren playing at the nearby cottages of the Prowse enclave.

McCardell instructed Pegram to drive to Toronto to pick up Knowles and the ransom. Then, contrary to the usual tense relationship between kidnapper and victim, McCardell, calling himself "Charlie," solicitously inquired if Labatt had slept well.

"Fairly well. How about you?"

"Not very good, either."

"I have a touch of indigestion," Labatt continued. No wonder, considering the large quantity of food he had consumed, as well as the tension he was suffering.

"Too bad. I could have given you some bicarbonate of soda. I had a little indigestion myself."

McCardell then asked, "How would you like a shave?"

"Fine."

"Just a minute while I get some water and a razor," McCardell replied. Labatt sat on the edge of the bed while McCardell shaved him with a safety razor. McCardell then inquired if he wanted to be bathed.

Labatt declined the offer. "It is hardly worthwhile, since I'll be going home soon."

"True," McCardell replied, offering to remove the tape from Labatt's eyes and bathe them if Labatt agreed not to look at him. Contrary to what many victims might have done, Labatt did not attempt even a single peek at "Charlie." "My guard was doing me a favour, so I felt honour bound not to look at him," he later explained. Besides, he had had a close-up look at the gang when they surrounded his car the day before because, uncharacteristically for kidnappers, they had been unmasked.

For his part, McCardell was behaving peculiarly for a kidnapper. Normally, a kidnapper would not take the risk of letting his victim see his face if he intended to release the victim alive. He also risked having

Labatt grab the razor with his free hand and brandish it as a potential weapon so as to force his release.

After brushing Labatt's hair, McCardell removed the basin of shaving water and the razor and asked, "How about a little breakfast?"

"What about you?" Labatt responded, in what was almost becoming an Alphonse and Gaston routine of "you go first — no, you go first."

"Oh, I was thinking of waiting until noon," McCardell said.

"I'll wait, too," Labatt answered.

"How about an orange meanwhile?"

Labatt accepted. McCardell then offered him a cigarette from a package Labatt had had in his pocket, lit one for himself and continued chatting. He speculated on the taxable income of the U.S. millionaire financier J.P. Morgan, then turned to his fervent desire to make money any way he could — provided it was illegal. He did not even mention the alternative of honest employment. "Some of the boys wanted to pick off your brewery payroll men," he told Labatt. "They wouldn't have got much," Labatt replied, "because the salaries are paid by cheque."

Only momentarily fazed, McCardell then inquired, as casually as if he were asking Labatt to recommend a good restaurant, "Do you know any other good payrolls in London?"

"No, I don't."

"It's just that things are getting tougher in our business all the time," McCardell explained wistfully, "business" being his euphemism for "criminal activity," reminiscent of Bessie Labatt's delicate reference to Labatt beer and ale as "the product."

Throughout the day, McCardell plied Labatt with food — eggs, sweet biscuits, toffee, honey, bread and butter, pretzel sticks, oranges and meat. This solicitude would continue throughout Labatt's captivity. So did the daily ritual of shaving him, bathing his eyes and chatting. Save for the neighbours in the cottage a short distance away, there were no outside sounds to break the summer stillness. Once, a boat passed by on which someone was strumming on a mandolin. For a while, the cry of a loon came intermittently across the lake. Not once did Labatt call out for help, even though he heard voices nearby. At ten o'clock each night, the two men went to bed.

Instead of keeping out of view of the other cottagers, McCardell went to the neighbouring cottage for water, dressed in city clothes rather than sportswear, in which he would have blended in with the real vacationers.

Conventionally for a kidnapper, McCardell had brought heavy-calibre revolvers and tear gas shells to the cottage — to subdue Labatt, if necessary, or to fire against the police if they discovered the hideout. But, peculiarly, he had stored the revolvers in the hollow posts of the cottage's verandah, where they would be out of reach if needed.

While the snatch itself had gone off smoothly, McCardell's post-snatch planning was singularly inept for someone who prided himself on being a criminal mastermind. No kidnapper with any common sense, or desire for secrecy, would have chosen to hold ransom talks at the Royal York Hotel, the largest hotel in the British Empire, filled around the clock with front desk clerks, porters, bellboys, guests, reporters on the lookout for a story, and house detectives. It was certainly not a place that lent itself to a quick handover of a ransom, followed by a speedy, unobserved getaway. An ordinary kidnapper would have taken into consideration the strong possibility that the Labatt family would have contacted the police, resulting in the hotel being placed under around-the-clock surveillance, both inside and out, by plainclothes officers and the tapping of the hotel's telephone lines.

The gang's quirky behaviour astonished the veteran criminal defence lawyer Charles Bell, who became part of the Labatt snatch saga during the trials. He expressed his amazement in his autobiography, *Who Said Murder?*, published in 1935.

> Many of the features of this strange affair were and are still quite inexplicable.
>
> The regular "Snatch" game is an antiquated affair, and is always marked by certain characteristics. In the first place, the victim is invariably snatched without warning. The advantages of that are obvious.
>
> There is no chance that the trail will be followed when he is taken — no chance of finding it fresh. The next step is to terrify the relatives so that they will scurry around to get a ransom. In the olden days, the popular

method was to send to the relatives a piece of the victim's ear, suggest that they recognize it, and then tell them that, if the ransom be not paid within a week or so, the ear will be followed by part of the victim's split nose. So it goes from step to step, until the relatives, in a frenzy over the sufferings of their lost one, do their utmost to raise the money and pay it.

Meanwhile, the victim is detained under conditions of the greatest hardship. He is put into some place entirely unfit for human habitation. He is half starved and terrorized. He is induced to write frantic letters for his release, explaining that his captors will kill him within twenty-four hours should the money not be available. He is kept in great agony of mind, threatened, browbeaten, terrified and probably tortured, in order that the frantic appeals resulting therefrom will produce the money.

When it becomes a question of payment of the ransom, the imprisoned man's friends are invariably told to go to some dark and secluded place, where, after raising a stone or looking into a hollow stump, or a discarded sewer-pipe, they find a note. This note directs them to go somewhere else, and probably after they have gone from place to place, three or four times, they contact the kidnappers. The purpose in all this circumlocution is of course that the kidnappers will be watching from some point of vantage, as the first note is unearthed, to see whether or not the victim's friends, proceeding to the second place, are accompanied by police. If they are, they don't get farther than the second note, because when they come to where the third one should be, it is not there. If, however, they come alone and unassisted, then they may go farther, to the end of the trail. In the Leopold and Loeb case of notorious memory, the persons carrying the money were told to throw it off the rear end of a fast train approaching Chicago.

Other such devices are common. But every rule must have its exceptions. The Labatt case, the first one ever to come to trial in Canadian courts, violated all well-established principles of "sound kidnapping" and created a situation which can never be accounted for in an ordinary way.

Chapter 2

THE MANHUNT

When London Inspector of Detectives Thomas Bolton gave the order, immediately after reading Three-fingered Abe's ransom note, that the Ontario Provincial Police and the Royal Canadian Mounted Police be contacted, it touched off a massive manhunt of a size unprecedented in Canadian history.

"Every available resource in the hands of the provincial police will be thrown into the task of apprehending the culprits and solving the mystery," Ontario's attorney general, Arthur Roebuck, pledged. "Kidnapping is one of the most dangerous crimes infesting a community and one which takes the meanest advantage of the affections which bind families together. To the extent that it is possible, no crime of this kind should go unsolved."

Ontario Premier Mitchell Hepburn — the youngest premier in Canada when he was elected in 1934 at age thirty-eight — called for life imprisonment for kidnappers rather than the twenty-five years recommended by Canada's Criminal Code. "We will stamp out kidnapping in Ontario," he vowed, adding, in a swipe at the rash of kidnappings that had been plaguing the United States, "We don't want an Americanized Ontario." He ordered all of the province's police forces into action and cancelled holiday leave.

The police searched every farmhouse, gas station, highway junction and wooded area from the Labatt summer home in Brights Grove to London in the east and Sarnia in the west in an effort to find clues as to where the abduction had occurred and the direction in which the kidnappers had taken Labatt. Numerous cars were stopped and examined —

all without result. The bridges and ferries to the United States, from Windsor to Detroit and Sarnia to Port Huron, Michigan, were carefully watched — also without effect. Roadblocks were set up in the Sarnia area. All these actions indicated that the police believed Labatt was stashed in southern Ontario or had been sneaked into the United States. Nobody guessed the kidnappers had headed north instead. McCardell's calculation that the police would not realize the direction they had actually taken had proved to be correct.

A Canada-wide hunt was also undertaken, and city, state and federal law enforcement officers in border states joined in the search and questioned gangsters they believed might be connected with the kidnapping.

London police drove Labatt's Reo from St. Joseph's Hospital to the huge garage of the Labatt brewery, where it was kept under police guard. They were relieved when no bloodstains were found in the car. Fingerprint expert Walter Harpur discovered a "good, clear" fingerprint on the car that he determined had been made by someone other than Labatt, and it was analyzed by police labs on both sides of the border to ascertain whether it matched those of any known criminal.

A public appeal for information that might be relevant yielded a number of tips. Mrs. Martin Burnley, who lived on the Egremont sideroad from which Labatt was kidnapped, told police: "I saw three cars travelling at breakneck speed down Egremont. The driver of the first car — Mr. Labatt — seemed to be fleeing for his safety with the other two cars in quick pursuit." She was wrong about the number of cars; there had been only two — Labatt's and the kidnappers'. And Labatt had stopped rather than fled. But she was the first person to provide definite information as to where the crime had occurred.

Charles Robertson, an employee at a service station ten miles east of Sarnia on the road to London, told police he had sold four gallons of gasoline the morning of August 14 to Labatt, describing him perfectly and giving the licence plate number of his car. His report contradicted Mrs. Burnley's, and the police spent considerable time investigating both leads to determine which, if either, was correct

One of the four maids the Labatts had taken to Brights Grove said she had noticed a car being driven slowly past the house three times on the day before the kidnapping. She described the driver as a man of medium build who was wearing tortoiseshell glasses.

Jack McGarrell of London's city engineering department told police that at about seven o'clock on the evening of the kidnapping, a man had stopped him near City Hall and asked him for directions to Labatt's home on Central Avenue. "After I gave him the address, he jumped into a car in front of City Hall driven by a second man," McGarrell said. He described the first man as "well dressed with a hardened countenance."

A man matching the description of one said to have been loitering outside the Labatt brewery two weeks prior to the abduction was reported as having been spotted in Sarnia on the morning of August 14. He was described as wearing a brown suit and a Panama hat, and it was reported he had purchased a case of beer shortly before 9:00 a.m. on the morning of the kidnapping.

Some residents in the Sarnia area swore they had seen Labatt being taken into a stretch of wasteland near Lake Huron. An intensive search turned up no trace of him. London police investigated the whereabouts of a former Labatt employee rumoured to have joined a gang of liquor smugglers. This lead also fizzled out into nothing.

The Labatt case was not the first or last in which purported eyewitness accounts by well-meaning, earnest citizens turned out to be unreliable — unintentionally hampering and slowing police investigations when speed and accuracy were crucial.

Coordinating all the Ontario police forces was not easy. Although they all wanted to help and did their best to cooperate, longstanding rivalries were difficult to overcome. As a result, there was some overlapping and confusion, prompting Attorney General Arthur Roebuck to call for an organizational overhaul. "This case points out a great weakness in our police system. There has been no unified control and no one who could dictate to every man in the various police forces what he must do or say," he noted. "While the Ontario government has no intention of taking over the responsibilities of local police commissioners, in such a crisis as this there should be some means whereby all forces may be mobilized into one unit." (This lesson would go unheeded. Sixty years later, the very same charge would arise concerning the investigation into the rape, torture and murder of two Ontario teenage girls for which Paul Bernardo was convicted.)

The Labatt snatch was a major challenge for Roebuck, who had been appointed attorney general as well as minister of labour only a month before Labatt was kidnapped. Born in 1878, Roebuck had a distinguished lineage. His great-great-grandfather was an inventor who collaborated with the Scottish engineer James Watt — who was credited with creating the first efficient steam engine — on smelting iron. His great-uncle was a British member of Parliament for more than forty years. But Roebuck himself grew up in hardship on a farm in central Ontario. To earn a living, he had to drop out of high school after attending for only three weeks. He made only a dollar a week operating a warehouse elevator; after five years, his salary climbed to $5 a week.

His meagre earnings did not quench his fierce determination to resume his education. In 1900, at the age of twenty-two, he crammed three years' worth of high school studies into six months, and passed. His goal was to become a lawyer, but he did not have enough money to attend law school. He trudged from law office to law office, asking to be articled. When that failed, he became a reporter for the *Toronto Daily Star.* He worked at the *Star* for five years, then managed weekly newspapers in northern Ontario for the next ten years, becoming owner and publisher of the *Cobalt Citizen* and *Temiskaming Herald.* But he had never given up his goal of becoming a lawyer; with the money he made from his newspaper career, he was finally able to attend law school at Toronto's Osgoode Hall. He graduated in 1917 at the age of thirty-nine, far older than his classmates.

Raised in a Conservative home, Roebuck became a Liberal due to the influence of a teacher in his hometown. Starting in 1911, he ran four unsuccessful campaigns in federal and provincial elections. On the fifth try, in 1934, he won as a Liberal candidate, representing a Toronto riding, in the provincial election that brought Mitchell Hepburn to power. During the campaign, he had charged that previous Conservative administrations had mismanaged Ontario Hydro and that huge profits had been made at the expense of taxpayers. In office, he renegotiated contracts that saved the public millions of dollars. To streamline court procedure, he dismissed a thousand justices of the peace and eighty-nine magistrates. His chief accomplishment as minister of labour was the 1934 *Industrial Standards Act,* which banned sweatshops and paved the way for binding contracts between employers and unions.

An article in *Saturday Night* magazine on July 28, 1934, three weeks after Roebuck became attorney general, praised him for his "tenacity, persistence and determination to overcome big odds, and inability to admit defeat. He is a man who gets things done." His determination was not always praiseworthy. For example, as a young man he was travelling on a train on a stiflingly hot day. The train conductor was unable to open the windows in Roebuck's car. At the next stop, Roebuck got off, found a piece of pipe and a brick, and smashed a hole in every window. Quite a reaction for somebody intending to be a lawyer!

Of medium height and with no grey in his brown hair even though he was in his late fifties, Roebuck wore clothes typical of the Victorian era — shirts with high wing collars, a black homburg hat, and gold pince-nez spectacles.

Hugh Labatt had implored reporters not to write about the kidnapping for fear that the publicity would make the kidnappers conclude he had double-crossed them by calling in the police and that they would retaliate by killing his brother. But what reporter can resist a scoop? All hope of keeping the kidnapping out of the press evaporated when an anonymous caller tipped off a reporter at the *London Free Press*. It was the scoop of a lifetime, and the paper raced to get the story into its evening edition of August 14, little more than half a day after the crime occurred. "J. LABATT KIDNAPPED," the front-page banner headline announced in a type size usually reserved for war news. To accommodate the word "kidnapped" in such enormous letters, Labatt's first name had to be truncated to just his first initial. The subheading, also much bigger than customary, read, "Gang Seizes President of Brewery Asking Payment of $150,000 Ransom before Giving Captive His Release."

In a sidebar adjacent to the main story, entitled "Mystery Telephone Call Tells Where Car Is Left," the *Free Press*'s typesetters made a humorous typo, saying that the caller had identified himself as "Three-fingered *Ape*" when asked his name. Subsequent stories in the paper correctly called him "Abe." The *Free Press*'s story destroyed police efforts to maintain a news blackout, and it wasn't long before so many reporters descended on the city to cover the sensational crime that the telegraph offices in

London had to bring in extra staff to handle the massive volume of stories being dispatched. Kidnappings had been rare in Canada; in 1928, Sam Low, a brother of a co-owner of Carling Breweries, had been abducted. And on the day Labatt was snatched, three men were committed to trial for trying to kidnap J.S. McLean, president of Canada Packers.

By August 15, the Labatt kidnapping was front-page news across Canada and the United States. The $150,000 ransom demand was triple the amount Charles Lindbergh had paid in 1932 for the return of his kidnapped baby, who was later found murdered. Labatt's snatch was a first in Canadian crime annals; that he had an attractive wife and young children added pathos to the story. In addition, there was the audacity of the snatch being carried out in broad daylight.

The electronic messageboard atop the *New York Times* building in Times Square, with its five-foot-high letters, blazed out the news of Labatt's kidnapping. In the paper, the abduction was the lead story on Page 1 under a six-tier headline, a treatment reserved by the paper for the most major of stories.

KIDNAPPERS SEIZE ONTARIO BREWER DEMAND $150,000

Abduction of J.S. Labatt the First Such Crime in the History of Canada

HE IS TAKEN FROM HIS CAR

Brother Is Named Negotiator by Note and Starts Work with Police in Toronto

AMERICANS ARE SUSPECTED

Authorities Declare the Federal Drive Has Sent Gangsters Scurrying over Border

The paper was impressed by the marked difference between the way kidnappings were handled in Canada and in the United States. "In contrast to the general practice in the United States, the Labatt family has not requested that the police not get involved," it pointed out. "There are useful lessons for Americans in how Canada's first known kidnapping is being handled. Canadian authorities start out with the advantage of a free hand against the criminals. British tradition, and presumably, colonial tradition, refuses to traffic with crimes."

The kidnapping also was big news across the Atlantic. *The Times* of London published it on its foreign news page.

A CANADIAN BREWER KIDNAPPED

FROM OUR CORRESPONDENT
OTTAWA, AUGUST 14
Mr. John S. Labatt, president of The Labatt Brewery, Limited, London, Ontario, was kidnapped today, while travelling by motor between London and Sarnia. Mr. Labatt's car was found outside a London hospital with a note which demanded $150,000 ransom and threatened harm to the brewer if the money was not forthcoming. No further details are known, as the police have instructed the family to maintain silence.

There was colourful, fanciful speculation by the press as to who had snatched Labatt, although all were certain the kidnappers must be American gangsters, since kidnappings were commonplace in the United States. Was it Alvin Karpis and Fred and Arthur Barker of the Ma Barker Gang, wanted for the kidnapping in early 1934 of the Minnesota brewer Edward Bremer? But their fingerprints did not match the one from Labatt's car. Or was it the Joseph "Legs" Lamar Gang, involved in a kidnapping in Detroit a few years earlier? Yet a third theory attributed the abduction to Detroit mobsters called the Purple Gang, whose specialty was kidnapping. Newspapers speculated that Labatt would have been targeted rather than an American because the U.S. government's crackdown on American hoodlums had forced them to relocate their criminal activities to Canada. As proof, the press cited a series of recent bank robberies in Ontario — half a dozen in the two months prior to Labatt's kidnapping. The scenario, according to the stories, was that the Purple Gang had spotted Labatt in Detroit when he was there on business on Saturday, August 11, followed him back to Brights Grove, and then waylaid him.

There were two schools of thought as to how the Purple Gang would then have spirited Labatt undetected into the United States. One group insisted the gang would have taken him in a plane they supposedly owned. For example, in its August 15, 1934, edition the *Toronto Daily Star* wrote: "The *Star* learned from a reliable source that police are inclined to believe the theory that a Detroit gang, possibly the famous Purple Gang, staged the kidnapping. It is well known that the Purple Gang has used aeroplanes in some of its missions and the fact that an aeroplane was sighted by residents of Port Huron at 7:30 last night leads to the belief that Labatt may have been taken from the country via this air route."

Other newspapers were equally adamant in declaring that the Purple Gang would have taken Labatt by rowboat across the Detroit River into the United States, just as bootleggers had smuggled beer during Prohibition.

With Bessie Labatt remaining in seclusion, journalists resorted to asking friends and relatives how she was coping with the excruciating stress of wondering where her husband was and whether he was still alive. Her few visitors reported that she was "calm and brave, although in a tense state, and has not broken down."

One of Labatt's sisters, Mrs. R.E. Balders of Halifax, gave a brief statement: "We have been reading of kidnappers in the newspapers and although dreadful, we never realized the full import of such a crime. Now that it has come right into our own house and taken one of the members of our family, it is so strange and horrible."

Bessie's seventy-two-year-old father, William Lynch, who lived in Ottawa, told reporters who came to his home that he was staying close to his telephone all the time, hoping and praying for word that his son-in-law was safe. "I wonder where he is now?" Lynch said in a low, quiet voice that gave reporters the impression he was trying to maintain control over his nerves. According to the *Ottawa Evening Citizen*, "the tension under which he was labouring was evident in the unconscious manner in which he continually moved his hands and glanced around the drawing room of his house."

"Oh, if we only knew where he is and could do something for him," Lynch continued poignantly. "Where do you think he can be? I hope he is all right."

He went on to speak of a visit he had paid to his daughter and son-in-law the previous month, and spent considerable time proudly talking about Arthur, his youngest grandchild. He told of how Arthur was being fed scientifically and of the nurse who was taking care of the baby. "That holiday meant so much to me," he said. "I had been ailing since last December and some months ago was knocked down by an automobile, injuring my back. I lost about eighteen pounds since the winter as a result of both health problems. But during the holiday the scales turned and I began to regain the lost weight."

Then he returned to the issue of his missing son-in-law, repeating again and again how anxious he was about John's safety.

As Charles Bell, David Meisner's lawyer, would point out in his book *Who Said Murder?*, "Kidnapping is one of the most cruel of crimes if for no other reason than the state of uncertainty into which the relatives of vanished persons are thrown. The hand of the kidnapper almost invariably descends upon inoffensive, kindly people. This case was no exception in spite of the courage with which John Labatt's relatives met the blow."

As is usual with high-profile crimes, there were some spectacle seekers and cranks. Celebrity watchers wanted to be a part of the action, even if only on the sidelines. They tried under various pretences to wangle their way into Hugh's hotel room. All were carefully questioned by the police, who were keeping watch from an adjoining room, and then sent on their way.

People who had planned parties at the Royal York Hotel hurriedly called them off for fear that overly zealous detectives might barge in on the chance the kidnappers had concealed themselves in the throng.

In London, cranks entertained themselves by imitating the ransom note and surreptitiously putting their versions into parked cars for the sadistic pleasure of watching the terror of the car owners as they discovered them. One prankster wrote threatening notes which he signed "Four X Spike," his parody of "Three-fingered Abe." Other cranks delighted in calling up the police and Crown officials and making fantastic threats.

On Wednesday, August 15, as McCardell was stuffing John Labatt with food and seeking his advice on prospective holdup targets, Hugh Labatt was frantic with worry, not having heard further from the kidnappers since the original startling call. Remaining in his bathrobe all day, he refused to leave his room for fear of missing the next call. He also wanted to avoid reporters. He requested that the hotel barber come to his room to shave him.

He was joined in his suite by Richard Green Ivey, a prominent London attorney of the law firm of Ivey, Elliott, Gillanders, which handled the Labatt company's legal affairs. A persistent reporter who had managed to breach the police cordon around Hugh's room asked, as Hugh greeted Ivey, if he had heard from the abductors. "Not a word since I left yesterday. I have no plans at all now. The only thing I can do is sit and wait and hope that I'll receive word some time today," Hugh replied disconsolately.

Meanwhile, Russell Knowles was waiting impatiently for Albert Pegram to arrive. He handled his worry far differently than Hugh did his. Hugh, one of Canada's wealthiest and most respected business-men, kept himself holed up in his room out of concern for the fate of his brother, and was so upset he could scarcely eat. Knowles, with a long record of past crimes, and currently one of the most wanted and hunted criminals in Canada, decided to pass the time by indulging in an epicurean repast, paid for with money gained from holdups, in the splendid dining room of the King Edward Hotel, where he had registered as "Mr. Tracey." The target of a massive manhunt by the police forces of two countries usually tries to be invisible, but Knowles' self-confidence would turn out to be well placed.

As he entered the dining room, the debonair, dapper Knowles was propositioned by an attractive woman who said her date was late and asked if she could join him for dinner. Admirably single-minded, Knowles recalled that a pretty face had been the reason the Bronfman kidnapping fell apart. "I was all business and shook off the flashy dame,"

he would proudly tell McCardell later. He also happened to be married
— to a pretty blonde — but the issue of marital fidelity apparently did
not occur to him.

Knowles noticed that the kidnapping was the only topic of conversation throughout the dining room. Nevertheless, he boldly followed
the maître d' to a table. An elderly man sitting alone nearby glanced up
as Knowles was passing and, smiling, told Knowles he had seen him
brush off the girl. He invited Knowles to join him. He started to talk
about the kidnapping. After a while he let drop that "I'm from the
RCMP and have been sent from Ottawa to help work on the kidnapping."
He had no idea that his dinner companion was one of the wanted men;
this was one occasion when the Mounties did not get their man. It was
all Knowles could do to retain his composure. "This town is getting
pretty well warmed up," he thought nervously while managing to keep
a poker face and calmly finish his dinner. This hard-to-believe but true
incident was yet another instance of the quirky comedy associated with
the Labatt snatch.

After dinner, Knowles went to his room and waited for Pegram. A
few blocks away, Hugh was waiting to hear from him. In Muskoka,
McCardell was waiting for Pegram to return with Knowles in tow. And
John Labatt was waiting for a safe and fast end to his ordeal.

Chapter 3
RELEASED

Wednesday passed without the kidnappers contacting Hugh. Alive or dead — over and over in his mind Hugh, sleepless, weary and alarmed, fretted about what the silence portended. Then, suddenly, the quiet of his hotel room was shattered in the early hours of Thursday morning by the shrill ringing of the telephone. Picking up the receiver instantly, Hugh felt his drooping spirits lift somewhat at the prospect of getting word about his brother.

His heart jolted when the caller said he was the kidnapper and promised that John Labatt would be released quickly in exchange for Hugh leaving the $150,000 ransom at Toronto's west-end Humber River bridge. This location apparently was named because it was a considerable distance from the Royal York Hotel and therefore less likely to be filled with police and reporters. The caller did not take into account that the police would naturally follow Hugh, and that alert reporters would follow the police.

As the police had advised him to do should he get such a call, Hugh stalled, saying he needed more time to collect the money, and asked the man to call back thirty-five minutes later. The police instructed Hugh to keep the man talking as long as he could in the second call so that they might be able to trace the number from which he was calling. When the call came, Hugh bargained back and forth, finally saying the man would have to accept $5,000 because that was all the cash he had with him. After some grumbling, the man agreed and hung up.

Somehow, a reporter from the Associated Press wire service overheard Hugh, took copious notes, and wired what he had heard of Hugh's end of the conversation to client newspapers throughout Canada and the United States in time for their Thursday editions.

> Something of the first conversation came to waiting newspapermen's ears. It indicated Mr. Labatt was being asked to keep a rendezvous alone. "It's 1:00 o'clock now and I can't get there until 2:30," he was heard to remark. "How can I get there alone? It's harder than you think with all these reporters around me."
>
> Following the conversation, detectives who had rested on their hotel beds half dressed arose and started to put on their coats and strap on their guns. But police were still in the hotel at 1:25 o'clock. The blind in Mr. Labatt's window was drawn for the first time this evening.
>
> Another telephone call came at 1:35 o'clock and Mr. Labatt seemed to have difficulty in hearing the person at the other end of the wire.
>
> Then came some reference to "twenty miles," which was taken as a reference to the location of the proposed meeting with the kidnappers.
>
> In this conversation he referred to 5:45, apparently his time of leaving the hotel or meeting the kidnappers. Then the other party hung up and silence enshrouded further activity.
>
> Labatt then spoke by telephone to a person he addressed as "General" — either Chief of Police D.C. Draper of Toronto or Provincial Police Commissioner V.A. Williams — and it was apparently decided a suggested rendezvous with the kidnappers would not be held.

Officers returned to their beds and Mr. Labatt went back to his room.

During the second conversation, the police were able to trace the caller's number to a service station. Shortly afterward, they arrested partly intox-icated twenty-two-year-old Edward Chard as he was going out the back door of his parents' home. He had no connection with the kidnappers, had no idea who they were, but thought he had come across a way of making some easy money. He was charged with attempted theft and extortion and pleaded guilty. Such cruel hoaxes are unfortunately not unusual in high-profile cases.

After the two Thursday-morning phone calls, there were no more to Hugh. As the hours crawled by, he became more and more frantic. It was too bad that he did not know that the kidnappers were also in despair.

The possibility that their dreams of sudden riches were about to fall apart had begun to occur to them late Wednesday night. Knowles had enjoyed outwitting his dinner companion, the RCMP officer who did not realize that the object of his pursuit was sitting right across the table from him in the King Edward Hotel's dining room. But as the hours passed with no sign of Pegram, Knowles's mood darkened.

He considered the possible reasons for Pegram's absence — all of them bad. He might have been caught by the police and "squawked." He might have gone to the police in the hopes of getting a reward. Or he might have headed back to the United States in "our only car and left us stranded." In fact, this was what Pegram really had done. Neither the kidnappers nor the police ever saw him again. The rest of the gang would always blame him — and never their own mistakes — for their troubles. Because of him, not only had they failed to collect the ransom, but they also were stranded — and $700 out of pocket in expenses. All they had got from Labatt was the $99 in his wallet. No wonder they always bitterly referred to Pegram as "that rat."

Stranded and almost penniless, Knowles could have followed Pegram's lead and fled. However, he remained loyal to McCardell, considering it his duty to warn his partner and then flee together before the police caught up with them. Since he did not have enough money to purchase another car, he took a bus to Bracebridge later that evening. Luckily for him, the police had no description of the kidnappers; thus, he was able to stroll brazenly through the police dragnet blanketing downtown Toronto, including the bus terminal. It was after midnight when he reached Bracebridge. There was no one around at that hour to ask for a lift to the hideout cottage, and even if there had been, Knowles would have considered it too risky. He wearily plodded the fifteen miles to the cottage along a stony road, the only light coming from the moon and stars — a lonely, eerie hike during which he had plenty of time to get angrier and angrier at Pegram, at Labatt, at the apparent unfairness of life.

Labatt and McCardell had gone to bed at 10:00 p.m., as usual. Since Knowles and Pegram had not arrived as planned, McCardell had thought, "It looks like they're not coming tonight." It was 2:20 a.m. on Thursday, August 16, when a footsore and enraged Knowles stormed into the cottage. As he began to loudly express his frustration and fury, McCardell warned him repeatedly to lower his voice to a whisper so as not to awaken Labatt and alert him as to what had happened. The warning was too late. Labatt was wide awake, although pretending to be asleep. He strained to overhear the conversation.

After being briefed by Knowles, McCardell tried to think of some way to salvage the situation. "We've got to get Labatt off our hands as quick as we can," he whispered urgently. "The coppers may be here any minute. We don't know but what Pegram may be leading them to trap us for some big reward that has been offered. First, though, we should try to drive the best bargain we can with Labatt so that we at least make some money."

Fiercely shaking the seemingly sleeping Labatt awake, Knowles yelled at him: "You're lucky to be alive. The boys wanted to do away with you. You're only a source of trouble. We can't collect the ransom because the Royal York Hotel is full of detectives and newspaper reporters. I spoke to your brother twice on the telephone and he said he was willing to pay $50,000 ransom." This was a lie, but Labatt had no way of knowing.

"What we should do is tie a stone to your feet and throw you into the lake," Knowles went on to threaten. "Your brother double-crossed us and notified the police and the press."

"That's no fault of mine," Labatt responded.

"The chief [McCardell] will let you go if you promise to pay us after you get free," Knowles continued. "Will you pay us $25,000?"

Under duress, afraid of being shot if he refused, Labatt agreed. Knowles then promised Labatt that he would be driven to Toronto and freed.

Without a car, however, nothing could be done. Fortunately for them, a solution was fairly nearby. A pal of McCardell's from the recent bootlegging era named Gerald Nicholson happened to be visiting his brother Joseph, who owned a hotel in the Bracebridge region. As the thirty-three-year-old Nicholson, a hotel worker in Windsor, had no arrest record, he would be able to borrow a car easily without arousing any suspicions. But as it was still the wee hours of the morning, nothing could be done for several hours. McCardell and Knowles had no choice but to wait. They passed the time smoking cigars, filling ashtrays to overflowing with ashes and butts.

Meanwhile, Labatt was fretting about whether they would kill him. "Charlie," he called to McCardell, using the fictitious first name McCardell had given him. McCardell went to the small bedroom, where Labatt was chained to the cot.

"Charlie, your fellows won't shoot me in my sleep, will they?"

"Oh, no," McCardell assured him. "Have a good sleep."

At daybreak, McCardell performed his usual routine of shaving and feeding Labatt. Leaving Knowles to guard Labatt, McCardell walked the fifteen miles to Bracebridge (after all, if Knowles could hike that distance, so could he) to ask Gerald Nicholson to borrow a car and bring it to the cottage that night. He said nothing about holding Labatt captive. Nicholson agreed to help.

Throughout the day at the hideout, Knowles and McCardell made preparations to leave, scrubbing the cottage, including the walls, to erase any telltale fingerprints. Then, after all this striving to get rid of incriminating evidence, they made a peculiar choice of where to dump three of their revolvers and the accompanying tear gas shells. Common sense should have dictated they be thrown over the nearby cliff into the depths of Lake Muskoka, where they would sink without a trace. Instead, McCardell and Knowles elected to toss them in the bushes on a nearby golf course, where any golfer might stumble across them and where the police were likely to scour for clues.

Around 3:30 p.m., in his persona of the generous host, McCardell gave Labatt a huge meal of pork and beans, eggs, cookies and oranges — most kidnap victims would have counted themselves lucky to get a sandwich. After the meal, the three men smoked cigarettes until nightfall. The kidnappers did not want to take the risk of departing in the daytime, when the nearby cottagers might spot Labatt and recognize him. His picture, after all, had been on the front page of every newspaper for two days in a row.

As dusk approached, Labatt's suit, shirt, tie and shoes were returned to him. The dog chain was removed from his wrist so that he could dress himself. McCardell handed back Labatt's watch, which he had kept running and on time — thorough as the most perfect valet in attending to his every need.

Throughout the day, Labatt had inwardly wondered if McCardell and Knowles had been sincere in saying they would drive him to the city, where his brother was waiting for him. It seemed extraordinary for two men who knew they were the target of a massive manhunt. Conventional kidnappers would have taken one of three courses of action: left Labatt chained to the bed for someone to eventually discover him; driven him to a lonely and secluded spot, miles from any houses, and left him there to make his way on foot; or, in the worst-case scenario, killed him. Any of these options would have given McCardell and Knowles a head start of several hours before the police might be alerted.

Around nightfall, as they were about to leave the cottage, McCardell gave Labatt instructions for the journey. "On the way, we'll pass one or two bad spots and might have to shoot our way through. If that happens, drop to the bottom of the car, as there'll be danger of your being hit. If you're asked your name, say James Cunningham and that we had just picked you up along the road." To disguise Labatt somewhat, McCardell put a straw hat on his head. So that Labatt would not be able to pinpoint for police the hideout's location or the route taken to Toronto, McCardell had him put on the goggles with the black court plaster on the inside that he had worn en route to the cottage. If he had prepared an explanation for the police, should they be stopped, as to why someone would wear a straw hat — normally used for protection against the sun — and dark glasses at night, he did not divulge it to Labatt. Given the kidnappers' unusual behaviour so far, it is entirely possible that McCardell did not take into consideration that the outfit would be regarded as very peculiar.

When McCardell and Knowles led Labatt out of the cottage to Nicholson's car, Gerald Nicholson realized immediately who he was. Driving him to Toronto would make him an accessory, yet he did not protest. After they were on the road, McCardell remembered that he had not wiped the kidnappers' fingerprints off of letters, Labatt's own glasses, and other items in Labatt's pockets; he requested that Labatt hand them over so that he could rub them clean.

These being the days before high-speed multilane highways, the drive to Toronto would normally have taken about three hours. However, because of detours they took to avoid detection, Labatt later estimated it might have taken twice as long. At about midnight, the kidnappers and Labatt arrived at the outskirts of Toronto. Nicholson drove down the city streets — including Yonge Street, Toronto's main street and its busiest north-south thoroughfare — past police stations, traffic cops, and motorcycle officers whizzing around in a fruitless search for the gang. Not a single policeman halted their car, even though random spot checks might have been expected. At 12:30 a.m. on Friday, August 17, Nicholson pulled up at the corner of St. Clair Avenue and Vaughan Road, several miles north and west of the Royal York Hotel.

Labatt was helped out of the car, and his dark glasses and hat were removed — but not the court plaster over his eyes. He was handed his own glasses. "You're free to go, but don't take off the tape until we're gone," he was warned. One of the kidnappers took his arm and thoughtfully pointed out the direction Labatt should follow to reach downtown Toronto. So that Labatt could take a taxi rather than have to walk, he chivalrously handed Labatt one dollar out of the $99 they had taken from him. Knowles later claimed that McCardell shook hands with Labatt. Then the car sped off. Labatt was free after sixty-three hours in captivity.

Peeling the plaster off of his eyes and staggering with shock and fatigue, Labatt made his way a few blocks east along St. Clair Avenue to the busier intersection of Bathurst Street and hailed a cab. Hard as it might be to believe, the driver did not recognize him even though his picture had appeared on the front page of every newspaper for days. At 12:55 a.m., Labatt reached the Royal York Hotel. Equally hard to believe, but also true, is that Labatt walked undetected, past the platoons of police and reporters in the lobby, to the reception desk. "I am John Labatt," he told the amazed night clerk. "Where is my brother's room?" To maintain Labatt's privacy, the hotel staff quietly took him through the pantry and up a freight elevator to Room 429 on the fourth floor, one floor below his brother's suite.

Hugh was notified of his brother's arrival, and he rushed down the stairs for a joyous reunion that reflected their devoted relationship.

Both were weary and haggard, John from the strain of his captivity and Hugh from the uncertainty about his brother's safety. After talking for a few moments, they went up to the seventeenth floor, where other Londoners, who had come to Toronto to provide Hugh with moral support, had rooms.

Although the police and reporters in the lobby had failed to recognize Labatt, Emerson Nichols, a London china importer who happened to be in the lobby, spotted him right away and immediately notified the *London Free Press*. Reporter Howard Broughton, one of a number of *Free Press* staffers assigned to the story, was despatched to the hotel for what would be the scoop of his career. After confirming that Labatt had been released, Broughton raced to London at seventy miles per hour, a very high and dangerous speed in 1934, especially when, as was the case in the early hours of August 17, there was heavy fog. At 3:15 a.m., only three hours after Labatt's release, the paper's first edition carried a one-line bulletin stating: "Labatt is reported released."

It was not until a half-hour after the paper announced his release that Labatt arrived back in London, even though he had hastily left the celebration with his friends at the Royal York. He and Hugh had exited the hotel via the back door, believing they would be undetected by reporters. They congratulated themselves — unaware of Broughton's sprint to London — that their subterfuge had worked. They were accompanied by family lawyer Richard Green Ivey, who drove them to London. At 3:45 a.m., they arrived at Hugh's apartment to an ecstatic welcome from an overjoyed Bessie. She would often recount in later years that her hair turned completely white in the three weeks after her husband's kidnapping because of the stress she had undergone.

Labatt's physician, Dr. W.J. Tillmann, hurried over to Hugh's to give John an immediate examination to determine whether he had suffered any ill effects. Tillmann was especially concerned about Labatt's weak heart. Satisfied that, although he was haggard and exhausted, his heart was all right, Tillmann said he would follow up with a further examination in the afternoon, when John Labatt would be more rested.

At 4:30 a.m., forty-five minutes after Labatt's reunion with Bessie, Claude Savage of the family's law firm, Ivey, Elliott, Gillanders, telephoned the *London Free Press*. "I have just had word that Labatt has been released and is now with his relatives. Further than that, I have no information at this time." The call was anticlimactic considering that the paper had announced Labatt's release seventy-five minutes earlier.

"Is Mr. Labatt in good health?" the *Free Press* asked.

"Yes, I believe he is," Savage answered.

Before 5:00 a.m., Bessie's parents, Mr. and Mrs. William Lynch, were notified of the happy ending. When a *Toronto Daily Star* reporter asked their reaction, Mrs. Lynch said: "We are very lighthearted this morning. We are keeping quiet, but both of us are very happy. We were overjoyed when we learned John was safe."

At 5:30 a.m., the *London Free Press* published a special edition, reporting, "The kidnapped brewery president was quickly smuggled in and out of the hotel without being detected." One hour later, at 6:30, in the regular morning edition of the paper, reporter Howard Broughton recounted his late-night trip from Toronto: "It was a speedy and dangerous journey, but it was well worthwhile. A newspaper man's dream had come true." That day, trains that normally sped through London made a stop long enough for passengers to pick up newspapers so they could keep posted on John Labatt's amazing release. The whole episode was turning out to be the most sensational story of the year — actually, of many years.

Labatt's nephew Richard Cronyn, the brother of up-and-coming actor Hume Cronyn, told reporters in Abingdon, Virginia — where he and his mother were visiting Hume, then the production manager of a local Little Theatre group — "We are greatly relieved. After hearing the news, my mother had her first sound sleep in days."

So intent had John, Hugh and Ivey been on getting back to London that they neglected to inform the police of their departure. This miffed the police greatly. General Daniel Draper, chief of the Toronto police, gave official notice of Labatt's release in a terse two-sentence statement: "Mr. Labatt was released by the kidnappers on the outskirts of Toronto. He had some experience, but is unharmed and, in the company of his brother, Hugh Labatt, is now in London."

It was left to Attorney General Arthur Roebuck to publicly, and sharply, rebuke the Labatts, doing so in the second paragraph of his statement about Labatt's release and returning to the theme in the sixth.

But the impact was somewhat blunted by the statement being issued via J.C. Elliott of the Labatts' law firm, Ivey, Elliott, Gillanders to which Roebuck telephoned his statement. It said:

> Mr. John Labatt was released in Toronto this morning about 12:30. He was blindfolded and had been continuously blindfolded since he was taken. He was left in the vicinity of Forest Hill Village. He took a taxi to the Royal York Hotel. He was immediately taken from there by his own friends by car to London.
>
> For some reason, those who took charge of him failed to notify either the Toronto or Provincial police on his arrival or departure, and the result of this lack of co-operation has meant that there is no hot trail of the abductors. It is most unfortunate and unnecessary that the Police Forces of both the Province and the City have been very seriously handicapped in their work by their inability to secure complete control of the situation.
>
> Labatt arrived at London about 3:45 a.m. At the time of his capture he drove around for a period which he estimates was twelve hours. He was in Ontario all the time. He has no knowledge of having passed over any water. At the time he was released, he drove between 5 and 6 hours, so he thinks, but his judgment is that of a man blindfolded. He also thinks they were killing time in the latter drive and were waiting for darkness.
>
> In this office, we have no knowledge as to what financial arrangements, if any, have been made between the captured man and the criminals. Whatever arrangements were made, if any, did not come through either Hugh Labatt or his solicitor, Mr. Ivey.
>
> Mr. Labatt says he was blindfolded with adhesive tape and glasses drawn down over the adhesive tape. When let out of the car, he was told not to remove either the tape or the glasses until the auto had moved on. There were 3 or 4 men in the car when he was released, in

addition to himself. When he was kidnapped, there were two men in the car.

You will observe that, owing to this exclusion of the police from the transaction in its closing hours, there is very little out of the incident upon which investigation can build. I have not told all the police know, nor indicated what is being done, and I am confident that in due season there will be a solution to this crime.

I am pointing out a great weakness in our police system. We have in Ontario a large number of municipal police forces and a very large one in Toronto. In a crisis such as that through which we have passed, there has been every desire to co-operate. You will remember that the minister of justice offered help of the Dominion police, but there has been no unified control and none who could dictate to every man in the various police forces what he must do or say. While the Ontario Government has no intention of taking over the responsibility of policing municipalities or letting its police force be entangled in municipal disorder or labour disputes or generally of taking the responsibility of local police commissioners, nevertheless in such a crisis as this there should be some means whereby all forces may be mobilized in one unit.

Following his Friday afternoon examination of Labatt, Dr. W.J. Tillmann announced: "Mr. Labatt has suffered a nervous collapse, but he is rational. He is very fatigued. He apparently suffered no violence at the hands of his captors. They seem to have looked after him well and, obviously, he was fed satisfactorily. His eyes are inflamed from wearing a bandage a long time. His heart is all right and he is in no danger. His condition is better than when I saw him this morning. It is difficult to say how long he must remain in bed after all the hardship he went through."

All day Friday, reporters, photographers and curious strangers milled about in front of Hugh's apartment building, hoping for a glimpse of Labatt. Throughout the commotion, Labatt's older children, watched over by a nursemaid, played happily on the balcony of their Uncle Hugh's apartment, oblivious to the excitement below. Later in the day, again overseen by the nursemaid, they merrily cleared up the litter that the crowd of strangers had left behind on the front lawn, still oblivious as to why so many people had been staring at them and at their uncle's apartment.

Labatt refused to speak publicly about his ordeal. When reporters turned to his lawyer, Richard Ivey, for comment, he replied: "If you were confronted with a matter that involved life and death to your family, what would you do?" The answer was, "Probably keep quiet." And Ivey responded, "Exactly."

In the absence of the facts, the media resorted, as it is prone to do about sensational events, to speculation. The *Toronto Daily Star*'s August 18 account ran under the headline, "'If Any of Us Caught, You Die,' Labatt Told When He Was Released." It went on:

> "After we turn you loose in Toronto — and you talk — and any of our gang are arrested, we will come back and kill you" — was the death threat given to John Labatt by his abductors when they left him on Thursday night in Toronto. This fact became known here today through channels close to the police and Labatt's family, The Star was informed.
>
> Labatt told the police he knows he was in a house, but has not the faintest recollection where he was. He was blindfolded all the time. But, The Star was also told that the kidnappers, on several occasions, even plugged his ears with cotton and taped them over when they were talking over certain angles of the case.
>
> The police think this extraordinary move was because the kidnappers did not want Labatt to get a chance to study their voices while they were holding prolonged conversations as to their plans so that if they fell into the hands of the police Labatt would not be able to pick out their voices.

The *Star*'s rival *The Globe* was also wrong in its August 18 story: "It was learned on good authority that negotiations with the kidnappers resulted in payment of less than $50,000, instead of the $150,000 originally demanded." Actually, no ransom had been paid, as the *London Free Press* had correctly reported on August 17.

Just as Labatt's kidnapping had received front-page coverage in the *New York Times*, so did his release. "LABATT IS FREED, SUFFERS COLLAPSE; RANSOM IN DOUBT," it headed its story on August 18. There was a secondary headline, "Brewer Is Released in Toronto and Goes Home with Brother before Police Learn of It," and a third, "Rumor of $50,000 Paid." The story occupied the entire far-right column on Page 1 and continued in two long columns on Page 4. It eclipsed an article on Page 4 on the kidnapping of a North Carolina evangelist whose abductors were demanding a $25,000 ransom from the famous American evangelist Aimee Semple McPherson. Indeed, the Labatt snatch had received so much publicity in the United States that, when Mrs. McPherson was notified that she had been sent a ransom letter about a kidnap victim, she immediately asked, "Who is he, the man that was kidnapped in Canada?"

On Sunday, August 19, the *New York Times* again placed the story on Page 1, filling nearly an entire column, but the continuation was placed further inside the paper — Page 20 — than on the previous day. "Labatt in Shack Heard Abductors Talk of Murder" was the main heading. The opening paragraph described Labatt's ordeal this way: "To sit for several hours Wednesday night and listen to a cold-blooded discussion of what steps should be taken to murder him and dispose of his body was the harrowing experience of John S. Labatt while he was held by kidnappers, it was learned from a source close to the family today."

The first part of the sensational Labatt snatch, in which danger and suspense had been incongruously intermingled with quirky humour, was over. The victim, happily, was safe, well, and back with his family. History had been made. Canada had recorded its first-ever kidnapping of an important Canadian for a large ransom. But the dramatic story had by no means come to an end. The perpetrators of the historic snatch remained at large. Attention now shifted to the imperative task of catching them with the greatest possible speed.

Chapter 4
THE SUSPECTS

The police had few clues. The only time Labatt had seen his kidnappers clearly was on the morning of Tuesday, August 14, when they snatched him, and in the shock and fright of the moment he had had little opportunity to indelibly memorize their features. Moreover, the kidnappers had been careful not to address one another by name, and McCardell had taken the further precaution of using the alias "Charlie" rather than give his real name — Michael.

There was a flurry of excitement on August 18, the day after Labatt's release, when a Labatt employee was found dead under mysterious circumstances. "LABATT EMPLOYEE IS FOUND DEAD," the *Toronto Daily Star*'s lead headline declared. For a brief time it was thought that the man's death might have some connection to Labatt's kidnapping. The employee, twenty-eight-year-old Gordon Mackenzie, who had worked at the brewery for only two weeks, was found lying unconscious on a London sidewalk by a taxi driver. The driver took him to the city's Victoria Hospital, where he died without making a statement. It was determined that he had died of a fractured skull. At first, it was thought that the fracture had been caused by a violent blow to his head, and there was speculation he had died of foul play. But an immediate autopsy found that he had fallen down some stairs to his death. In a written statement, Coroner J.C. Wilson said, "In view of the fact that there are many rumours regarding the death of Mackenzie, and at the request of the Crown Attorney, I wish to state that the evidence is conclusive that there is no connection whatever between the Mackenzie case and the kidnappings."

Crown Attorney Norman Newton also maintained there was no evidence of foul play, adding that a check of Mackenzie's movements over the two weeks of his employment at the Labatt brewery had proven to his satisfaction that he had had nothing to do with the kidnapping.

The two men who had been the captain and first lieutenant of the snatch — Michael McCardell and Russell Knowles — were back in Detroit. Taking the precaution of travelling separately, McCardell rode a bus, while Knowles took the train. They must have thought they were leading a charmed existence; not once had any policeman on either side of the border suspected who they were. Their quixotic gesture of driving Labatt to Toronto had not had any dire consequences.

Determined to capture the kidnappers, Attorney General Arthur Roebuck asked J. Edgar Hoover, the director of the U.S. Federal Bureau of Investigation, to assign some G [government] men — as FBI agents were then colloquially called — to assist with the search south of the border in case they had fled there. Hoover agreed. Various state and municipal police forces also took part. Meanwhile, the Ontario Provincial Police were energetically at work.

On September 6, it was announced that the police had located the Muskoka cottage where Labatt had been held captive. They had been contacted by Horace Prowse, the owner of the cottage, after receiving a tip from a neighbouring tenant who believed that the men he had seen in mid August were the kidnappers. The police also found the kidnappers' guns on the golf course.

"Did you have any suspicions that they were kidnappers when they rented the cottage?" a *Toronto Daily Star* reporter asked Prowse.

"Not at all. They seemed to be well dressed, typical business-like tenants, nice, affable men." Not even their putting down a deposit in a combination of American and Canadian currency had made him suspicious, because he often rented to Americans.

"As a matter of fact, they still have the key to the cottage," he added.

With permission from Prowse, the *Star*'s reporter went inside the cottage to browse around. He saw a number of empty food tins — with both American and Canadian labels — and ashtrays filled with cigar ashes and butts. Outside the cottage, he found more cigar butts, an empty wine bottle and a heap of eggshells. All the debris had apparently been left by the kidnappers, as the cottage had not been rented since. Their thorough scrubbing of the interior to remove telltale fingerprints was utterly wasted, considering that they left behind so much garbage that was covered with fingerprints. Still, it was typical of their peculiar behaviour.

Also on September 6, the Ontario government offered a $5,000 reward for information leading to the capture of the kidnappers. The money had been provided by the Labatt family. John Labatt was asked to look at about forty mug shots of known American criminals, which the RCMP and OPP had obtained from the Detroit Police Department and the Michigan State Police Identification Bureau. Without hesitating, he picked out husky Albert Pegram as the driver. As he continued to leaf through the mug shots, Labatt stopped suddenly at a picture of a man with a long, pointed nose and big ears. "That's him; that was my chief guard and the gang's leader," he said adamantly. Ironically, the picture was of David Meisner, the Kentucky gambler who had turned down McCardell's invitation to take part in the kidnapping.

On September 11, Fred Frahm, the chief of detectives for the Detroit Police Department, announced that two of Labatt's kidnappers had been identified as Albert Pegram and David Meisner. Pegram, also known to the police by his aliases Albert Leon and Jack Snead, was described by Ontario Attorney General Arthur Roebuck as "an American desperado with a record." A Toronto gambler acquainted with Pegram told the *Toronto Daily Star* that Pegram "has quite a reputation as a rough-and-tumble fighter among the police of Detroit and the boot-legging fraternity of the Sunnyside district near Windsor. I was with him in Detroit one night when he licked three policemen, and it took six others to get him into the patrol wagon." A former Detroit taxi driver, Pegram was known to the police for rum-running in the Windsor–Detroit area during Prohibition.

Meisner was described by the police as "43 years of age, 5 feet, 6 inches tall, weighing about 145 pounds, with brown hair, hazel eyes, an American flag tattoo on his right forearm with an additional tattoo sign of crossed hands also on his right forearm." In actuality, Meisner was fifty-five and weighed 118 pounds. In any event, in his affidavit, Labatt had described his "chief guard" as standing five feet, nine or ten inches, and weighing about 175 pounds.

Had Meisner informed the police of McCardell's plan when it was proposed to him, McCardell and his crew probably would have been arrested and the kidnapping would not have occurred. On the other hand, Meisner could very well have been killed out of revenge by cronies of the gang.

A native of Brantford, Ontario, Meisner had circulated for many years on the fringes of the underworld in Covington, Kentucky, located across the Ohio River from Cincinnati and in those days a cesspool of vice and corruption. Charles Bell, who became Meisner's defence lawyer in the Labatt case, wrote in his 1935 book *Who Said Murder?*, in a chapter entitled "Ditching David Meisner,":

> Taxi across the bridge from Cincinnati for a few minutes or take the trolley and you are there. You will see wretched collections of shacks and shebangs, giving an outlet for many things in which residents of Cincinnati indulge but are unable to do so in their own bailiwick. Covington bears the same relation in the middle West of the United States that Hull, Quebec, bears to Ottawa, Ontario, excepting that Covington can give cards and spades to Hull and then shoot them out of Hull's hands with a riot gun, for Covington is a plague spot, nothing less.
>
> Its pleasing little industries are the maintenance of speakeasies, brothels, gambling houses, and nests of unmentionable vileness. Around the gambling tables to be found in all parts of the town, cluster night and day hard-faced men and hard-boiled women who come from Cincinnati and many other points where they cannot ply their vicious trades as they can in fair Kentucky.
>
> Cardsharpers, pimps, roulette players, unnatural creatures of both sexes, who are essentially of the underworld and spend most of their time under-ground, flourish there. To them there is no such thing as daylight, nor yet cleanliness, physical, mental or moral. They fit well into their surroundings, creatures indigenous to the soil. If they have not police protection

in many quarters, they at least claim to have, and the thugs that come to Covington for what they are wont to call a good time feel that anything goes there.

Meisner was a small-time gambler, racetrack follower and bookie. "Whatever charges had been laid against him during his career, he was never convicted of anything more than a picayune offence," Bell wrote. "Meisner came down to an insignificant stooge game. It consisted of looking over the automobiles parked outside well-known Covington gambling houses at night; where there was a woman sitting in the car, her escort was generally willing to hand over a few kopeks when he came out of the dive and joined her."

Meisner lived with a young woman whom he called his common-law wife in a rooming house whose owner, an old man, was drunk much of the time, though never so drunk that he forgot to collect their rent. Meisner always paid promptly.

From time to time, Meisner drifted to the gambling dens of Detroit, where many of the big shots of the underworld operated. He met a number of hoodlums, including Michael McCardell, never dreaming of the misfortune he would suffer as a result of that acquaintance.

In the early part of 1934, Meisner's left eye began to pain him. A Cincinnati oculist he consulted told him he was developing a serious cataract growth, and that if left untreated the other eye might also become affected, resulting in total blindness. Meisner had no money for an operation, but he hoped to win enough at the racetracks during the summer to finance surgery that September, or October at the latest. By June, the cataract had spread to such an extent that his eye looked like a white bulb, even to casual observers. Meisner's desperate need for cash for the operation was probably why he accepted McCardell's June 1934 invitation to meet with him and hear his "little proposition." But he was not so desperate that he accepted.

Although there was some slight similarity in Meisner's and McCardell's facial features, there was none whatsoever in their height and weight. Meisner was short and frail, weighing only 118 pounds (the press always described him as "the little Kentucky gambler"); McCardell was tall, weighing 170. Unlike McCardell, Meisner's left eye was clouded by the cataract. Meisner's hairline was receding, while McCardell's hair flopped over his forehead. Meisner was fifty-five, McCardell was forty-two.

For a week, there were no new developments in the hunt for Pegram and Meisner. The silence was broken on the 19th, when Roebuck, annoyed at speculation that the lack of disclosure signified a lack of progress, tried to squelch that impression. "A very great deal has been accomplished, and the Provincial Police are to be highly complimented," he said in a written statement. "The suspects have been located and named. Best of all, by most vigorous activity, the kidnapping has been made unsuccessful. Police work forced the kidnappers to release Labatt; it was the police who learned of the hideout, and they would have caught the gang if they had stayed at Muskoka Lake another twenty-four hours."

On the morning of September 20, readers of *The Globe* saw on Page 1 a Canadian Press dispatch dated the 19th that reported: "The search for one of Labatt's kidnappers was concentrated in this section of northern Ontario tonight. Inspector James Gardiner of the Ontario Provincial Police and Chief of Detectives Fred Frahm of the Detroit police were in Timmins attempting to find trace of David Meisner, one of the men identified as a kidnapper of Labatt."

Events on September 20 would show that Gardiner and Frahm were in the wrong place; on that day, hundreds of miles to the south, David Meisner voluntarily surrendered to police in Detroit. Hard to believe but true, he was accompanied by Russell Knowles, whom he had regarded as a good friend for seventeen years. Knowles was confident that he personally ran no risk because, just a few days earlier, he had been taken into custody by Windsor police, questioned about the kidnapping and released for lack of evidence. Some friend he was to Meisner!

Knowles was not the only kidnapper who had decided to ditch him. Having seen Meisner's picture in the papers, Jack Bannon, in his role as police stool pigeon, had led Detective-Sergeant Ted Weeks, the lead RCMP investigator on the case, through the maze of the Covington underworld, doing all in his power to build up the case against Meisner. In return for what was thought to be genuine help, he received $500 of the $5,000 reward being offered by the Labatts via the Ontario government.

It was arranged between the Covington and Detroit authorities that Meisner would surrender in Detroit, because the police there were overseeing the investigation in the United States. Meisner had agreed to surrender voluntarily after the Detroit police promised he would only be held until he could be viewed by people claiming to be eyewitnesses in Muskoka at the time of the crime. Meisner was unconcerned, confident that he could quickly clear his name. He adamantly told reporters, "I didn't have the first thing to do with this kidnapping." That was true. "I don't know who pulled the snatch and I don't know the first of the details," he continued. He may not have been certain, but, based on his June meeting with McCardell at which they discussed McCardell's "little proposition," he must have had an inkling.

"I want to get out from under this indictment," Meisner said. "It isn't that there would be deliberate unfairness, but the kidnapping has been a big thing over there [in Canada] and they are anxious to put someone away for it. I don't want to be burned to satisfy somebody's political ambition."

He insisted he had a rock-solid alibi that he wasn't even in Ontario when the kidnapping occurred. "I was at my home in Cincinnati the whole time. I've got all kinds of witnesses — all the witnesses in the world. I can even bring up policemen to prove I was in Cincinnati. I have a perfect alibi."

But, according to records from the Attorney General's office and the Ontario Provincial Police, held in the Archives of Ontario and obtained by the author under the Freedom of Information and Protection of Privacy Act, it is clear that, behind the scenes, the machinery was being set in motion to charge Meisner. On September 21, the day Meisner surrendered, the acting consul at the British Consulate in Detroit — signing himself only by his surname, Smith — wrote Attorney General Roebuck, informing him, "I have obtained a provisional warrant for his arrest from the U.S. commissioner. He has remanded him until the 5th October for a hearing of the extradition proceedings. Meisner has refused to cross the boundary on the grounds he would be unable to obtain readmission to the U.S."

The next day, the 22nd, Rendle Stone of the British Consulate Office telegraphed Roebuck: "Present at examination Misner's [sic] eye. Personally satisfied process is under cornea. Two police doctors diagnose cataract at least year old."

Also on September 22, according to OPP records at the provincial archives, Inspector E.I. Hammond wrote a memo to the OPP's chief inspector, John Miller, that some of the Muskoka witnesses could "positively" identify both Meisner and Pegram from police mug shots, while others could only identify one or the other, and that more of them were certain about Pegram than about Meisner. "There is no question regarding those who have said they positively identify either one," Hammond wrote. "Their identification was immediate, there was no hesitancy on their part." Then he added a caveat. "It will be noted, however, that Meisner's identification is not as complete as that of Pegram. This is owing to the fact that Pegram did all of the talking and Meisner was the 'silent partner' and naturally more notice was taken of Pegram." But he ended on an upbeat note about Meisner's identification. "Mrs. Louise Eveleth talked to Meisner about her dog. He wanted to get it, claiming that his own dog had been killed, and she got a first-rate chance to identify him."

With Meisner in police custody, it was wondered whether Albert Pegram would follow Meisner's example and surrender, too. It seemed unlikely, as the *Star* reported in a September 22 story headed "Pegram Sees Meisner Tricked":

> Pegram has decided, according to well-informed circles, to take no risk of also being hurried to Canada as the result of extradition proceedings. He intends to continue in his hiding place for the present. But police, working on the case, have hopes of apprehending him at any minute in spite of his friends.

The story concluded by focusing on what would become a major issue: Meisner's cataract.

> The marked cataract on Meisner's left eye is undoubtedly to be a big factor in the identification proceedings for the six persons in Muskoka who picked his picture out of the 40 and more police record photographs secured by the Royal Canadian Mounted and provincial police

from the Detroit police and Michigan state police identification bureau. None of these people apparently noticed anything the matter with the eye of the man they identified from the pictures. Yet Meisner insists that he has been suffering from this defect for over three months and can prove it by doctors at Covington, Kentucky, whom he has repeatedly consulted. For three months or more he has been wearing the darkened lens over his left eye, so noticeable a feature of his glasses, he claimed, when he was arraigned yesterday afternoon.

Following Meisner's surrender, the question arose of whether extradition proceedings would have to be undertaken to bring him to Canada for face-to-face identification by Labatt and the Muskoka witnesses. (Otherwise, the witnesses would have had to go to Detroit.) Extraditions between Canada and the United States were routine, provided that there was sufficient evidence that an offence had been committed and that there was a possibility the accused committed it. An accused person could fight extradition, but the chances of success were slim. Considering the severity of his alleged crime, Meisner was ordered extradited.

While an appeal of the extradition order was being considered, legal authorities remembered that Meisner was a Canadian citizen. That settled the question and Meisner was brought to Canada to the Middlesex County Jail in London. A very unconventional identification was then conducted in the prison yard.

A number of prisoners were rounded up to stand alongside Meisner in a lineup. The witnesses who had picked Meisner's picture from amongst the police mug shots were taken, one by one, to look through a slit in a tarpaulin that had been hung before an open gateway. While the prisoners, like Meisner, wore civilian clothes, theirs had been supplied from bags into which they had been stuffed, leaving them very much crumpled. Meisner's suit, however, was neatly pressed, a conspicuous difference. All the witnesses singled out Meisner.

In *Who Said Murder?*, Meisner's attorney, Charles Bell, argued that this procedure blatantly disregarded the usual identification methods. "Whether this really led to any identification that would not otherwise have been made, it is impossible to say, but it is certain that, in the matter of identification, the regulations in force in London, England, and especially in New Scotland Yard, were grievously violated in many particulars. In fairness to the Sheriff and to the Governor of the London jail, it should be added that they were not responsible for this, as their instructions came from higher authority." Bell then outlined the regulations for such lineups as they existed in London, England.

> No. 620
> METROPOLITAN POLICE
> Identification Parades
>
> Persons whom it is proposed to put up with others for identification are to be informed:—
>
> (1) That they will be placed among a number of people of similar age, height, general appearance and class of life as themselves.
> (2) That they may stand in any position they choose among them; that they may, after each witness has left, change their position if they so desire, and that they may object to any of the persons selected or the arrangements made.
> (3) That any such objection should be made to the officer conducting the identification.
> (4) That they may, if they so desire, have a solicitor or any friend present at the identification, but that it must be distinctly understood that such persons may not interfere by action or words with the proceeding.
> (5) That no intimation as to their identity will be given to the witnesses.

Bell continued: "It will be noted that, according to the regulations enforced in London, England, the prisoners are *to be informed* of all five of the above conditions. It was proclaimed by the prosecution subsequently that no fault was to be found with the identification test as made in London, Ontario. Scotland Yard would be grieved to hear of this. To think that in thousands of cases covering a long stretch of years the Yard has observed a series of wholly unnecessary precautions and put itself to such a great deal of trouble, all for nothing."

After the identifications, Meisner was retained in the Middlesex jail to await the convening of a grand jury to weigh whether he should go on trial. His family became increasingly worried about his fate. His brother, Richard — who spelled his surname "Misner," as did their mother, while David used the original spelling of the family surname — was a Detroit businessman in the chemical industry. Their mother and a sister, Mrs. Lantis, lived in Windsor. On December 8, 1935, a family friend, M.W. Howell of Goderich, Ontario, wrote Roebuck on their behalf:

"Grandma Misner is quite elderly, over ninety. She is a very sick woman. To all appearances she has not long to live. The fact that her son Dave is behind prison bars, falsely accused of a crime, is a continual heartbreak to her and it has doubtless contributed to shortening her days. Mrs. Lantis said her mother is getting little rest and it is expected that the lung will fill and all will be over. The family are hoping that the mother will live to see Dave at liberty. She questions one member of the family then another for any news regarding Dave being set free. The family say Dave was not in Canada and had not been for some years prior to the kidnapping."

The attorney general's department hired a handwriting expert, Arthur Black Farmer of Toronto, at a fee of $25 to compare Three-fingered Abe's printing to that of a "Frank Blaine" — conceivably a pseudonym for Meisner. On October 31, Farmer wrote the department, "Blaine does not appear to be the writer but might easily be a brother or close associate."

Meanwhile, Michael McCardell, the real mastermind of the kidnapping, was fuming that Labatt had not honoured his pledge, made on the day of his release, to pay the kidnappers $25,000. Just before Christmas, he decided the time had come to take action. From his viewpoint, a deal was a deal and Labatt should keep his word, even if given under duress. Then in Detroit, McCardell wrote two letters: one to Bannon, with instructions as to how to proceed, the other to Labatt, demanding the money.

Too cowardly to do so himself, he instructed Russell Knowles — also in Detroit and always willing to do McCardell's bidding — to take the letters across the border and hide them under the cushions in the lobby of the Prince Edward Hotel in Windsor. It did not matter to McCardell that he was placing Knowles at possible risk of being captured. Next, McCardell telephoned Alex Colvin, the Labatt company's agent in Windsor, and told him where the letters were and that Jack Bannon, as the intermediary, would join him at the hotel.

When Colvin and Bannon found the letters, they saw that one was for Bannon, the other for Labatt. Bannon's said that Labatt was being asked to pay him a first installment of $5,000 and that he should then travel to Montreal, check in at the Windsor Hotel and carry the money on a daily walk along Sherbrooke Street in downtown Montreal. On one of these walks he would be contacted to hand over the cash.

McCardell's letter to Labatt demanded that he give the $5,000 to Bannon and threatened dire repercussions if he alerted the police. "I believe you are going to listen to the police until you get killed," it said. "All the bodyguards in the world won't save you. When we get ready to act we will mow them down with you."

Although Bannon had been one of the plotters of Labatt's kidnapping, he had not actively participated in the snatch, so Labatt had no way of knowing his connection with the crime.

In an atmosphere of extreme tension, Bannon's confrontation with Labatt took place December 24, 1934, at his brother Hugh's apartment at 860 Waterloo Street in London. In addition to John, Hugh and Bannon, Alex Colvin and RCMP Sergeant Ted Weeks — the Mountie whom Bannon had led to Meisner through the Covington underworld — were in attendance. Because a number of people had already harassed him, claiming to be one of the kidnappers and attempting to collect the $25,000 payoff, Labatt fired a number of questions at Bannon to verify that he did indeed represent the real kidnappers. For his part, Bannon gave Labatt McCardell's letter.

A follow-up meeting, with the same participants, was held at Hugh's on January 3, 1935. Once again, Bannon demanded the $5,000. Outraged, Labatt refused to pay. "I won't do it," he firmly declared. "You'll have to kill me!" That defiant statement ended the brief, electrically charged discussion.

At the same time Labatt had picked out Pegram and Meisner from the mug shots, he had pointed to the picture of a third man, Kingdon "Piccolo Pete" Murray, identifying him as another of his kidnappers. ("Piccolo Pete" was a nickname derived from a popular tune of that era.) Murray lived in Covington, where David Meisner spent much of his time. Murray was arrested without resistance on January 14. Newspaper accounts of his background differed. The next day, the *Toronto Daily Star* reported that he had been in state prison in 1922 on a charge of obtaining money by false pretenses and had subsequently been arrested for operating an illicit still. The same day, *The Globe* reported that "Murray has a criminal record. He is wanted by American authorities in connection with his escape from the Kentucky State Reformatory in 1921. He had been sentenced there in 1920 on conviction of receiving stolen goods. Murray also has admitted a conviction in Columbus, Ohio, on grand larceny.... Files in the Cincinnati City Bureau of Identification said the arrested man was variously known as Kent P. Dayton, Albert Murray and Piccolo Pete."

Murray was thirty-five years old, blond, slight and boyish-looking. "He is mild and inoffensive to a degree; weak might be a better word to describe him," *Toronto Star* reporter Frederick Griffin wrote. Murray gave his occupation as a door-to-door rug salesman.

"What do you know of the Labatt kidnapping?" Griffin asked Murray.

"Absolutely nothing. I'm absolutely innocent. They've got the wrong man. You can bet on that."

"Did you know John Labatt?"

"Never heard of him. Never saw him. How could I when I was never in Ontario, never in Canada in my life?"

"Do you know David Meisner?"

"I may know him to see, but I never had anything to do with him."

Murray's wife told Griffin, "My husband was not out of Covington in August 1934." Griffin wrote about her, "She is a blonde, smart, fashionable, smooth-legged woman in a collegiate coon coat. Tears from her brown eyes ran down through her high makeup."

Murray's slim dapper looks bore a faint resemblance to Russell Knowles. Murray was arrested and extradited from Covington shortly before the grand jury in London was scheduled to meet about Meisner.

On January 29, 1935, in a closed hearing, the grand jury that met on the third floor of the Middlesex Courthouse in London indicted Meisner on evidence presented by only one witness: John Labatt. Having gone to the county jail and confirmed his identification, Labatt reiterated to the grand jury that Meisner had been the kidnappers' ringleader. Three charges were laid against Meisner: kidnapping, robbing while armed, and unlawfully imprisoning John Labatt. His trial was set to begin the very next day, Wednesday, January 30, the opening day of the winter session of the Middlesex Assizes Court, held in the county seat (London) on a quarterly basis for trials of serious offences punishable by death, life imprisonment or a long prison term.

More history was about to be made in the Labatt kidnapping. It would be the first kidnapping case in Canada to go to trial.

Chapter 5

THE CROWN AND THE DEFENCE

The double sensations of Labatt's abduction and Meisner's trial thrust London, Ontario, into the national and international spotlight as nothing had done before.

Located midway between Toronto and Windsor, London was established in 1792 by Colonel John Graves Simcoe, the first lieutenant governor of Upper Canada. He lobbied for it to be made the capital of Upper Canada, replacing Niagara-on-the-Lake, but instead that honour was conferred on his second choice: York, later known as Toronto. London's ties to Great Britain are evident not only in its name but in the names of streets such as Piccadilly, Oxford and Pall Mall, and of its river, which Simcoe had renamed the Thames, replacing the Iroquois name Askunessippi. Because of a program introduced in the nineteenth century to plant a thousand trees annually, it is known as the Forest City. It is also the home of the University of Western Ontario, founded in 1878.

Even as late as the mid 1930s, the city had a reputation for strict Victorian morality. For example, around the time of Labatt's kidnapping, a thirty-seven-year-old man was fined $7 plus costs after pleading guilty to acting in a disorderly manner in a city park — his crime had been swimming in the Thames River in his underwear.

Fittingly for a case with so many unconventional aspects, Meisner's trial took place in a courthouse far different from the traditional buildings constructed in the Greek or Roman architectural styles. In 1826, the legislature of Upper Canada designated London as the district town (county seat) for its area, requiring it to set aside four acres for the construction of a courthouse and jail. Opened in 1831 after three years of construction at a cost of £4,000, the courthouse, amazingly, resembled a Gothic castle. One hundred feet long, fifty wide and fifty high, it overlooked the Thames River near what became the downtown intersection of Dundas and Richmond streets. It had octagonal towers fourteen feet in diameter, crenellated turrets at each corner, Gothic-style windows ending in a point, and brick walls plastered over with cement to simulate the stuccoed appearance of the rough-hewn stone typical of Gothic castles.

Designed by John Ewart — who was also the architect of the original part of Toronto's Osgoode Hall, the headquarters of the Law Society of Upper Canada — the courthouse intentionally resembled Malahide Castle in Ireland, north of Dublin, the boyhood home of Colonel Thomas Talbot, a leading developer of London and one of the five commissioners appointed to oversee the erection of the courthouse.

Although Talbot lived in an unpretentious log cabin in London, he was a strong supporter of elitist aristocratic rule in Canada, in the style of the British feudal lords in their castles. It was thought that this was why he requested Ewart to design the courthouse as he did.

The design was quite controversial; Londoners either loved or hated it. Those in favour described it "as the finest building in the province" and "the glory of the townspeople." Detractors disparagingly called it "an ugly fortress."

Originally, there was a jail in the basement and dungeons further underground. The dungeons were only seven to ten feet square, and on occasion as many as twenty prisoners were crowded into the cramped space. The individual cells were also extremely small, with a tiny, diamond-shaped opening in the door through which food was passed to the prisoners. There was no plumbing then, and since no chamber pots were provided, the only place inmates could relieve themselves was in a corner of the cell. Indignation over the deplorable condition of the cells resulted in a separate jail being built just seven years after the first one. The new jail was connected to the courthouse on its west side.

In 1850, the district of London became Middlesex County and the courthouse was renamed the Middlesex County Court House. The legal community loathed it. It was too small for the increased volume of trials, and furthermore it had no water and no toilets. A judge angrily called it "a pest house. The jail with all its faults is better than the disease-producing courtroom."

After two decades of complaints, an expansion was undertaken which was completed in 1878. With the exception of the north, south and west walls, the courthouse was torn down and rebuilt, although Ewart's architectural concept was preserved. An eastward extension doubled the space so that the original eastern corner turrets became half-turrets in the centre of the north and south walls. Even so, over-crowding continued to be a problem. By 1967 it was so severe that the Middlesex Law Association felt it had no choice but to sue the city and county for better facilities. The result was a replacement — a fifteen-story courthouse that opened in 1974. The old courthouse was converted into the Middlesex County Building.

Meisner's trial was held in the second-floor main courtroom. The atmosphere was impressive and sombre. Moderate in size, the seats in the public spectators' gallery rose, as in an amphitheatre, in tiers. The prisoner's dock, a rectangular enclosure, was located in the centre. As at the famous Old Bailey — the central criminal court in London, England — the prisoner's dock was reached by a narrow stairway from the cells below that terminated right beside the dock.

Facing the prisoner's box there were long tables for the prosecuting and defence lawyers. There were two jury boxes — the one on the left was for grand juries of up to two dozen people whose responsibility it was to determine whether there was enough evidence for an indictment; the box on the right was for "petit" juries, commonly called "trial" juries. The door to the left of the judge's dais led to the judge's retiring room ("chambers") in the massive rectangular entrance tower of the building.

Jurors were selected from a panel assembled from the assessment rolls. Their names were pulled at random from a black box by the clerk of the court. During recesses and deliberations, they withdrew up a flight to a third-floor room that was furnished with only a plain table and chairs. It had a five-sided alcove that was formed by a corner tower of the building.

Although David Meisner and John Labatt were the key players in the drama about to unfold, the calibre of the judges and lawyers also attracted much attention.

In the judicial pecking order, judges at the higher levels of the court system — the Supreme Court and the Court of Appeal — are called Justices and greeted as Mr. (Madam) Justice as a courtesy. In court, based on British tradition, they are addressed as My Lord (My Lady) or Your Lordship (Your Ladyship), in contrast to Your Honour at lower courts and Your Worship for justices of the peace.

A now retired, greatly respected former treasurer (a title equivalent to president) of the Law Society of Upper Canada, who was later a justice of the Ontario Court of Appeal, graciously provided the author with comments, which he was making for the first time ever, about the lawyers and judges who participated in the Labatt trials, all of whom he knew. He also spoke about the legal system and issues and behind-the-scenes politics. He wished to remain anonymous.

Ontario Supreme Court Justice George Frank McFarland (known by his second name, Frank) presided over Meisner's trial. Born in June 1880, he was two months younger than Labatt. During the trial, McFarland was photographed as he jauntily strode along, swinging a cane. Inscribed canes were regarded as a symbol of judicial office and were a popular gift from members of the bar (the legal profession) to judges.

Two years before Meisner's trial, McFarland had been appointed a justice of the Supreme Court of Ontario. Previously, he had served as a deputy judge advocate (legal staff officer) in the Canadian Army at General Headquarters in Ottawa, been solicitor for the University of Toronto, and was in private practice handling litigation for the Toronto law firm of Davidson, Paterson and McFarland.

Interested in the arts, he supported the Hart House quartet at the University of Toronto. A noted dog lover and breeder, he frequently acted as a judge at prestigious dog shows held at Madison Square Garden in New York. His favourite breed was the bull terrier.

When he died in 1950, McFarland was highly praised by the then chief justice and a fellow justice. the *Globe and Mail* quoted the chief justice as describing McFarland as a "man who applied himself with great diligence to his judicial duties"; the other justice praised him as a "man with a most genial personality, a lovable friend with a broad and versatile experience." But the retired justice of the Ontario Court of Appeal who spoke with the author is of a different frame of mind. He says, "Justice McFarland was not well regarded by the bar. He had a reputation for being lazy with a short attention span. Among the judges of the trial division of his day he would have been regarded as towards the bottom of the list as far as ability was concerned."

McFarland made small quips from time to time during the Meisner trial, not standard for a judge. "Jokes are an alternative to hard work," the former justice says.

Although McFarland lived in Toronto, he was presiding over the Meisner trial in London because trial justices of the Supreme Court of Ontario moved around the province to preside at assizes sessions.

It was called "going on the circuit." In late May or early June, trial judges would draw up assignment lists, determining who would go where. The most senior judge got first choice, and usually picked Toronto. The circuits were divided by geographical district: for instance, North Bay, Sudbury, Timmins and Sault Ste. Marie were on the northern circuit, while London, which ranked fourth in size among Ontario cities, was on the southwest circuit. London was a popular choice with the travelling judges, which may or may not have been because it was one of only two cities in the province that had cocktail bars. Windsor was the other.

The prosecutors at Meisner's trial were Middlesex County Acting Attorney Norman Fisher Newton and Crown Counsel John Claude Manley German (known either by his initials, J.C.M., or as Jack). The term "counsel" applies to a lawyer engaged to give advice in a legal matter or to conduct a case in court.

Norman Newton was appointed Acting Crown Attorney for London and Middlesex County on August 13, 1934, the day before John Labatt was kidnapped. Newton was born in 1894 at Strathroy, Ontario, about thirty kilometres west of London. His father was a carpenter. As was common at the time, he began his law studies immediately after matriculating from high school, enrolling at Osgoode Hall in Toronto. In 1915, one year after the outbreak of World War I, Newton at the age of twenty-one enlisted in the Middlesex Light Infantry and served in France and England, where he married the daughter of an Oxford alderman.

On returning to Canada, he set up practice in Parkhill, a village near Strathroy. He served on the board of education and as a councillor, then was mayor of Parkhill from 1927 until 1928. In 1930 he moved to London and started a private practice; two years later, he was elected a city alderman. Seven weeks short of his forty-first birthday at the time of the Meisner trial, Newton was the youngest lawyer involved in the case. Newton, who was in the army reserve, had ramrod-straight military posture.

Although the Labatt trial occupied most of Newton's time as Acting Crown Attorney, he had a very busy caseload over and above. He also had to prepare four manslaughter trials, even though Justice McFarland had agreed to postpone all other criminal cases until the next assizes to clear the way for what was expected to be an extraordinarily long trial for Meisner. He had also just completed a case against a family of black-mailers made up of a father, his ex-wife, their son and daughter-in-law who operated in the London area.

Jack German, the youngest lawyer after Newton, had celebrated his forty-sixth birthday three days before the Meisner trial was due to begin. He had a blueblood background. He was the fourth generation of a United Empire Loyalist family descended from Jacob German, a bugler in the British Army during the American Revolution. Both his father and an uncle were prominent lawyers and parliamentarians. His father, William Manley German, practised law in Welland, Ontario. Over a forty-year period he defended almost every person charged with murder in the vicinity. In 1909 he represented one of the three men accused of attempting to dynamite the Welland Canal, which crosses the Niagara Peninsula about thirteen kilometres west of Niagara Falls and provides passage for cargo ships between lakes Ontario and Erie. It was one of the few cases William German lost; his client was sentenced to life imprisonment.

A Liberal, he represented Welland in the House of Commons from 1891 to 1892. In 1894 and 1896 he was elected to the Ontario Legislature for Welland. In a successful effort to break the American power-generating monopoly at Niagara Falls, he managed to kill a proposal to lease power rights for a period of ninety-nine years to U.S. interests. In 1900, he was returned to the House of Commons and continued there until 1925, becoming one of Liberal leader Sir Wilfrid Laurier's closest friends.

Jack's uncle, Angus Claude Macdonell, ten years younger than Jack's father, represented the riding of South Toronto in the House of Commons from 1904 to 1917, overlapping much of the period William served in it. Later he became a senator. In addition to law and politics, Macdonell was interested in journalism and sports. He was one of the founders of the *Catholic Review*, later merged with the *Catholic Register*, and was an associate editor of the *Canadian Law List*. He excelled in rowing and was a president of the Association of Amateur Oarsmen.

Although Jack German listed himself as an "insurance lawyer" in the *Canadian Who's Who*, he was in fact a generalist who was primarily a defence lawyer but who also represented the Crown from time to time. "He was somewhat tempestuous in nature and involved in controversy from time to time," says the retired Ontario appellate justice. "His judgment as a lawyer was suspect at times. He would ride out a particular course of action which wiser people would have realized was a losing approach."

German probably was appointed Crown counsel in the Labatt case for two reasons: volume of work and political connections. In the 1930s, most Crown attorney's offices were overloaded and understaffed, with two or three lawyers all told. Swamped with work, Middlesex Acting Crown Attorney Norman Newton likely appealed to the Ontario attorney general's office for assistance. "He probably didn't want someone who would come in and become the leader, or he would have asked for somebody better than German to be appointed," the retired justice comments.

At that time, the Liberal party was in power both in Ottawa, under Prime Minister William Lyon Mackenzie King, and in Ontario under Premier Mitchell Hepburn. German had connections at each level both through his forbears and his own efforts. He was on the executive committees of the federal and Ontario Liberal parties and was chairman of the speakers' committee for both.

Because of these connections, it can safely be surmised that his appointment to the Labatt case emanated from the attorney general's office in Toronto and not from a request of Norman Newton. Attorney General Arthur Roebuck was combative and would not look kindly upon a defeat in the Meisner case. In theory, a Crown counsel is not out to win or lose, but rather to fairly present all evidence pro or con and leave it up to the jury or judge to decide the case. As a result of this impartiality, the perfect Crown counsel does not feel glad or sorry after a verdict.

In reality, however, Crown counsel are human beings, and their characteristics vary from person to person. Some are respected by the bar almost to the point of being loved. Others are regarded as difficult. Some come to be regarded as overzealous in trying to secure a conviction.

The Labatt case was very high-profile, not because it involved intricate legal technicalities that would have an impact on the future of Canadian law, but because it was of great interest to the public, and Roebuck wanted the Crown to win because a victory would radiate glory on the government. Therefore, he selected German as the Crown counsel because he had a talent for deft sarcasm and fireworks. German may not have been the leader in preparing the case, but as chief counsel he did much of the questioning and delivered the Crown's closing statement.

Over at the Crown attorney's table, along with Newton and German, were John Labatt's uncle, Major General Mewburn, in his capacity as a lawyer, as well as Labatt's lawyer and friend Richard Green Ivey, who had driven him and Hugh back to London after his release by the kidnappers. Besides being a foremost London attorney, Ivey was a power in the business community as a part owner of the Northern Life Assurance Company. He was one year younger than Labatt.

Of all the lawyers in the four trials arising from Labatt's kidnapping, Charles William Bell, who represented Meisner for only a token fee, was the most renowned in reputation and the most unique in background. Called "Charlie" by his friends, Bell was regarded in Canadian legal circles as the nation's foremost criminal defence lawyer of the era.

Brilliance in law was just one of his talents. He was also a popular politician who many thought would make a fine prime minister and a playwright whose farces were performed on Broadway and on tour. His success on Broadway was a tribute to his skill; very few plays make it to this pinnacle of the theatre world, and Canadian-authored ones would have been unlikelier still in those days to succeed.

At the time of Meisner's trial, Bell was two months short of fifty-nine. After graduating from Osgoode Hall in Toronto, he joined Bell &

Pringle, a Hamilton law firm established by his father, William. Until Charlie became a member, Bell & Pringle was a sedate outfit specializing in corporate law. Charlie, however, decided he wanted to practise criminal law. Not long after he settled into the family firm, he defied his staid father by defending a man in a criminal case. This horrified the elder Bell, who, like many of his contemporaries, regarded criminal law as unworthy of a dignified law firm. But Charlie persisted.

His fee on the case amounted to only seventy-five cents. "The case was turned over to me by a man who didn't want to be bothered," he told the *Star Weekly* in a November 1932 interview. "I took it in fear and trembling." He lost, seemingly an unpromising beginning.

But it turned out to be a misleading omen; from then on, Charlie Bell was a success. His clever conduct of the defence attracted the admiration of lawyers, judges and reporters. "Charlie came into his father's conservative quiet office with a bang. He was the most exciting happening in many years," a Hamilton journalist fondly wrote of this period. Reporters flocked to cases Bell was handling because they knew he could be counted on to give them some startling turn that would yield a good story.

Bell usually gave jocular reasons as to why he had broken with family tradition to venture into criminal law. It was in his genes. "My grandfather was a wild Irishman from the Protestant North of Ulster." He "wanted money and criminal law was a convenient way of making it." He did live comfortably, owning a handsome house in Hamilton and a summer home on a beach nearby. But much of his income came from royalties on his plays. His explanation that he was in criminal law for the money was met with skepticism because Bell charged impoverished clients a minuscule amount — just enough for a small retainer. In a serious moment, Bell conceded his real motive was neither money nor rebelliousness, but rather humanity. "I would far rather fight for a hide than for money," he said. "If you believe a man ought to have a defence, don't stop to haggle about money."

The retired justice says of Bell: "He was a well-known figure and very highly regarded in legal circles as an excellent trial counsel. To be an excellent trial counsel, a lawyer must be personable, able to cross-examine, and able to manoeuvre when the weight of the evidence shifts, as it frequently does at trials. Unexpected things happen all the time, and a good trial counsel rolls with the punches." Certainly, the unexpected arose many times in Meisner's 1935 trial.

By 1935, Bell had defended twenty-one people charged with murder, and had obtained acquittals for all of them. Little wonder that the profile of him in the *Star Weekly* was called "The Man Who Gets All of Them Off" and that he titled his legal memoir, published in 1935, the year of Meisner's trial, *Who Said Murder?*

"How do you plan your campaign when defending a murderer?" a *Saturday Night* magazine reporter asked Bell for a November 1935 article.

"A murderer?" Bell replied in a surprised tone.

"Yes, a murderer."

"But I have never defended a murderer," Bell answered gravely, demonstrating his legal agility.

"I mean a person charged with murder," the reporter apologized.

With neither the senior Bell nor Pringle at the firm any longer, its name had been changed to Bell and Yeates; Ralph Howard Yeates was Charlie's partner. Bell and Yeates had a mutual admiration society. "Any little success I've had has been due to the most bloodthirsty man I've ever been associated with, Ralph Harwood Yeates," Bell affectionately told the *Star Weekly*. "Regard him. He prepares all the cases and believe me, he prepares them well."

"Don't you believe him," said Mr. Yeates, positively blushing. "He wins because he is the best criminal defence man in Canada."

"By gorry," said Mr. Bell, now blushing in turn and becoming Irish in his confusion. "He's pulling your leg."

Bell took cases throughout Ontario as well as in his hometown of Hamilton, but only occasionally in Toronto, which had many fine criminal lawyers of its own. Between the 1930s and the 1960s, all law firms outside Toronto had to have a registered agent in the city on whom documents could be served in their stead. Bell and Yeates's agency was the prominent Toronto law firm of Mason, Foulds, Davidson, Carter and Kellock (now WeirFoulds), which had a large agency practice.

Bell was so famous as a defence lawyer that it was little known that he occasionally acted as Crown prosecutor in capital murder cases. He was as successful in those cases as he was as defence counsel, but he avoided those assignments, preferring to represent the underdog. "I don't like the Crown side and I might say I don't take it for money for there is little money in it," he told the *Star Weekly*. Nor did Bell relish it when an accused whom he had successfully prosecuted was sentenced to death. "It upsets me terribly but I figure I am only an instrument of the law, like the judge and the people whose duty it is to put the sentence into effect."

Despite his success, Bell did not flaunt it in his office in the Sun Life Building in Hamilton. A master of stagecraft, he decorated his office simply, aiming not to overwhelm his clients, many of whom were poor. Only a handful of pictures hung on his walls: a print of the Fathers of Confederation, an engraving of Sir John A. Macdonald and a court scene from Charles Dickens' *The Pickwick Papers*.

There also was a framed cluster of signatures, a memento of the first acquittal Bell had obtained in a murder case. As the *Star Weekly* recounted the tale:

> He walked over to the framed cluster of signatures. "Let's see if it's dated," he said. "No, it isn't, but that was my first murder case. Jimmy Bruce was charged with causing the death of Rosie Zeipe, in Hamilton. He always protested his innocence and I believed him. This was a poison case. It was alleged by the Crown that he had bought strychnine and put it in chocolates to poison his wife who was in the hospital. Rose had eaten them by mistake, it was claimed, and died. The Crown had to prove possession of poison.
>
> "Here you are," he said, pointing to the framed signatures. "This was one from the poison book. Then there are these other signatures. The Crown's theory was that Jimmy had started to write 'Bru—,' that is, 'Bruce,' and had then changed it to 'Bruwn,' an attempt at 'Brown.' That was the theory. He always protested his innocence and I always believed him."
>
> "Did you get him off by proving it was not his signature?"

"Partly. That and other things. I still insist the woman did not die of poison. I insisted then and still think she died of tetanus."

"Was that what struck the jury?"

"We did not know, as we never know, what decided the jury. We were only interested in the verdict."

Also hanging on the wall was a sardonic quotation from Chaucer's *The Canterbury Tales* about the law: "For half so boldely there can be no man swere and lyen as a woman can."

"Is that true?" the *Star Weekly* reporter asked Bell.

"There is nothing half so true," Bell replied. "Face a woman in the witness box with something that should cause her to revise her testimony and she will persist, 'It's as I said.' Shake a man's testimony and he will admit, at least, that he might have been mistaken."

"Why?"

"Ask God to explain that."

Bell was not alone in his opinion. It was shared by Joseph Sedgwick, another distinguished lawyer, who was the Crown counsel in the third trial related to the Labatt kidnapping and associate Crown counsel in the final trial, the fourth in the case.

Bell did not believe in intimidating witnesses unless absolutely necessary. "I never proceed on the basis that I may get a witness to break down and say he is lying," he told the *Star Weekly*. "I don't browbeat and hammer unless I feel a witness is an infernal liar. I try to behave with common decency and common sense."

His playwriting sharpened his trial skills. "One of the essential rules in playwriting was to watch the play on the opening night and then the audience for the next three nights. From their expressions, I was able to learn what situations and words caused reactions, and the nature of each, and I have applied that knowledge in court," he explained to the *Star Weekly*. "The theatre has no time for extraneous matter. One must go right to the heart of things. I have kept that rule in court."

Bell's experience in analyzing theatregoers' facial expressions helped him to quickly size up a witness and adjust his questioning accordingly. In addition, it provided a useful background for the preparation of eloquent, persuasive addresses that would have a favourable impact on a jury. He knew how to make every word count, as well as how to win over antagonistic members of an audience, and therefore how to make jurors listen and get them to share his belief that the accused person he was defending should be acquitted.

"This, it seems to me, is the great secret of Mr. Bell's success at the bar," concluded R.E. Knowles Jr. in his November 1935 *Saturday Night* profile. "He combines an intellect that is penetrating, analytical and facile with a temperament and intuition that makes a great dramatist or impresario. He is able, therefore, to grasp at once any flaws in his opponent's case; and — more important still — he is able to utilize them with the most telling effect. Without the judge or jury being conscious of it, he can bring the artifices of histrionics to his aid."

Of his three careers, playwriting was Bell's favourite. "I'd rather write than anything else," he told a reporter from the *Canadian Magazine* in October 1927. In 1904, when he was just twenty-eight, Bell's first play, *Prince of Zanzibar*, was produced. It had an unusual history. After failing for two years to convince anyone on the Canadian or American theatre scenes to look at it, Bell sent it to literary agents in England who had it translated into German and sold it for performance in Germany. It flopped, but Bell persevered. "There are three requisites for success in authorship: the first is courage, the second is courage, and the third is courage," he later recalled when he had had many successes.

His second play, *The Heart of a Charlatan*, a comedy about patent medicine fraud artists, was staged by a stock company at the Old Savoy Theatre in England and did sufficiently well for Bell to use it as a springboard to Broadway. Over the years he wrote — and frequently directed — many successful farces: *The Dislocated Honeymoon*; *Her First Divorce*; *Parlour, Bedroom and Bath*; *Elsie*; *Thy Neighbour's Wife*; *Paradise Alley*; and *When Rogues Fall Out*. *The Dislocated Honeymoon* is historically significant because of its connection with the famous songwriting team of George and Ira Gershwin. In 1921, the title was changed to *A Dangerous Maid*, with music and lyrics by the Gershwins, then in their early twenties. At that time, Ira wrote under the pen name "Arthur Francis," based on the first names of their brother Arthur and sister Frances.

It was the first time the brothers had teamed up to write a full musical score. Unfortunately, the show died en route to Broadway, but one of the songs, "Boy Wanted," became a standard.

For Bell, who rose at 2:00 a.m. to write his plays so that they would not interfere with his legal work, the comedies provided a form of rest and relaxation because he was not interested in the conventional pastimes of golf and bridge. But the plays must also have strained his health, because on more than one occasion while directing rehearsals in New York, an urgent call from Hamilton would request him to return at once to defend a client. Racing to and fro by jet was not an option in the 1930s; a lengthy train trip was the only way to make the journey. Bell would spend the time in transit working on a play or a court case.

Bell's first big success on Broadway came in 1913 with *Her First Divorce*, in which husband and wife Ethel and Harry Wilmot are lawyers. When Harry, a famous corporate lawyer, declines to represent a family friend in divorce court against her drunken husband, Ethel — a general practice lawyer — takes on the case. Angered at Harry, Ethel flounces out of their house and moves in with the would-be divorcée. Much of the humour in the play revolves around Ethel's attempts to examine a witness with a bad memory and her efforts to reverse the testimony. Considering that it was produced in 1913, *Her First Divorce* was considerably ahead of its time, both in terms of its subject matter and in having the heroine be a lawyer. It starred Laura Hope Crews, one of Broadway's most popular leading ladies.

The New York *Herald Tribune* gave an enthusiastic review: "Here is one of the best things of a long theatrical season, coming with ripples of laughter, provoked by legitimate comedy, clever lines and ingeniously planned situations, not by the broader methods of barely distinguished farce."

By contrast, the *New York Times* was lukewarm. "An amiable farce … a considerable amount of brightly written dialogue with occasional laughter-provoking situations but the main idea wears thin by the middle of the second act," it commented.

Thereafter, Bell avoided writing plays about the law because "fact murders imagination and the people who write the best crook plays are often those who never knew a crook."

Bell's most successful play was *Parlor, Bedroom and Bath*, which opened Christmas Eve, 1917. While most of his plays ran six to eight weeks, *Parlor* lasted eight months on Broadway. The plot concerns the humorous dilemma of Reginald Irving. His adoring wife Angelica loves him primarily because she believes he has a lurid past and an even worse present. Reggie, however, actually has an unsullied past and is utterly faithful — "all the passion of a clam," as Bell put it. But because he wants to hold onto his wife, he believes he must live up to the unsavoury reputation she has projected upon him. Thus, he resorts to writing love letters to himself, signing them "Tootles." Farcical complications heap up, culminating in Reggie registering three times in one night at the same hotel — with three different women — to make his wife believe he is the ultimate scoundrel. Then he scurries between the three rooms trying to keep each woman from catching onto the presence of the other two. A further complication is that, unbeknownst to him, one of the women is a gossip columnist. Everything is straightened out in time for the final curtain, and Reggie and Angelica live happily ever after.

The *New York Times* gave a rave review. "While the humour is extremely broad at times and the plot more than a little suggestive, the play has some situations that are excruciatingly funny," its drama critic wrote. "The theatre rocked with laughter."

Bell's third career — politics — was not of his own seeking. In 1924, three days before its nomination meeting for the upcoming general election, the Conservative party in the riding of Hamilton West still had no candidate. Someone was inspired to ask Bell to run. On election night, he won by twelve thousand votes and was serving in Parliament at the time of Meisner's trial. But he had little taste for politics. "It's the dumbest of my three jobs," he frequently said.

It is rare for the press to wholeheartedly praise someone, but Bell was one of the few to receive constant accolades. For example, *Saturday Night* wrote in its November 1935 story:

> One might suspect that a long career at the criminal bar, where a lawyer is continually being reminded of the vicious, the depraved and the sordid, would make him a cynic or a misanthrope. It has not done this to Charlie Bell for more so than most men, he loves life and seems to enjoy every minute of it with zest. His legal work has

brought him into contact with unexpected and amazing instances of unselfishness and integrity that have
confirmed his faith in human nature and the funda-
mental goodness of things.

The *Canadian Magazine* was equally effusive. In its October 1927
article, *Is Versatility an Asset?*, it asked the rhetorical question, "Can a man
be a brilliant lawyer, a playwright, and a political figure at one and the
same time?" Its conclusion: absolutely.

He is popular but it is not because he follows popular
fetishes. He knows that it is a fine thing to be yourself,
and he goes on his happy way urbanely, humorously,
brilliantly, but withal doggedly and courageously being
himself, a man who has once again proved that versatility
may be, not a liability, but a great asset, and that a well
rounded personality when it is the flowering of fine
character, fine mind and fine gifts is more to be desired
than any of those achievements which are merely the
milestones marking its path through life.

Bell was grey-haired with a ruddy complexion and a rugged frame.
His most notable facial features were keenly observant dark eyes and a
deep cleft chin. Although somewhat theatrical in court — not an unusual
trait for criminal defence lawyers — offstage he was a mixture of quiet
dignity, affability and good humour.

David Meisner was very lucky to be represented by this foremost
criminal lawyer of the era, a man who had won an astounding number
of murder cases. How would Meisner, a "nobody," have gained access to
the famous Charlie Bell? He was probably introduced by the Detroit
lawyer who accompanied him when he surrendered so confidently to
the police there. When the lawyer realized that Meisner had fallen into
deep trouble, he would have referred him to a big-time Canadian
criminal defence lawyer and Bell was the most "big-time" in Canada.
While kidnapping is not as grave an offence as murder, it is a very serious
charge, especially when the victim is wealthy, well known and respected.

For his part, why would Bell have taken on such a seemingly hopeless task? For the same reason that a lot of trial lawyers take on difficult cases: it sounded interesting and was a challenge. "The challenge of litigation is one of the things that drives the best lawyers all the time. I once remarked that, 'Litigation is not a profession but a disease that, once developed, is never lost.' It was a facetious comment, but there is an underlying truth to it," the retired Ontario Court of Appeal justice says.

Bell definitely had the "disease." As he put it: "Criminal law calls for fast headwork. That lends excitement to many a case. A new situation, an uncounted factor, and unforeseen evidence may bob up like a flash of lights."

Based on his years of experience, Bell believed intuitively in Meisner's innocence. He agreed to defend him virtually for free. Meisner could only afford to pay $400. Of that amount, $200 was spent on investigative expenses and for Bell's partner, Ralph Howard Yeates, to travel to the United States in search of evidence to support Meisner's case. Bell's young London-based associate for the trial, Howard Cluff, was paid a retainer of $75. That left Bell with just $125. "You might say, when the man sent for me in his extremity, I took the case without any hope of remuneration," he said during the trial. "I had one reason. I remembered the barrister's oath I had taken thirty-five years ago as a youngster in Osgoode Hall in Toronto. I stood up and took that oath, which says, 'You shall refuse no just cause.' And I have faithfully kept that oath all through the intervening years."

Chapter 6
THE WRONG MAN

As Meisner's trial date approached, both Crown Attorney Norman Newton and defence counsel Charles W. Bell had been the targets of crank calls and letters containing dire predictions of what would happen should the trial proceed. Some of the cranks tried to intimidate scheduled Crown witnesses; others made threats against Bell for defending Meisner. He tossed the letters and telephone messages in the wastebasket. "I have always believed that the place to try a case is in the courtroom," he remarked.

The newspapers had warned that few spectators would be allowed into the courtroom; thus, there were no crowds lined up for seats in the gallery on Wednesday, January 30, the first day of the trial. On the other hand, the press's interest in covering the trial, the first of its kind in Canadian history, was so intense that a room in the courthouse was set aside to accommodate twenty reporters and was fitted up with telegraphic equipment for them to transmit their stories. Just before 10:00 a.m., Meisner entered the prisoner's dock. Suffering from a severe throat infection, he looked frail and ill. The cataract in his left eye shone like a beacon.

The first day was devoted to choosing a jury and the opening statements of both sides. The testimony did not begin until the second day. The Crown began with its star witness, John Labatt. As Labatt made his way to the witness stand, he limped and used his cane because of the boyhood injury to his left leg. He had a bad cold and was on the verge of laryngitis. Crown Counsel John German asked Justice McFarland to allow Labatt to sit during his testimony because "he has a lame leg and is suffering from a cold." McFarland assented and a chair was put in the witness stand for Labatt. During the short recesses throughout his day-long testimony, he was protected by three burly private bodyguards, even though he did not leave the courthouse but only went to a room elsewhere in the building. One bodyguard kept in front of him, one followed and one was at observation points. According to the *London Free Press*, Labatt was "taking no chances on any gun play," but it did not say whether he had received any threats.

His face revealing little of what he was thinking, Labatt detailed his kidnapping and captivity. He recounted that the kidnappers had told him they had intended for several years to kidnap him. He described how they threatened to tie a stone to his feet, "rip me up and throw me in the lake." He said they had referred to the $25,000 he had agreed to pay for his release as "your debt."

"I didn't ask what they would do to me if I didn't agree," Labatt testified. "I thought I had better agree to anything. He tried to instill as much fear in me as possible. I didn't feel very comfortable, so I agreed."

Throughout his testimony, Labatt implicated Meisner: "Meisner told me the two cars — mine and theirs — were going to pass"; "Meisner told me the third man was taking my car to London"; "Meisner told me of the $150,000 ransom to be demanded"; "Next morning, Meisner asked me if I had slept all right." Meisner watched intently, sometimes with a wry smile.

Bell began his cross-examination by asking Labatt his age.

"I am fifty-four."

"Is your brother Hugh younger or older?"

"He is younger."

"How long did it take you to get from St. Clair Avenue to the Royal York Hotel after you had been released?"

"About ten minutes."

Bell then asked Labatt about his claim that he was able to see through a slit in the court plaster covering his eyes.

"I take it that, coming back, you had no vision until you were left on the Toronto sidewalk?"

"Not of anything I could identify again. Only the silhouette of heads."

"When you took off the pieces of adhesive material, did you keep them?"

"I put them in my pocket."

"Where are they now?"

"I don't know."

"They would have been helpful if preserved. You didn't give them to your brother Hugh?"

"I don't think so."

Bell then turned to the issue of the ransom. "You didn't think it difficult for United States kidnappers to come to Canada and possess themselves of $150,000 in Canadian bills and be able to dispose of them?"

"Yes, I did."

"I suggest to you that under any circumstances it would be an impossible proposition. The money would be useless to them. They couldn't handle it in the States."

"No," Labatt replied.

There was a noticeable startled reaction in the courtroom. Labatt then added, "I think they could, come to think of it. They need not dispose of it at once."

The day ended tensely as Bell swung to Labatt's identification of Meisner as one of his kidnappers.

"Did you see Meisner clearly?"

"I'll never forget that face as long as I live."

"Why not?"

"Would you?" At this retort, the spectators began to laugh.

"Order, order!" demanded McFarland. "We won't have this turned into a burlesque."

"With a revolver staring at you, do you mean to say you were looking at Meisner's face?" Bell continued.

"Yes, I was."

"Well, then, you are the only person that ever would."

At this dramatic point, McFarland adjourned court until 10:00 a.m. the following day.

When the session of Friday, February 1 opened, Labatt returned to the witness stand for further cross-examination by Bell. As the *London Free Press* put it, "During the night, Mr. Bell had thought up a lot of new questions to fire at the president of the Labatt brewery."

Bell began by returning to the tape Labatt said had been stuck over his eyes. Holding several rolls of tape to demonstrate the difference, he asked whether the tape had been made of narrow pink court plaster that allowed Labatt some movement of his eyes and to see through a slit in the strips, or of wide, sticky adhesive tape that would have kept him in total darkness.

"It was court plaster that stuck only in spots to my eyelids and enabled me to see out of one eye," Labatt insisted.

"Could you move your eyelids?" Justice McFarland interjected.

"Oh, yes. I took good care to keep moving them so it wouldn't stick."

"There seems to have been no end to the kindness of your kidnappers," Bell remarked sarcastically. "They even used court plaster so you could wriggle your eyelids."

"I don't think we need to go into this at very great length," the judge declared, once more coming to Labatt's aid.

Next, Bell questioned Labatt about his claim that he could see through a slit in the tape covering his eyes.

"There was a perceptible slit?"

"Yes."

"But a person sitting beside you wouldn't observe it?

"Yes."

"Why?"

"Because I was wearing goggles."

"In order to put the goggles to your eyes, whoever did that had to come close and look at what he was doing."

"I didn't think so. There was no close inspection."

Bell walked up to Labatt, stood before him and asked, "Supposing he were as close as this to put on glasses; can you suggest how he might have missed that aperture?"

"If he had a blind eye?"

"Oh, if he had a blind eye?"

"I said if he did."

"You gave evidence for the extradition hearing and in the police court and you did not mention his blind eye."

"I didn't see it."

"How many times have you gone over this story?"

"What story?"

"The story of what happened."

"Once at the extradition, once at the preliminary, and now again."

"Oh. And the police knew nothing about it?"

"I told the police."

"You said that Meisner allowed you to bathe your own eyes on Wednesday, August 15, the second day at the cottage. Was the covering taken off?"

"Yes."

"You and he were alone?"

"Yes."

"Did you look at him?"

"No. The basin was in front of me and I was bending down over it. I could see his trousers. I felt I didn't have the privilege of looking at him. He might resent it."

"It was a matter of courtesy and honourable feeling?"

"Yes."

"That is, you might have been able to look at him and subsequently identify him?"

"Yes."

Bell then moved on to Labatt's insistence that Meisner was his chief guard and the gang's ringleader, reading from Labatt's description in his affidavit.

"'The first man, we'll call him Number 1. He became my guard. He was five feet, nine or ten inches, medium build, athletic type, 175 pounds, thirty-eight to forty years of age, dark complexion, hair black, thin face. His talk was mild, nothing about his voice to distinguish it from a Canadian's.' Is that the identification you made of David Meisner?"

"Yes, sir."

Bell turned toward where Meisner sat in the prisoner's dock. "Stand up," he beckoned to him. "Let's see your 175 pounds, your athletic build."

Meisner rose to his feet. The discrepancy between him and Labatt's description of "Number 1" was obvious. He was more than ten years older (fifty-five), slim (118 pounds), short and frail rather than athletic in

build. The Toronto *Evening Telegram* described the excitement of the
moment this way:

> "There, I want you to see your 175-pound athletically
> built man," said Mr. Bell, turning to Labatt. The witness
> admitted he had made a very bad guess.
>
> The incident was over in a minute, but had a sudden
> effect on the jury, court and audience. Even the lady
> who surreptitiously knitted must have dropped a stitch.
>
> "It must have been a shock to you when you saw in
> the newspaper portraits the marked infirmity in the man's
> eye which is not in the photograph?" remarked Bell.
>
> "No, it wasn't. I have said I did not see it myself."
>
> "Do you say you didn't see it when you were face to
> face with the man?" asked his Lordship.
>
> "I did not see it."

The *Telegram* wound up its story by commenting, "And thus again
was Bell's score on behalf of his client repeated."

Next, Bell read Labatt's affidavit description of kidnapper Number
2 — "a man over 200 pounds."

"Could that by any stretch of the imagination apply to the prisoner?"
Labatt: "No."

Pointing out that Labatt had at first told police that he was unable to
describe kidnapper Number 3, then said he could but that the description did not match Meisner, Bell asked, "Have you changed your mind
about Meisner's 175 pounds?"

"Yes, I made a bad guess there."

Bell recapitulated this exchange in the chapter "Ditching David
Meisner" in his book *Who Said Murder?*, published some months after
Meisner's trial. "And so he made a bad guess. It might have been more
nearly excusable if he hadn't wanted to say there were several occasions
when he saw Meisner through the slit. But the more he claimed to have
seen of Meisner, the less justifiable the attempted identification became.
And the more evident it was that if it really was Meisner he saw, his
failure to see the growth on the blind eye was absolutely inexplicable."

Neither German nor Bell referred to an ailment that Labatt had told police "Meisner" suffered from. C.R. Magone, a solicitor in the attorney general's office, had written the Ontario Provincial Police about it on October 15, 1934. "Labatt said, 'Meisner told him that every morning he coughed up phlegm and until he did so he felt rotten.' This apparently is an indication of catarrh of the stomach, and I think it might be advisable if you made some inquiries at the gaol to ascertain if the prisoner was suffering from this ailment." Apparently, this was not in Labatt's affidavit. If it had been, it could have been raised at the trial that the real Meisner did not have these symptoms, a fact that might have helped his case.

The February 1 evening edition of the *London Free Press* summed up Labatt's testimony this way in its Page 1 story:

LABATT ADMITS HE DID NOT SEE CONSPICUOUS FEATURE AND DEFENCE SCORES POINT

Wealthy Brewer States Accused "Created Picture in My Mind I'll Never Forget" but Admits He Missed Essential Feature Characteristic in Appearance of Kentucky Gambler

IN OTHER POINTS EXECUTIVE'S EVIDENCE STANDS UP UNDER RELENTLESS GRILLING BY BELL

Sticks to Story, He Could See out of One Eye Sufficiently Well to Be Able to Identify Accused Later; Moved Eyelids so as to Preserve Sight Though Bound with Court Plaster

David Meisner's case may rest on a "blind eye."

Despite the fact that Meisner has a cataract in his left eye which seems to be his outstanding feature, John S. Labatt admitted under cross-examination today that he "didn't see it."

John Labatt said he would never forget the face of the leader of the kidnap trio who held him for three days in a Muskoka cottage while unsuccessful attempts were made to collect $150,000 ransom. He told the court yesterday that man was David Meisner. "He created a picture on my mind I'll never forget," the 54-year-old brewer told a hushed courtroom.

Yet today John Labatt admitted he didn't see Meisner's blind eye.

The admission was the greatest victory the defence has secured since the opening of the trial.

In other points, John Labatt's evidence stood up well under the relentless pounding of Defence Counsel Charles Bell. He refused to let the wily lawyer trap him in telling his story.

When the trial resumed on Monday, February 4, Bell waived the opportunity to continue his cross-examination of Labatt because of Labatt's laryngitis. Labatt insisted he was all right, but Bell stuck to his decision. In a brief re-examination, Crown Counsel John German moved to undo the damage Bell had done to the prosecution's case on Friday by casting doubt that Meisner was the right man.

Handing Labatt a picture, he asked, "Do you recognize that as Meisner's photograph?"

"I do."

Labatt was then allowed to leave the witness stand, and his brother Hugh was called. German asked Hugh to describe the events of the day of his brother's kidnapping from his own perspective: John's failure to arrive at the 10:30 a.m. appointment with their uncle, Major General Mewburn; the telephone call at lunchtime informing him that John had been kidnapped; his hasty drive to Toronto and registration, as instructed, at the Royal York Hotel.

German then asked Hugh to recount telephone calls he had received at the hotel.

"There was a phone call after lunch August 15," Hugh started to answer when Bell rose to protest the conversation being entered as evidence. "It would be prejudicial to the defence because there was no way of verifying who the caller was beyond who he said he was," Bell argued.

Again and again, German tried to ask further questions about the call, as well as about another at 2:45 p.m. the same day, and again and again Bell rose to object. At last, Justice McFarland intervened.

"Do you know who was calling?" he asked Hugh. "Did you recognize his voice.?"

"No."

"Did he say who he was?"

"Yes."

"You had no way of identifying him beyond what he said.?"

"No."

"I'm sorry, Mr. German, but the rules of evidence are quite clear," McFarland said.

As a result, Hugh's time on the witness stand was short.

Knowing that the Crown was about to call people who would say they were eyewitnesses who saw Meisner in London or Muskoka prior to the kidnapping or at the Muskoka cottage during Labatt's captivity, Bell tried to draw attention to the fact that the Crown had announced before the trial that it would produce thirty or forty people to identify Meisner as a participant, but in the indictment against him had listed only twelve. Realizing how damaging this shortfall could be to the Crown's case, Newton moved hastily to forestall Bell. He asked Justice McFarland to instruct the jury to leave the courtroom, then explained that the extra people were intended to identify alleged blackmailers who had been in the same lineup as Meisner. He asked that Bell therefore not be allowed to refer to the seeming discrepancy in the number of witnesses. McFarland ruled in his favour.

While Bell had his frustration, unbeknownst to him, so did Newton. According to a February 2 memorandum from the acting chief inspector of the OPP to the attorney general, Newton and the provincial police suspected that Meisner had been involved in a 1928 kidnapping, but Newton could not say anything about it during the Labatt trial because there was no corroboration. The memo said:

The following is the story, as I have been able to gather it, of the Burns Kidnapping Case. This matter was never reported to the Police. There had never been an investigation into the matter and only by degree had the story leaked out. Burns is a Racketeer and I believe he is now serving a term in jail.

In the year 1928, two men walked into Loew's Theatre in London and invited Burns to come outside. This he did and he was taken at once to his apartment, where he was told he would have to produce $35,000. This amount of money, I am led to believe, was actually paid over to three men. The three men who are alleged to have participated in this kidnapping were the present man on trial, David Meisner, Albert Pegrim [sic], for whom we have a warrant now in connection with the kidnapping of Labatt, and Jack Bannon of Windsor being the third man and the man who drove the car. As there had been no investigation into the matter, the facts were never published in the press.

It is the opinion now of Mr. Newton that if he had the evidence of Mr. Manning, the Bank Manager who was asked at the time of the Burns Kidnapping to secure for him the $35,000 and bring it to his apartment, that he could place David Misner [sic] on trial for the Kidnapping of Burns, but unfortunately Mr. Manning dropped dead a few months ago and the only witness to the case would be Burns himself.

The parade of people who claimed to be eyewitnesses began with William Brent of Adelaide Village, a small community near London. He testified that he had seen Meisner in picnic grounds at Brights Grove, near Labatt's summer home, nineteen days before the kidnapping in the company of two other men in a car with American licence plates.

"Do you recognize anyone who was in it?" German inquired.

"That man over there," Brent responded, pointing at Meisner.

He stood by his story, even when Bell pounded home the point that he had only identified Meisner as the person he saw after seeing Meisner's picture in the newspapers.

John Graham, a London bill collector, maintained that he had seen Meisner "nervously" pacing Talbot Street near the Labatt brewery nine days before the kidnapping.

"I saw him walking up and down about eleven o'clock in the morning in a rather sharp manner," Graham said. "He was on the east side of Talbot Street, which faces the door of the brewery."

"Have you seen him since?" Crown Attorney Norman Newton asked.

"Yes."

"Where?"

"Once, in the jail. I picked him out of a lineup of fourteen or fifteen men."

"Do you see him now?"

"I do."

"Where?"

"The man in the prisoner's box looking at me right now."

The questioning was then turned over to Bell, who implied, as he had with Brent, that Graham's identification had been influenced by seeing Meisner's picture in the newspapers.

"How many pictures of him had you seen?"

"Just one."

Next, Mrs. Mary Lythe of Toronto was called to the stand. It had been touch and go as to whether the 68-year-old woman, who had once worked at St. James's Palace in London, England, for King George V and his family and now lived on a $15-a-week pension, would be well enough to testify. She had been scheduled to have a major operation at the time of the trial, but felt it was her duty to postpone it in order to testify. She testified that, five days before the kidnapping, two men — one of whom she said was Meisner — had negotiated with her to rent a cottage near where Labatt was held captive.

"Your place is secluded?" John German asked her.

"Quite secluded."

"Do you remember August 9 of last year?"

"Yes. Two men spoke to me for twenty minutes about renting the cottage at $25 a week."

"Do you see either of those two men now?"

"Yes, sir," and she pointed at Meisner.

"Did you notice anything about him?"

"I noticed something the matter with one of his eyes."

Under cross-examination, she admitted that the man had been too far away from her, "standing at the window," for her to tell what was wrong with his eye. "I couldn't tell whether it was a cast or a cataract or what it was," she told Bell. But she, too, denied that her testimony had been influenced by pictures of Meisner in the newspapers.

The ordeal of travelling to London and testifying in her weak condition caused her to fall ill with pleurisy and pneumonia. OPP Inspector E. I. Hammond accompanied her as far as Cooksville, a town west of Toronto (now part of suburban Mississauga), where she went to stay with a friend. Her condition worsened, and she died in early March.

George Bannister, a clerk at Hanna's hardware and appliance store in Port Carling, about twenty miles from Bracebridge, followed Mrs. Lythe as a witness. He was prepared to testify that Meisner was one of three men who had bought a dog chain "strong enough to hold a savage dog" from him in August 1934. For a while it seemed as if he would not get a chance to speak, as German and Bell fought fiercely over the admissibility of his testimony.

"Do you remember in August 1934 selling a dog chain?" German began.

"I object," interrupted Bell, jumping to his feet.

"Overruled," Justice McFarland declared.

"I repeat the question. Do you remember in August selling a chain?"

"Yes. It was in August that three men came into the store and asked for a dog chain."

"Objection," interrupted Bell once more, jumping again to his feet. "The conversation cannot be introduced without proof that the accused was present."

"Are you able to identify anyone who came in?"

"Yes, that gentleman in the prisoner's box," Bannister said, pointing at Meisner. "He was one of the three men. The biggest one said —"

He was interrupted for a third time as Bell shouted "Objection!" jumping yet again to his feet. This objection, coming so soon after the others, prompted the spectators to burst into laughter. Bell turned and scolded them. "It may be very funny to you but it means a lot to the man in the dock."

The rebuke worked; the spectators were silenced.

"Was there any conversation between you and any of the three when the accused was close enough to hear what was said?" German continued.

"The man in the prisoner's box was standing beside a Beatty washing machine. He was about six feet back when the big man asked me whether the chain would hold a savage dog. I told him, 'Any dog.' I remember the conversation because I wondered why the men needed a chain, since I had never sold one to a man before, only to women. The chain cost 35 cents and I remember that the big man paid with a quarter and a dime."

Bell sought to undermine Bannister's claim of a perfect memory regarding the entire day by asking him about every sale he had made. Bannister remembered many, but not all.

Subsequently, Matthias Harrison, a workman at the Prowse cottage enclave, testified that he had seen Meisner on the site on the day Labatt was kidnapped. "He was within twelve feet of me. I noticed he walked peculiarly. He passed by me and walked up to the Prowse cottage."

Harrison's cross-examination was handled by Bell's young London associate, Howard Cluff. He got Harrison to admit that he had recorded the date in different pencil from other entries and that he had taken only a "casual look and gone on with my work."

A number of people who had vacationed at the Prowse cottages then testified that they had seen Meisner in the vicinity of the hideout with two other men. They said all three had seemed out of the ordinary because they had American accents, wore suits instead of sports clothes, and weren't interested in the usual vacation pastimes of boating and fishing. Of this group of witnesses, Albert Douglas Crews of Toronto, the nearest neighbour to the hideout cottage, was on the stand the longest. Crews, an executive with General Motors Products of Canada, had, along with his wife, two children and a maid, occupied a cottage about forty to fifty yards away.

"Did anyone occupy the Prowse cottage during your holidays?" German asked.

"Yes. Three men."

"Do you know who any one of them is?"

"Yes. The prisoner in the box over there."

"Do you know how long the cottage was occupied?"

"Yes. They moved in on Monday, August 13. They were away all day Tuesday, August 14 [the day Labatt was kidnapped]. They were there again on Wednesday, August 15. I know because a big man came to our cottage for water. He was uncommunicative. On Wednesday evening around dusk, a man I have since identified as Meisner came for water."

"What conversation did you have?"

"He said, 'Where do you get the spring water?' I showed him and instructed him to keep the dirty bucket out of the spring so that the water wouldn't be polluted. But he put the dirty bucket in, so I explained once more. He seemed excited and anxious to get away. He had little to say otherwise."

"After you saw Meisner, did you see someone else?"

"The big man came for water on Thursday."

"And next?"

"We naturally wondered who our neighbours were, because they never went swimming or fishing to enjoy the outdoors that people go to Muskoka for. For instance, one time we were burning some brush and the fire got out of hand. They didn't come out and lend a hand with a pail of water as another neighbour might."

On cross-examination, Bell returned to the night of August 15, when Crews said he had met "Meisner" briefly.

"How long did you speak to him?"

"About three minutes."

"It was dusk?"

"Yes."

"Yet you could see him quite distinctly?"

"It was lighter by the spring than it was in the dark."

Bell had cast some doubt on Crews' identification of the man he had met; but all told, thirteen witnesses had testified that Meisner was one of the kidnappers — a number that would impress a jury.

"Some of these witnesses were grotesquely impossible, but others were 'poison' for the defence," Bell wrote in "Ditching David Meisner." "It was the *bulk* of it that told. Naturally the jury felt some of them *must* be right. In all there were thirteen who professed to identify Meisner, and allowing for the absurdity of some of the 'identifications,' several were reasonable enough, and none could be said to have been made in bad faith."

The prosecution rested its case at 3:45 p.m. on Tuesday, February 5. The outlook for Meisner was mixed at best. As preparation for his defence, Bell had had his partner R.H. Yeates do the legwork to check out Meisner's "perfect alibi." Yeates had gone first to Cincinnati, where he interviewed the oculists who Meisner said had diagnosed his eye problem as a cataract. "They were men entirely above suspicion and in a position to prove what Meisner had alleged about the condition of his eye," Bell wrote in "Ditching David Meisner." "But their fees [to appear at the trial and testify] were quite out of reach for anyone not possessed of a very substantial bank account, and of course they could not be made answerable to a Canadian subpoena. Thus the hope of getting the necessary evidence lay through the two Covington, Kentucky, detectives, who were in a position to know whether or not Meisner actually was in Covington during the month of August, when the kidnapping was said to have taken place.

"My partner was under instructions to contact these men only through the Chief of Police in Covington and to ascertain if he would vouch for them, and these instructions were carried out to the letter. The Chief summoned the two men, [Leroy] Hall and [Albert] Seiter, to his office, and there in his presence they both declared emphatically that they had kept tab on Meisner every day in August 1934, and that beyond question he had not left Covington at all. They also were both positive that the condition of the growth over his left eye was very much in evidence as far back as the preceding June. In the light of these assertions the necessity for bringing the oculists was not so great. Assuming the reliability of the detectives, their story should be equally right for acceptance on all points. They explained they could get a good car by which they would motor to London, and it was arranged that we would wire them forty-eight hours in advance of the time when their evidence was likely to be needed. For gasoline and incidental expenses they asked only a small amount, which we were able to arrange to have taken care of out of the remainder of Meisner's money, supplemented by what a relative of his raised for his assistance."

Bell called Detective Hall as his first witness. Hall spoke in what the *London Free Press* described as "a deep southern accent with a slight nasal drawl."

Bell began by asking, "Your occupation?"

"Detective in Covington, Kentucky."

Justice McFarland interjected, "Private detective, or official police force?"

"Official police force, sir."

"For how long?" Bell continued.

"Four years."

"Do you know the man in the dock?"

"Yes, sir."

"How long have you known him?"

"About two years."

Again McFarland interjected, "Under what name?"

"Under the names of Davis and Morrison," Hall replied.

"What is his occupation?" Bell asked.

"To my knowledge he has none."

"Do you know anything about his activities?"

"He hangs around gambling houses."

"Do you know where he was last summer?"

"Yes, he was at Covington and Newport, Kentucky."

"And to what extent have you kept track of him?"

"Well, we are on night force duty, and take in all of the noted places, such as saloons, dance halls, and the like, and we keep a pretty close watch on the noted characters."

Once more McFarland interrupted: "Is this man a noted character?"

"Yes, sir," Hall answered.

"Why?" Bell asked.

"Because he hangs around the gambling joints."

"Is there any other police officer associated with you in keeping track of these things?"

"Detective Seiter."

"Tell the court how closely you kept track of this man in the month of August 1934," Bell directed.

"Well, he returned to Covington in the latter part of June. He was missing from his regular haunts for ten or fifteen days in June. When he returned, he had a black patch over his left eye. About 7:30 at night, Detective Seiter and I ran into him the first night he was back. We asked him why he had the black patch on his eye. He said his eye was getting worse, and he raised the patch to show us. He had a white growth on the eye."

"Did you see him in July?"

"Yes. He was missing four or five nights in July. Never more than one night at a time, though."

"Take August. Did you see him then?"

"He was in Covington in August. On August 2 or 3 we stopped at Johnny Gates's place where he used to hang out. The boys in there were talking about putting on a chicken dinner. There was Meisner and George Greene and Johnny Gates and some others. I remember that night because we were working on the case of a coloured man who shot a night watchman."

"After that, what track did you keep of him?"

"Well, from August 5 to August 16 we worked on an automobile ring. We searched around Gates's place, and Meisner was there every day at Gates's saloon. I saw him there."

"What about August 17?"

"Well, on August 17, we received a call from Louisville, Kentucky, that two men had escaped from a hospital, and they were passengers on a train coming to Covington. They asked us to take them off the train. We went down to meet the train at Latonia, Kentucky. There were seven or eight of us. I had a machine gun. These two men that escaped were on the train. We stayed on the train and sent word on to Covington for an ambulance to meet us. When we got off the train, there were three hundred or four hundred people there at the station. I saw Meisner and Johnny Gates at the station. It was about 9:20 p.m.

Meisner was in Covington all the month of August. We never missed him one night."

Hall had provided what seemed to be the "airtight, perfect alibi" about which Meisner had been so confident, as had Bell and Yeates, after Yeates's interview with the two men. It seemed the case against Meisner was now in doubt. But Crown Attorney Norman Newton looked remarkably unconcerned as he rose to his feet to cross-examine Hall.

"What are the names of those two captured prisoners you were bringing to Covington on August 17?" he asked.

Seeming a little surprised, Hall answered, "I can't remember. I left the papers regarding them in my briefcase."

Newton ordered him to get the briefcase from an adjoining room where Seiter was waiting to be called as the next witness.

Newton asked to see the papers. Hall handed them to him. Newton began to smile.

"Just what I thought!" he exclaimed. "The date is September 17, not August 17."

This surprising development suddenly made an utter shambles of Bell's defence strategy. He was experiencing the completely unexpected element that he had once told a reporter "lends excitement to a case. A new situation, an uncounted factor, and unforeseen evidence may bob up like a flash of lights. Criminal law calls for fast headwork." Certainly, "fast headwork" was going to be necessary now.

Newton then waved his hand at two men sitting among the spectators. He beckoned for one of them to stand up.

"Do you recognize this man?" he asked Hall.

"Yes, I recognize his face. He's a United States Department of Justice agent."

"In other words, a G-man," Newton said.

"Yes."

At this point, Bell leaped to his feet in an effort to stave off further disaster in what was turning out to be a series of unanticipated twists and turns, the sort that can suddenly jolt a trial, making it wonderfully thrilling for spectators and an adrenaline-pumping challenge for a lawyer.

"Your Lordship, you ordered all witnesses from the courtroom during the trial except when they were testifying, but these men have stayed during the entire trial," Bell protested. "It is standard procedure for witnesses to be excluded from other witnesses' testimony so that they do not influence one another."

"That is right," McFarland agreed.

Newton was ready for this complaint.

"We have closed our case," he said suavely. "I don't know whether we will call him in rebuttal or not."

"You cannot evade it that way," Bell retorted fiercely. "His Lordship's direction was clear."

"Certainly he should not be in the courtroom listening to the evidence," McFarland said.

"Then I will have him go out," Newton replied. "But before that I will ask the man next to him to stand up." He beckoned to the other man as Bell seethed in frustrated indignation.

"Do you recognize this man?" Newton asked Hall.

"Yes. He posed as a reporter in Covington."

McFarland then ordered the two men to withdraw from the courtroom. Reporters clustered around them in the corridor outside the courtroom and asked them to identify themselves. "H.D. Harris of the United States Department of Justice," one said. "Sergeant Ted Weeks of the Royal Canadian Mounted Police," the other said. Weeks was the RCMP officer escorted through Covington by Jack Bannon in his guise as helpful police informer so as to frame Meisner.

This unexpected bombshell had come about as the result of some quick work by Newton, in conjunction with the OPP, just days earlier, on February 1. First, OPP Chief Inspector John Miller sent a memorandum marked "Urgent" to then Deputy Attorney General I. A. Humphries. ("D.A.G." stands for "deputy attorney general.")

Message from Norman Newton, London, 1.25 p.m.

"Have been trying to get in touch with D.A.G. Require Mr. Harris, Department of Justice, Cincinnati, U.S.A., as witness at Labatt trial on Tuesday next. Mr. Harris to bring with him certified court record of the conviction of LeRoy Hall, and it will be necessary for Mr.

Humphries to get in touch with Dept. of Justice at Washington, to get permission for Mr. Harris to be here. Mr. Newton states this is very vital."

Humphries immediately sent a telegram to Washington.

```
CONFIDENTIAL
TELEGRAM
                              TORONTO 5
                              FEBRUARY 1, 1935

THE MINISTER OF JUSTICE,
DEPARTMENT OF JUSTICE
WASHINGTON, D.C., U.S.A.

IMPORTANT THAT MR. HARRIS OF YOUR
DEPARTMENT AT CINCINNATI BE PRESENT
AT  LONDON  ONTARIO  IN  CONNECTION
WITH  TRIAL  NOW  GOING  ON  OF  DAVID
MEISNER CHARGED WITH KIDNAPPING AND
TO  PRODUCE  CERTIFIED  COURT  RECORD
OF  CONVICTION  OF  LEROY  HALL  STOP
MR.  HARRIS  TO  BE  IN  LONDON  TUESDAY
MORNING FEBRUARY FIFTH STOP CAN YOU
PLEASE ARRANGE THIS STOP WIRE REPLY
STOP

                              I.A. HUMPRHIES
   IAH/MSJ        DEPUTY ATTORNEY GENERAL
```

These messages, now in the Archives of Ontario, were why Newton was smiling when he rose to cross-examine Hall.

While the press huddled around Harris and Weeks, in the courtroom the beleaguered Bell lodged a final objection to any move by Newton to put the two men on the stand.

Holding a fistful of papers, Newton returned to the cross-examination of Hall, who was waiting apprehensively. So were Bell and Meisner.

"How long have you been a detective on the Covington force?"

"Four or five years."

"You were suspended at one time?"

"Yes."

"For how long?"

"Until the Court of Appeal reversed the decision of the lower court."

"You were suspended eighteen months?"

"No, sixteen months."

"Recall March 7, 1932. You were at that time living on Main Street, Covington?"

"Yes."

"You were arrested that day?"

"Yes."

"And charged with burglary and defacing automobile markers?" ["Markers" was a common term in those days for licence plates.]

"Yes."

"And you a detective!"

At this point, Bell leaped to his feet. "Objection!" he shouted. "I demand that this line of questioning be followed out." It is a long-established rule of practice that a suggestion of wrongdoing must be followed to its conclusion, not left dangling in the air.

"What became of the charges?" McFarland asked.

"You were indicted by the grand jury?" Newton went on. "And your case never came to trial?"

"That wasn't my fault."

"Maybe it was because of your uncle?"

"What uncle?"

"Your uncle on the police force."

"I have several uncles on the police force." This remark gave rise to some titters of laughter in the courtroom, where the tension had been escalating during the dramatic confrontation between Newton and Hall.

Newton then produced a stack of newspaper clippings about the kidnapping. After displaying them, he asked Hall, "How is it that as soon as Meisner was arrested, you sprang to his defence?"

Once again Bell protested Newton's methods of introducing evidence.

"Your Lordship, the Crown should first produce the reporter who wrote the stories or the publisher in court."

"If my friend would not be unduly perturbed," Newton remarked urbanely.

"That's a falsehood. I am not unduly perturbed," Bell retorted.

"Well, then disturbed," Newton said, goading Bell as a toreador does a bull.

"That is another falsehood and it is not proper to comment on my conduct in court," Bell responded, struggling to keep calm.

Newton ceased, then slightly revised his approach about the newspaper clippings. "Have you given newspaper interviews?" he asked Hall.

Once again, Bell objected.

At this moment, Judge McFarland spoke out. Complimenting both the defence and the Crown on their "admirable conduct up to this date," he suggested that both sides get together and see if they could reach an agreement regarding the submission of the newspaper clippings. When they failed to do so, McFarland adjourned the trial for the day, since it was the usual adjournment time of 4:45 p.m.

Just one hour had elapsed since Hall had taken the witness stand, but in those sixty minutes the momentum had shifted dramatically from the expected beneficiary — the defence — to the opposite side. Newton, almost twenty years younger than the acclaimed Bell, had sprung a trap on the very accomplished veteran lawyer. "CROWN SPRINGS SENSATION," the *London Free Press* reported in summing up the astonishing drama.

Newton's bombshell caused Bell to think back to remarks he had made in 1932 in his interview with the *Star Weekly*. "You don't know in advance what is coming from the Crown?" he had been asked. "No, you may know a great deal, but never all. That's what gives a case interest and keeps you on your toes, since you don't know where the next punch is coming from."

"What about alibis?"

"Don't trust them. Once when Sir Francis Lockwood was congratulated on a highly successful alibi, he said, 'Yes, it was a good one, but we had two others equally as good.' An alibi is a dangerous thing to play with. If you depend on it and it flops, you're sunk. You see, an alibi, at best, means shifting the proof which, strictly and properly speaking, rests with the Crown."

Meisner's alibi had flopped. Had his case been struck a mortal blow?

Chapter 7
THE RUNAWAYS

Bell left the courtroom with very mixed feelings. As he later wrote in "Ditching David Meisner": "disgust naturally was one. That Hall, although not shown to have ever been convicted of a crime, was very different from the kind of police officer [that] responsible police officials in Covington had induced us to believe him to be, was obvious.

"But there was a much more serious side to it: what was the connection between him and someone belonging to the prosecution?

> For on the questioning of the two detectives in Covington, Mr. Yeates had limited the period to be gone over to the time between August 11 and August 20, 1934. That is, he took the period of three days before the date of Labatt's abduction, until three days after he returned to his home, each way, so that that period was specifically covered. No other date than those dates in August was mentioned, but Hall produced a report sheet purporting to deal with the machine gun episode and it was just one month out! And that was *the first thing the Crown Attorney asked for!*
>
> There were some things I was determined to know about *that*. "Just what I expected!" cried the Crown Attorney when he looked at the report sheet. Why? Who told him to expect it? Who told him Hall had come prepared with the report sheet bearing a date in September instead of the month he had talked about to

us? And why had Hall brought all the way from Kentucky a report sheet dealing with a month outside the month of August altogether? It looked like a smart trick for a rig on the part of someone in Kentucky. But smart tricks and rigs have no place in a British court of Justice. However, Hall's cross-examination would be completed next day, and I'd take him for re-examination. And I resolved to find out who was responsible for the rig if it took me the rest of the week.

Outside of this one episode I had solid cause for satisfaction. By whose mistake had the G-man and the Mounted Policeman been "planted" in Court listening to the evidence of other witnesses? If the Crown, after what had occurred, should succeed in getting leave to call them in rebuttal, we would have grounds for a new trial, if we should ever need it. On the other hand, if these policemen were not called after all the hullabaloo over their appearance… Well, one can imagine what we were prepared to do about the omission.

Considerable time would pass before Bell would learn whether his conspiracy theory was valid. The answer to this mystery would be found in another strange but true development, one that was not at all what might have been anticipated.

Having talked himself into "a very hopeful frame of mind," Bell arrived back at his hotel, the Hotel London. As he was entering, he noticed the Detroit attorney who had represented Meisner in the extradition proceedings coming out to a cab, followed by a porter who was carrying his bags.

It struck Bell "as odd that he should be leaving when Hall had not completed his evidence and Seiter had not been called. However, that was his business. We had not exchanged half a dozen words at any time and it really made no difference to us whether he was there or not." Dismissing this incident from his mind, Bell concentrated on a transcript of Hall's evidence by his secretary, Mrs. E. E. Thornley, who had sat at the counsel table with him and taken it down in shorthand. The more Bell reviewed it, the more confident he was that Meisner's case had not been dealt a mortal blow.

Bell was not the only major figure from the trial staying at the Hotel London. So were Detectives Hall and Seiter. As Bell read Hall's transcript with increasing optimism, he was distracted by a commotion around 6:00 p.m. on the sidewalk below, as a crowd gathered to watch two men race down the street. Word of mouth quickly filled Bell in on what was happening. It was extremely bad news: the two men running down the sidewalk were Hall and Seiter. They had dashed into their car, which was conveniently parked near the hotel, and sped away toward the U.S. border. Shortly afterward, the Ontario Provincial Police took after them in hot pursuit, but did not catch up to them. The OPP did not alert border authorities to stop the two men, and they were soon in the United States, racing toward Kentucky.

It was a catastrophe for Bell and his client, David Meisner. "Gone all in one swoop was my chance to force from the mouth of Hall the next day the information as to how he had come to bring that September 17 report, and at whose request, and how someone connected with the prosecution apparently knew beforehand that he was bringing it, and what it would contain when produced," Bell recalled later in "Ditching David Meisner." He stayed awake the rest of the night, anxiously awaiting word as to Hall's and Seiter's whereabouts. Near dawn he learned that they had vanished across the border.

"Who ran the Covington men out?" he wondered in "Ditching David Meisner." "Did someone terrify them with threats of prosecution for perjury so that I would be unable to get the real truth the next day? I suspected strongly that was what had happened, but proof was absent — I could do nothing but wait for what the morrow would bring."

Hall later contended to reporters in Covington that "I took the judge's comment 'That will be all' when I finished my testimony on Tuesday to mean that I was finished and could leave for home." For someone in law enforcement with a knowledge of court procedure to have made that inference stretched credulity. "Anyway, Meisner never had a chance," Hall insisted, overlooking that he, Hall, was a major reason why.

The "morrow," Wednesday February 6 — the sixth and what would turn out to be the final day of the trial — began with the sensational news of Hall and Seiter's flight spreading like wildfire through town. Londoners, who had previously refrained from trying to gain entrance to the trial because they had been cautioned about the courtroom's limited seating capacity, now began to throng outside it, pushing and shoving, clamouring for admittance. They were so keen that they ignored the frigid temperature of eight below zero Fahrenheit as they waited. And most were to be disappointed, as there was room for very few.

Meisner knew nothing about Hall and Seiter's disappearance until just before the session began at 10:30 a.m. Howard Cluff, the local lawyer who was Bell's associate counsel, walked over to where Meisner was sitting in the prisoner's box and whispered the bad news. "They have ratted on you," he told the little bookie. Tears came to Meisner's eyes. It took him about ten minutes to control them.

Bell did not intend to call Meisner as a witness in his own defence, reasoning that "an innocent man is often his own worst witness." In general, Bell had no firm rule about putting an accused person on the stand. "I make a decision in this regard based on the course of the trial and the general circumstances," he explained. "I have read of a great English counsel who used to submit to the prisoner a piece of paper on which he wrote, 'Do you wish to testify?' and left it to him. But I feel I'm a much better judge of that than he."

As Justice McFarland entered the courtroom and took his seat, Charles Bell was, atypically for him, not in an optimistic mood.

"The prosecutor was cross-examining a defence witness," McFarland said, opening the session. "Where is he now?"

One of the worst moments in Bell's career was facing him. Rising to his feet, he explained: "I have learned that the defence witness who was on the stand when the court rose last night has left the Hotel London without notice to any of us. A man went with him who was also to have testified. I have had no contact with these men outside the courtroom. I saw Detective Hall for the first time yesterday when he took the witness stand. The other man was Detective Seiter.

"There is nothing we can do. If these two witnesses had not crossed the border into the United States, I would have sent a sheriff's officer after them to bring them back on the strength of the subpoenas we served on them. However, those subpoenas are worthless on the other side of the border."

McFarland asked Bell if he had any other witnesses.

"No, my lord."

"Does the Crown wish to call any witnesses in rebuttal?"

"No, my lord," Crown Attorney Norman Newton responded.

McFarland then instructed that closing arguments begin after a fifteen-minute adjournment requested by Bell to "assemble some notes."

During the recess, lawyers and law students eager to hear Canada's most famous defence lawyer make his address to the jury in this landmark case crowded into the courtroom. There was a hush as he rose to speak.

Bell spoke for ninety minutes in what the *London Free Press* described as "a beautifully dramatic appeal. Those privileged few who listened to Bell's dramatic address heard one of the most brilliant appeals the veteran defender had made to a jury."

Bell attacked John Labatt's testimony from every angle. He claimed the Crown had failed to show there really was a kidnapping and ridiculed Labatt's story in all aspects, especially his failing to see Meisner's cataract despite having said he would never forget his kidnapper's face. "The question is whether or not the story you have heard bears out the allegation there was a kidnapping, there was a robbery, there was a detention," Bell said. "It is up to the Crown to prove there was a kidnapping. It is not to be taken for granted. If a kidnapping is not established beyond any reasonable doubt, then this case should go no further.

"Did you hear John Labatt, a gentleman born and bred, a distinguished manufacturer of this city, a man of honour, a man who wouldn't soil his hand by the smallest act of dishonesty, say he was asked, 'Do you know where there are any payrolls?' What does this mean? It means that John Labatt was asked to give his assistance to rob with arms some place of business where there is a payroll and where thugs could come in and take that money. Any man who would give that information becomes an accomplice. And the man who has John Labatt a prisoner asks him, 'Do you know where there are any good payrolls?'

"Do you think that was ever said? Yet he swears to it. Explain it? It is not for me to explain. It is for you to consider how valuable that evidence is to prove there was a kidnapping.

"And later on we come to the place where John Labatt says the men stopped to get gas. What on earth prevented John Labatt from raising an outcry then? If they were to shoot him, they would destroy all possibility of getting a cent from him and they would of a certainty hang by the neck until dead.

"Later on the men who have Labatt are so murderous, so villainous, that when they hear a constable is coming, they get away as fast as they can, these bold, bad brigands. And when they stopped for groceries, Labatt didn't call for help. I don't know what everybody would do, but if I were in that position they could have heard me from here to Woodstock."

Bell's quip produced a ripple of laughter from the spectators. Woodstock is about forty kilometres east of London. "Order," Justice McFarland demanded. "Order." The spectators quieted down.

Bell then attacked Labatt's story from the aspect of whether kidnappers would be so stupid as to choose such public places for their hideout and for their rendezvous with Hugh Labatt. "With all the possible hideouts available to people desiring to use them, these ingenious kidnappers take Labatt to a place where he can hear children playing about. What do you, the jury, think? Was there really a kidnapping?

"And his brother gets a note which says to meet the kidnapper at the Royal York Hotel. The Royal York, with all those servants, guests, elevator men, and detectives in easy reach. Did you ever hear of a kidnapping when the suggestion was not to meet in some unfrequented place?

"I ask you: is this a genuine kidnapping? 'Meet me at the Royal York,' the kidnapper says. Why not on the steps of the City Hall with a brass band?

"And when they decide to release him, they don't take him back to where they picked him up or to the outskirts of London. No, they take him to the heart of Toronto where pursuit would be swift.

"Labatt writes a note to his brother. Look at it. See if it portrays fear and agony of mind as would be the case with you and me if we were in such a position as he was said to have been in.

"John Labatt was never kidnapped before. He is in fear. He thinks of the anxiety of his wife and children. Yet he sleeps peacefully. He calls to the man he says was Meisner. 'You wouldn't shoot me, would you?' he asks. The man says, 'Of course not.' He says 'That's fine' and turns over and goes to sleep. That's a kidnapping, is it?

"Oh, W.S. Gilbert, you died before your time." (An allusion to William Gilbert of the musical comedy team of Gilbert and Sullivan.)

"I say to the Crown, take all the facts and assemble them and then prove that there had been any kidnapping. Until that is proved the whole case for the Crown collapses."

Bell then turned to the sudden disappearance of the two defence alibi witnesses, Detectives Hall and Seiter. "May it not be the truth that those who deserted yesterday had really come here as a kind of blind to protect the real kidnapper who is hiding?" Bell suggested. "May they not have been hoping this man would be sent to jail for virtually the rest of his life so that their own friend could go free?"

Drawing near the end of his address to the jury, Bell drew a parallel to the simultaneous trial of Bruno Hauptmann for the 1932 kidnap-murder of Charles Lindbergh's infant son. "I want you to bear in mind that the first thing John Labatt did when he came into the court was to say, 'Yes, that's the man.' I am glad to say he didn't point at him. It would remind us of another trial where everybody was pointing — the trial of Bruno Richard Hauptmann. What value is that evidence? It may easily be wrong." Bell's objective was to make the jurors feel the same doubt about Meisner's guilt as many Americans and Canadians felt about Hauptmann's. There was a widespread belief that Hauptmann was being railroaded so that American law enforcement authorities could claim they had solved the Lindbergh case. Although Bell did no go so far as to charge that the same injustice was happening in the Labatt case, he hoped his inference would leave the jury no choice but to make the connection.

Bell then reminded the jury that Meisner had voluntarily walked into a Detroit police station and surrendered. "He wasn't any fugitive from justice."

"That isn't evidence," Crown Counsel John German interrupted.

"I am very sorry. I thought it was in evidence," Bell said with feigned astonishment. Then he employed a favourite tactic of courtroom lawyers.

"Members of the jury, I am going to ask you to blot from your minds that this man walked into a police station and gave himself up."

Bell concluded: "A man with an eye like Meisner's would never take part in a kidnapping. No doubt you all know what will happen to that eye in a few years. With one cataract, another comes. If you restore him to his poor life there is still a chance for him. What chance has he in a penitentiary, walking in partial or total blindness day after day, month after month and year after year?

"Even if he is only a poor innocent little bookmaker, deserted by those who have ratted on him, you must not allow yourselves to drift into the error of taking this man and putting him in a penitentiary because he is the only one within reach."

Bereft of solid defence witnesses and an alibi for Meisner that could be backed up with evidence, Bell had done his eloquent best for his client. When he finished it was noon. Justice McFarland called for a recess until 2:30. German then gave the summation for the prosecution in just twenty minutes, less than one-third of the time Bell had taken.

One by one German attacked Bell's argument that there had been no kidnapping, his ridiculing of Labatt's failure to call for help, and his assertion that Meisner was the wrong man.

"To say there is even the suggestion that it was not a kidnapping is absurd. This was not a joyride, a little jaunt in the country for a businessman with a kindly man with a gun. Mr. Labatt was not robust. He was not husky. You all saw him in the witness box here. He was lame and had to carry medicine for his heart with him. You gentlemen of the jury are all robust, but if any of you had been sitting in that car, with that little gambler beside you with a gun, you wouldn't have called out.

"Mr. Labatt had as much chance of escaping as a dead man. Why should a man try to escape at the risk of his life? My friend Mr. Bell said the kidnappers wouldn't shoot for fear of being hung by the neck until they're dead. Well, they kidnapped him, didn't they? And they discussed killing him. They were ruthless.

"My friend speaks about Mr. Labatt's ability to sleep. Well, a man can't be awake forever."

German then tackled the issue of why Labatt hadn't noticed Meisner's cataract. "I have been sitting in this courtroom for the past week and I couldn't tell how many of you jurymen are bald. People don't see the same things, and having seen them, don't recollect the same things.

"You all know that a cataract is something that grows." Showing the jury a picture of Meisner, German continued, "This picture taken last September doesn't show his eye in the condition it is today. It isn't even in a terrible condition now. Witness Graham testified that he saw it and witness Mrs. Lythe said she noticed a twitching of the eye."

Finally, German refuted Bell's charge that there had been a rush to judgment against Meisner. "The defence seems to be arguing that you have a duty of charity to perform. One excellent way to have some of your friends kidnapped is to allow kidnapping to go on. You owe no charity to that man. You owe a duty to yourself.

"If the Crown can't prove its case on the evidence which has been produced here, I believe we won't have much success in prosecuting criminals in this country hereafter," German concluded.

After a momentary pause, Judge McFarland began his charge to the jury. He reminded the jurors that they had three charges to consider: kidnapping, illegal imprisoning, and robbing while armed, a reference to the $99 taken from Labatt.

"The only evidence of robbing is the story of John Labatt himself. If you believe him, you should bring in a verdict of guilty on this charge.

"Your duty on the other two charges is not as simple. First of all, you must decide whether or not there has been a kidnapping. Then you must decide whether the defendant was actually concerned in it."

McFarland then reviewed the evidence of the witnesses, starting with Leroy Hall, the defence's sole witness. "As far as the evidence of Detective Hall is concerned, I do not believe a word he said. This is the only comment I am going to make on it." Having tersely disposed of Hall, McFarland turned to the evidence of the Crown's Muskoka witnesses.

"Their stories seem to dovetail and there are no serious inconsistencies. All these witnesses must be presumed to have no personal interest in the matter. In fact, many of them would rather have had nothing to do with it."

Next, McFarland addressed the issue of whether Meisner had had a fair trial. "A good deal has been said about the enormous forces at the command of the prosecution by the lawyer for the accused, while the accused had no money and no help. I think every facility was offered this man for his defence. He has had for chief counsel one of the most brilliant counsel Canada has ever produced. This man has not been persecuted and no unfair advantage has been taken of him. The case for the Crown has been very fair.

"The only thing for you to decide is whether or not this man is guilty. You must bring in a separate verdict on each of these three charges."

The judge's comments had taken thirty minutes, ten more than German's summation. It was 3:30 p.m. as the jury left the courtroom to deliberate. The jurors took only one hour to reach a decision. They returned to the courtroom at 4:45 p.m.

"We find the defendant guilty on all charges," foreman Simon Bright announced.

McFarland enumerated each charge to double-check.

"Do I understand you to find the prisoner guilty on the charge of armed robbery?"

"We do," Bright responded.

"Do you find him guilty of kidnapping?"

"We do."

"And do you find him guilty of illegally imprisoning?"

"We do."

Crown Attorney Norman Newton had punctured Charles Bell's record of "getting all of them off."

Meisner slumped in despair. He had become the first person convicted of kidnapping in Canada, a historic first in Canadian crime annals.

McFarland then asked Crown Counsel German what punishment he recommended. German asked for the harshest possible penalty.

"I ask your Lordship to give the prisoner life and lashes for armed robbery and the maximum sentence of twenty-five years on each of the other two charges."

Lashes, also referred to as "whipping" or "flogging," had been imported into Canada from England as a punishment for a broad range of crimes such as rape, attempted rape, indecent assault on a male, breaking and entering a house with intent to commit theft or another crime, and robbery. In 1938, the Criminal Code was amended to provide that the last of any whippings should be administered just a short time before a prisoner was released, the intent being that it would have a salutary effect on him to mend his ways. Opponents, however, maintained that whippings would make criminals even more of an enemy of society. Whipping remained on the statutes until July 6, 1972, when it was eliminated under an omnibus bill of amendments to the Criminal Code. If Meisner were whipped, it would be another first: the first time lashes would be used on someone convicted of kidnapping.

Meisner turned white with shock, horror and despair. His perfect alibi had been shredded into tatters. He had been convicted for a crime he hadn't committed. Since he was fifty-five, a twenty-five-year sentence would in all likelihood condemn him to spend the rest of his life in jail. Considering his ill health, he could very well die behind bars. Moreover, he was too frail to withstand lashes. His mind whirled in bewilderment over the nightmarish, ever-downward spiral in which he was trapped.

He was jolted out of his state of shock by the sound of McFarland's crisp voice.

"What have you to say, Mr. Cluff?" McFarland asked the associate chief defence counsel. (Charles Bell, who was a member of Parliament, had left for Ottawa for a session the next day.)

"Your Lordship sees the state of the accused's health, including his blind eye, and you have watched his quiet deportment during the trial. With all due respect, I submit the end of justice would be met by a much lighter sentence," Cluff pleaded.

"How old is your client, Mr. Cluff?" McFarland asked.

"Fifty-five," replied Cluff.

McFarland pondered briefly, then ordered Meisner to stand for sentencing.

"You have been found guilty of three of the most serious crimes possible," he declared. "On each of two of these you could be imprisoned for twenty-five years. On the third you could be sent to prison for life and given lashes. I can relieve your mind at once. I am not going to impose lashes for two reasons. The first is your physical condition and the second is that John Labatt was not injured."

Meisner looked momentarily relieved, but continued biting his lip nervously.

The judge resumed. "The jury has found you guilty, and I think rightly so, on the evidence. I think the sentence I am going to impose will be a deterrent to others. I sentence you to fifteen years' imprisonment on each of the three charges, the terms to run concurrently — at Portsmouth." Portsmouth was verbal shorthand for the Kingston Penitentiary, located in the village of Portsmouth immediately west of the city of Kingston, Ontario.

While fifteen years is certainly more lenient than twenty-five, it is no less horrendous if, as Meisner was, the accused is innocent. If Meisner were to serve the full term, he would be in jail until 1950, when he would be seventy years old — and likely blind, if Bell's dire prediction about his threatened eyesight were to come true. As the guards started to take Meisner down a private stairway to the jail, his brother Richard, who had come from Detroit to attend the trial, ran up and tried to grasp his hand to comfort him, but other guards held him back. Later, Richard was allowed to visit his brother in his cell, but for only a few minutes. Meisner's common-law wife did not attend the trial, probably because she could not afford to travel from Kentucky.

As associate defence counsel Howard Cluff left the courthouse, a *London Free Press* reporter asked, "How does Meisner feel about the case?"

"He believes he was double-crossed," Cluff replied.

"Do you mean by the two Covington, Kentucky, detectives who were to have testified for him?"

"Meisner said the moment Detective Hall got on the stand he knew something was wrong."

"Double Crossed, Meisner Believes," the *Free Press* put it in a February 7 headline.

On February 10, four days after the verdict, Meisner wrote Bell a touching letter of gratitude.

> I was very sorry I did not have the opportunity of thanking you, in my poor way, for the very brilliant manner in which you conducted the defence of my case, before you left London.
>
> The verdict was not a surprise to me, inasmuch as it was such a terrible uphill battle for you, right from the

start, and then to be given such a damnable jolt, right when you should have been getting all the aid there was to be had!

I presume it was my fault in selecting those men as witnesses. However, I am not at all satisfied that there wasn't some tampering in some way, but unfortunately, I have no proof. As soon as the man got into the witness box, I knew there was something wrong, but what, I could not imagine.

At any rate, I have been reading some of the things he has since caused to be published, and I want to say I think it is a rotten, low-down trick for either him or his partner to do, and I consider it no less than a subterfuge to cover up their own dirty tricks. All I wanted anyone to do, was to come up here and tell the truth, nothing more. It was all the chance I had, and it failed miserably.

I want to state here and now, I had as fair a trial as anyone could wish. Everything was conducted on the highest order, and, on the evidence produced, the jury had no alternative but to find me guilty. My defence was conducted wonderfully, and I cannot thank you and your associates enough.

I have had visitors ... who have expressed their firm belief in my innocence. I *am* innocent, regardless of the evidence produced. But I know I can't prove it — especially in here. Thanking you again, and hoping some day I may be able to repay my obligation...

Labatt recuperated from the stress of the trial by vacationing in the West Indies. Two of the Muskoka witnesses complained about what they regarded as inadequate compensation for expenses: $1.50 per day and twenty cents a mile one way, with special allowances possible under Section 13 of the *Administration of Justice Expenses Act*. Displaying monumental self-centredness, Albert Lee — who had lived in the same house as Mary Lythe for fifteen years and accompanied her to Muskoka, testified at the trial and was her trustee — submitted a claim on behalf of her estate, much of it for unrelated expenses, with a most unusual, memorable last line in his itemized statement.

```
train fare return ...................................................$7.50
30 meals   ............................................................. 18.00
tip to girl  ............................................................. 0.50
phone calls re. case   ........................................ 0.30
to take care of her dog while away  ........ 5.00
damage to plumbing (burst pipes)
in house closed up through
absence, owing to bad weather  ................ 25.00 (unpaid)
trained nurse (5 days)   ..................................... 20.00 (unpaid)
doctor's bill (at hospital)   .............................. 39.00 (unpaid)
second doctor   ..................................................... 6.50
hotel bill at London   ......................................... 25.50
Why Go Any Further   ....................................
```

The other complaint came from Mrs. Louise Eveleth, who had been the sole support of her family since her husband, who made children's school desks and chairs, had lost his job. They had a son who was high-school age. To make ends meet, she paid four women one dollar each per day plus carfare to go door to door trying to sell housedresses and aprons at between forty-five cents and three dollars each. She wanted to be reimbursed for two return trips by railroad ($16); six nights at hotel ($15); meals for ten days ($22.50); and time lost at five dollars per day for ten days ($50.00).

John German returned to his law practice in Toronto. He billed the Ontario government $1,449.12 for fees and expenses, saying he had spent a total of twenty-four days on the case, including fifteen days of preparation spread over two months. Bell "returned to the thrilling debates in Parliament over what Farmer Jones didn't get for his wheat last year or how the contractors were chiselling regarding the new Post Office," as he sarcastically wrote in *Who Said Murder?* Considering his attitude, there was no surprise when he decided not to run for re-election in the 1935 general election. "I find politics dreary and colourless, and the House of Commons the dullest grind I know of," he had told *Saturday Night*. "It's miserable compared to the glory of a battle in a criminal case, and that in turn is dull compared with the delights of the theatre."

Bell continued to believe wholeheartedly in Meisner's innocence. He was determined to reverse what he was certain was a terrible miscarriage of justice. He began his campaign by adding the chapter "Ditching David Meisner" to his book *Who Said Murder?*, published shortly after Meisner's conviction. By far the longest chapter, it was highly derisory of Labatt.

He described the drive to Muskoka as "one of the strangest in history," in which "everything was done to make Labatt feel quite at his ease." Regarding Labatt's first night in captivity, Bell wrote, "One might have expected that Labatt would have tested the other end of the chain to see if it could not be removed from the head of the bed but he stated that he did not do so. Instead he lay down and peacefully went to sleep." About the generous portions of food, he gibed, "If Labatt failed to find the surroundings satisfactory, he at least had no reason to complain of the service."

Not all his scorn was for Labatt. He was also indignant about the "wolves" in the seamy Covington underworld who he was certain had made Meisner a victim of the "law of the jungle." "Wolves have ever been ready to detect the first sign of lagging in their number and to turn and rend him. Such was the calamity that overtook David Meisner.... The big shots had decided that any usefulness he possessed was fast waning and he was to be ditched at the first convenient opportunity. Because of that decision he landed in Kingston Penitentiary."

Bell concluded in the eloquent style for which he was acclaimed:

> But one thing stamps itself indelibly on my memory. The lofty vault-roofed ceiling of the fine old London courtroom with the trial going on, the late afternoon sun peering in for a minute through one small window before disappearing for the night, and the troubled, haunted face of David Meisner with the white blur of what was once an eye standing out every time I turned to look at him. How could John Labatt have ever believed that such a thing as that eye could have escaped his notice? It passes my understanding.

While Bell seethed about the verdict, Deputy Attorney General I.A. Humphries sent a thank-you note on March 29 to FBI director J. Edgar Hoover. "On behalf of the Attorney General and his Department, I wish to extend to you our appreciation for the courtesy and assistance that has been rendered to officials of this Department by two of your agents, namely, H.D. Harris and N.B. Klein of Cincinnati. I might also mention Mr. Larsen, who is the Agent in charge of the Criminal Investigation Branch at Detroit. It is indeed most gratifying to have such excellent co-operation from these gentlemen."

Hoover replied on April 4: "I am indeed pleased to learn by your letter of March 29, that the work of the Special Agents of the Federal Bureau of Investigation was of assistance to you in the Labatt kidnaping [American spelling] case, and appreciate your thoughtfulness in expressing your appreciation of their efforts. It is a pleasure to work with the law enforcement officers of Canada in our many mutual problems. The effectiveness of co-operation and the exchange of ideas is, I believe, helpful to all."

Chapter 8
THE BIG HOUSE

Meisner was kept in his three-lock cell at the Middlesex County Jail in London for a month after the verdict, then was transferred to the Kingston Penitentiary. Grim as the London jail's "steel cage" — as newspapers described it — had been, the penitentiary, nicknamed the "Big House," was infinitely worse. Canada's oldest prison had the most fearsome reputation for harsh prison conditions. Even hardened criminals found it almost intolerable. For an innocent man like Meisner, who had never been in prison and had only been convicted of a "picayune" — to use Bell's word — offence in the past, being sent to the Big House was a terrible fate.

Also known as the "Kingston Pen" and "K.P.," the prison marked its centennial in 1935, the year Meisner was sent there. It had cells for 805 male inmates; a separate jail, opened in 1934, had room for 100 female prisoners. It was called a "penitentiary" rather than a "prison" or "jail" because part of its original purpose was to provide an opportunity for penitence through meditation, rigid adherence to a long list of regulations covering daily routine, and hard labour.

Kingston Penitentiary: The First Hundred And Fifty Years, 1835–1985, published by the Correctional Service of Canada, credits Hugh Thomson, a Kingston businessman, editor, and member of the Upper Canada Legislative Assembly, as being, in 1826, the first advocate in British North America of a "penitentiary." Hitherto, the sole purpose of jails had been to hold persons awaiting trial and retain convicted criminals. It took Thomson many years to gain public support for what was regarded as a radical idea.

The turning point occurred in 1831 after a number of convicts escaped from overcrowded jails. The public feared crime was out of control. Thomson and fellow Kingstonians Christopher Hagerman, a judge, and John Macaulay, a merchant, were commissioned by the Upper Canada Assembly to come up with a solution. They recommended a reforming prison — a penitentiary — to be built at Kingston. The Assembly approved the proposal in 1832, allocating £1,000 for the purchase of 100 acres of land at Hatter's Bay on Lake Ontario, a short walk from Kingston, near the village of Portsmouth. Thomson would not live to see his dream realized; he died in 1834 as the project got underway.

Portsmouth had large quantities of strong limestone that was suited to the construction of a prison that would be as tough to break out of as anything on earth. The quarries were also a place where convicts could be set to work chiselling the limestone, thereby satisfying their obligation to perform hard labour.

Starting with Thomson, punishment was regarded as more important than reform. As Thomson put it, "A Penitentiary, as its name implies, should be a place to lead a man to repent of his sins and amend his life. If it has that effect, so much the better, as the cause of religion gains by it. But it is quite enough for the purpose of the Public if the punishment is so terrible that the dread of repetition of it deters him from crime, or by his description of it, others."

In keeping with the term "penitentiary," the prison was designed in the shape of a cross with four cell blocks (wings) joined together by a circular rotunda. The "Dome," as it came to be known, enabled close scrutiny of prisoners walking around it. At first, the cells were stacked five stories high in double rows that ran the length of each wing. Each cell was a mere twenty-seven inches wide and six feet, eight inches long. A thin bunk was hinged to the wall. When it was lowered for the night, there was no space to stand except at the end of the cell where the waste bucket was located. Close confinement in tight spaces was regarded, both then and later, as an essential part of the penitential process. A small window provided a little air but no light.

Criticized as "mail slots for human bodies," these tiny cubicles were replaced between the 1890s and the outbreak of World War I with cells that were twice the size, each of which contained a folding cot, a toilet, a sink, an electric light bulb and sufficient room for a small table for writing paper and books.

Despite the renovations, conditions continued to be deplorable: overcrowding; punishment more excessive than what the rules called for; improperly cooked food; lack of both recreation time and facilities for them; insufficient lighting in the cells; poor medical care; lack of family visits; an allowance so small (five cents a day) that it was difficult to buy tobacco — one of the few comforts of prison life — candy or magazines.

The prison "school," which operated for only thirty-five minutes per weekday, was attended by only 15 percent of the inmates. The library's books were mostly dilapidated cast-offs from schools. There were scarcely more than a thousand books in good condition, an average of roughly one per inmate — by no means the 15,000 that prison officials boasted about in the early 1930s.

The regimentation was mind-numbing. Symbolic of the rules and precise scheduling of the day and events was the bell in the Dome, which signalled the beginning and end of all activities. The first bell of the day, the wake-up call, struck at the command of the deputy warden in charge of operations and security, rang at 6:45 a.m. By 7:15 a.m. the prisoners were expected to have shaved, washed, dressed — in thinly striped shirts, light-coloured pants, dark brown jackets with numbers on the back and heavy boots — folded up their beds and pushed them and their writing tables against the wall.

Then the breakfast march began, with the occupants of one cell block following those of another to ensure a steady flow to the kitchen. The prisoners would be famished, having last eaten at 4:15 p.m. the day before. After receiving their meal, they returned with their plates to their cells.

Here is how a *Star Weekly* reporter in the 1920s described the routine that came after the wake-up call, a routine that was still adhered to when Meisner was there (and thereafter).

> Then the prison comes to life. The Deputy Warden
> pulls the gong again. Keys rattle. Guards move swiftly.

Range barriers swing open. The windlasses on each side line of cells throw every bolt into gear. The gong again. The first cell of each line opens. The inmate, the *tapper* as he is called, runs to the far end of his line of cells. The gong again.

From away up on the top of Range A comes the sound of a man running and a quick tap-tap-tap as he speeds along. As he runs, he strikes each protruding bolt a blow with his open hand as he passes. In seconds, he unlocks the line of cells. The inmates are all standing at their cell barriers at this point and when the sound of the tapping stops, they all open their doors, form a line and proceed to their place of work. They do this silently. No staff speak either. Except for the gong, there is no sound but the shuffling of feet.

In the Keeper's Hall adjacent to the Dome area, a complex and intricate tote board was maintained to constantly keep track of the location of each of the hundreds of prisoners. The *Star Weekly* described it this way:

On the wall is the check board. On this board is a hole corresponding to every cell in the place arranged according to location in tiers and ranges. An empty hole means, at a glance, an occupied cell. A red plug means a man in hospital.

A blue plug means a man in punishment. And so on. Every cell in the penitentiary must be checked by the guards on this board and totals made to tally before the all-clear signal rings at night and the prison is sealed tight as the tomb of Tutankhamen.

The prisoners came to hate the Dome bell, which symbolized all that they loathed about the dehumanizing regimentation within the Big House. Roger Caron, who served many years in the penitentiary and won a Governor General's literary award for *Go Boy!* (published in 1978) about his prison experiences, summed up the hatred for the bell this way:

To the guards who were always grouped around it, the bell took on the proportions of a cherished symbol of authority. To the cons it was an object of repugnance and outrage, an unjustifiable punishment, a brass monster that we were convinced had been designed solely to shatter our nerves with its loud and strident ringing. Its grating sound controlled all our movements: woke us up, sent us off to work, to lunch, to supper, to secure the count, dictating when we must dummy up and when we must go to bed.

Its clang reverberated throughout the cavernous dome 127 times a day! Multiply that by 365 days a year and it is not hard to imagine how the damn thing could drive a man stir crazy.

Tobacco was supplied by prison officials as a reward and withdrawn as a punishment. This means of control met with limited success, as visitors smuggled tobacco into the Big House; it was also offered as an incentive by private contractors using prison labour. Guards were so poorly paid that they sometimes risked dismissal by trafficking in tobacco. In the 1920s, the warden cut off the supply of cigarette paper after two convicts were found shooting craps and recording their bets on the papers. For ten years afterward, inmates had to roll their cigarettes in toilet tissue. Since matches were hard to come by, prisoners improvised with a "punk box": a small metal disc (the "zipper") was struck against a flint-like stone in order to set off sparks that would ignite the punk (carbonized cloth), which would light the cigarette.

In the early days, prisoners were not allowed to speak at any time. They grew so accustomed to the silence that, as the story goes, one inmate asked to be removed from his job in the kitchen, a coveted assignment, because his "nerves couldn't stand the noise of banging metal trays, shouting, steam hissing, and all the rest of it."

Many jailhouse slang terms, such as "screw" (a guard) or "fish" (a new convict), have entered the popular lexicon. But while six is just another number in the outside world, within the "Big House" it has always had a special meaning, according to *Kingston Penitentiary: The First Hundred And Fifty Years*.

"Got you, six," is a greeting from the Tower guard to the keeper as he walks the yard at mid-shift, just before the last count of the day is taken at 11 p.m. Six times a day, from morning to night, correctional officers must count every inmate and report the total to Keeper's Hall. If it does not tally, they go back and do it again. And if it still is not right, the search starts immediately.

The senior man on duty at night will usually be a CX-6, Correctional Officer Six. He is the keeper and the boss. To "stand six" is to watch out for the boss coming. To "call six" is to warn of his approach. The inmates are always on the alert for authority, and any guard is "boss," but "six" has special meaning.

From the Big House's early days as a supposedly enlightened place of reform, punishment was harsh for even the most trivial offence. In the early days there was the "shower": a prisoner's head and arms were pinioned in wooden stocks so that his head, tilted forward, fit into an open-topped container. A barrel of cold water was emptied over his head into the container until his head was submerged, making him feel he was about to choke to death. The water would slowly seep over the container and run down his body, enabling him to lift his face and gasp for air.

The most prevalent form of punishment throughout the Big House's first century was whipping. In the early years, whipping was performed in the Triangle, so called because of the shape of the device to which the convict was attached. His ankles were strapped to the base and his wrists at the top. He was stripped to the waist and struck with a cat-o'-nine-tails, a whip with nine knotted lines fastened to the handle.

By the time Meisner arrived at the Big House, the Triangle had been replaced by the "strapping bench." A convict's legs were immobilized by ankle slots at the base of the bench — actually a high, rectangular table. With bare buttocks he bent over the table so that his upper body could be strapped onto the top of the bench, and he was whipped with a leather paddle. This was the dreadful punishment Meisner so feared and which he escaped only because of his frail build. The strapping bench was used at the Penitentiary until the 1950s.

From time to time, governments of the day established commissions to recommend ways of improving the Big House. This had happened in 1921 with the appointment of a three-person committee consisting of lawyers O.M. Biggar and William Nickle and labour leader Draper. Their report was highly critical of the Penitentiary.

> Beyond food and clothing, the convict is without rights, and the conduct prescribed for him is that of an automaton; he is prohibited from feeling, or at least from exhibiting, any human emotion. It is not part of the purpose of imprisonment that the spirit of prisoners should be broken or that they should, when they have completed their terms, as almost all of them sooner or later will, be worse citizens by reason of their punishment.

The report went on to recommend a set of elementary rights for prisoners, none of them in the least radical.

- A convict shall have the right to be brought before the warden to complain in person of his treatment by an officer or to make any other request which he may desire to make the warden.
- Every convict shall instantly obey any order ... but nothing in this paragraph shall prevent such convict from complaining to the warden of his having been compelled to obey any order.
- To receive in the presence of a guard once in every two months a member or members of his family.
- To write at the public expense once in every month to some member of his family.
- To receive all letters on personal, family or business matters.
- To receive from the library one volume and one magazine weekly.
- To exercise himself outdoors if the weather permits in such proper manner as he desires for at least fifteen

minutes in every twenty-four hours.

- To be supplied with pen and pencil, ink and paper, in reasonable quantities, both for purposes of correspondence and of study and training.

- To receive two ounces of tobacco weekly and to receive materials for its use at the public expense until a system of remunerating convicts has been established and thereafter at their own expense.

- To receive from the publisher at his own expense, such newspapers and articles as are not expressly prohibited by the warden.

- To subscribe and pay for such courses as he may desire at any correspondence school approved by the warden.

The recommendations were ignored. Family visits, for example, continued to be so constricted by bars and screens and interventions by monitoring guards that the visits were upsetting rather than comforting. Although complaints could be made personally to the warden, his reception of them was usually hostile, consisting of a tongue-lashing and peremptory dismissal.

The prisoners' frustrations grew to the point that they decided to hold a peaceful demonstration on October 17, 1932, to air their grievances. Their demands were actually quite innocuous requests: a request for cigarette papers (they received tobacco but were still without papers since the craps game incident years earlier) and more recreation. They scheduled their protest for 3:00 p.m., but the acting warden, Gilbert Smith, learned of the plan and had the doors to the workshops locked with the convicts still inside. Those in the mail bag shop managed to climb out a window, obtain an acetylene torch and cut the locks from the doors of the other shops.

The prisoners then poured into the Dome. Their spokesmen outlined their grievances, asking Smith to pass on their complaints to the federal government. Smith overreacted, not only refusing to call Ottawa, but calling in soldiers from the military base across the Cataraqui causeway.

Smith's decision touched off the first major riot in the Big House's nearly one-hundred-year history. When the inmates learned that the army was on its way, they seized some guards as hostages and barricaded themselves in the mail bag shop. Shots were fired into the room by either a soldier or a guard, and a number of sewing machines used to make the canvas mail bags were shattered. At this point, Smith agreed to meet with a committee of the inmates and to forward their grievances to Ottawa, and the prisoners returned to their cells without further incident.

It seemed as if the excitement was over. But the unrest and grievances of the prison population were stoked by Communist Party of Canada leader Tim Buck, who had been sentenced, along with eight other known communists, to the Big House for sedition.

Between October 17 and October 20, the tension grew. On the afternoon of the 20th, some of the prisoners began "acting up" in their cells — prison slang for causing a disturbance. Once more, soldiers were brought from the nearby army base and within minutes they had stationed themselves inside the prison grounds. Guards at the Big House were not armed unless stationed at an observation post, such as the walkway overlooking the Dome and the cell ranges radiating from it, or in a tower. But on this day they were issued rifles, revolvers and shotguns and ordered to go into the narrow ducts between the cells. The ducts had peepholes through which the guards could see what was going on in a cell while remaining undetected. Even though the inmates were securely locked inside the cells, the officers had been ordered to shoot into those cells where they considered inmates to be acting up. Many shots were fired during the night of October 20. One prisoner struck in the shoulder did not receive medical treatment for twenty-two hours. Seven shots were fired into Buck's cell, but he was not hit. Many cells were damaged.

In the days following the riot, questions were raised in Parliament as to why and how a peaceful demonstration had escalated into violence. Although Acting Warden Gilbert Smith was replaced, the riot did not lead to better conditions at the penitentiary. There was a lack of government and public interest despite the publication in 1933 of a stunning exposé by ex-inmate O.C.J. Withrow, *Shackling the Transgressor*. He wrote:

> The militarism of the system was apparent even in the
> outer trappings. The guards wore khaki uniforms with a
> military cut. The under officers were required to salute

the warden and his deputy whenever they might appear and a fine would be imposed if this order were not scrupulously obeyed.

The pay [for security staff] was quite inadequate to the type of service which should have been rendered. Most of the officers had no real interest in their work. They knew nothing and cared less. Of the constructive principles of rehabilitation or reform, they knew nothing and cared less. As I watched sentinel on the northeast tower one day [from Withrow's vantage point as an orderly on the third floor of the hospital], I thought what a colourless, aimless, lazy and devastating experience.

A convict hospitalized with severe symptoms of syphilis, stated that the dishes from the hospital patients were washed three times a day in a bathtub in the hospital, which tub was also used by inmates for bath purposes. Dishes used in the hospital are not sterilized, but are washed with hot water in the two bathtubs, and no provision is made to keep those of infected patients from entering the large white bathtub in the same batch with those of patients with a clean sheet.

A few of the guards supplement their meagre pay by trucking and trading for the convicts. Money finds its way from friends [of convicts] directly into the hands of these guards who deliver a portion of the value in goods for inmates. If a guard is caught carrying on such traffic, he is immediately dismissed.

When I entered the prison the food was not good — insufficient and badly cooked. Rotten fish could be thrown between the bars [of the cells where the prisoners ate their meals] to the cell block floor and on the days when fish was served, the stone floor would be strewn deeply with decaying debris. The steward had to feed the men on nineteen cents per day per man. The food supplied was merely fuel for our bodies.

When Meisner was transferred to the Big House, conditions were as bad as ever. Along with two other prisoners, he was placed in charge of a storeroom where sheets were kept. He became convict #3737. His name slipped out of the headlines. Most people felt that justice had been done. His future seemed utterly dismal. Yet he kept hoping for a miracle that would extricate him from his nightmarish quagmire.

Chapter 9
COMEUPPANCE

David Meisner's conviction did not end the Labatt case. Labatt had said there had been three kidnappers that he knew of, and the police search for the rest remained a top priority. Still, despite their best efforts, the trail appeared to have gone cold.

When a gun battle between police and two robbers — one of them calling himself James Parker — erupted outside Chicago on June 22, 1935, nobody on the Labatt case paid it any attention.

"Parker" and his accomplice had been trying to evade arrest after robbing a produce truck making a run from Detroit to Chicago. They were racing through Hammond, Indiana — on the southern outskirts of Chicago — when the police started chasing after them, perforating their car with thirty bullets. After two blocks the gangsters jumped out of their car and started to run. The police opened fire at them. Parker was wounded in the arm and lost the trigger finger of his right hand. He was captured by the police. But it was not James Parker they had nabbed; it was Michael McCardell, the "brains" behind the Labatt kidnapping. He had undertaken the robbery immediately after spending four months in hospital for serious neck injuries sustained when his car overturned in a ditch as he sped at eighty miles an hour in an effort to escape police.

McCardell later maintained that he had no idea it was the police who were chasing him on June 22. "If you had been around Chicago as much as I have, you would have attempted to escape also," he said. "I thought it was someone trying to take me for a ride. If I had thought it was the police, I might not have run away."

When McCardell was taken to the Hammond hospital and treated for his gunshot wounds, he gave his name as James Parker. Later, he was transferred to the jail in Crown Point, Indiana, a short distance southeast of Hammond, where he was registered as Parker.

When news of James Parker's arrest became known, stool pigeon Jack Bannon sensed an opportunity to make a bundle of money. He knew that Parker was one of several aliases used by McCardell. Already the recipient of $500 from the Ontario government (out of the $5,000 reward being funded by the Labatts) for his purported help about Meisner, he hoped to get a much larger chunk now. He approached a Toronto policeman with whom he was acquainted in his role as stool pigeon.

"You know that reward for the Labatt kidnapping?" he asked.

"What of it?" the policeman responded.

"Is it still good?"

"I'll find out."

Shortly afterward he told Bannon that a "substantial portion is still good." Bannon then squealed on Parker/McCardell. He was put in touch once again with RCMP Detective Sergeant Ted Weeks, to whom he had been so "helpful" about Meisner and who was one of the two policemen involved in Crown Attorney Norman Newton's "surprise" at Meisner's trial. The two prepared to go to Crown Point for an in-person identification of McCardell.

Meanwhile, McCardell was being questioned by Captain Singer of the Hammond police about the Labatt kidnapping. He admitted nothing. He had carefully read the newspaper stories about Meisner's trial and was well aware that Labatt and the Muskoka witnesses had identified Meisner as the man he knew was actually himself. McCardell had also subsequently read of Meisner's conviction for the crime he had committed, and therefore felt "pretty safe" in feigning ignorance. When Singer showed him a picture of Russell Knowles and asked if he knew him, McCardell replied that he did not.

Singer then showed McCardell a telegram stating that Albert Pegram had been arrested in Nashville, Tennessee, and had named Knowles and McCardell as his "companions in the crime." McCardell denied it. He knew from the underworld grapevine that Pegram had not been arrested and realized that Singer was trying to trick him into confessing.

A few days later, Bannon and Weeks arrived at the Crown Point prison. A lineup of prisoners was arranged and Bannon identified James Parker as McCardell, aka "Three-Fingered Abe." Not long afterward, an FBI agent approached McCardell and said, "Hello, Mac." With that remark, McCardell realized his real identity was known to the police. He surmised that either Bannon or Knowles had squealed on him. Subsequently, McCardell was questioned about the kidnapping by Sergeant Weeks, Ontario Provincial Police Inspector Hamar Gardner, a Canadian government immigration official, and the FBI agent. He admitted everything, implicating Bannon and Knowles. At this point, he said Meisner was innocent. It had taken McCardell a long time to tell the truth, and his admission was to have no instant happy repercussions for Meisner.

On July 25, John Labatt was brought to the prison to confront McCardell. He was accompanied by Norman Newton, the crown attorney in Meisner's trial. "Hello, John," McCardell insouciantly greeted the beer tycoon. It was a startling, highly unsettling moment for Labatt. McCardell matched exactly the description Labatt had given in his sworn affidavit at the time that Meisner's extradition was being arranged: "The first man, my guard, was five feet, nine or ten inches, medium build, athletic type, 175 pounds, thirty to forty years of age, dark complexion, hair black, thin face, nothing about his voice to distinguish it from a Canadian's." After a lengthy recitation by McCardell of details of the crime that were not public knowledge, Labatt concluded he had been "my guard" and told Gardner and Weeks so.

Labatt had genuinely believed Meisner was guilty. Now he began to worry that he had picked out the wrong man, condemning him to fifteen years in jail for a crime he hadn't committed.

This was one occasion when Bannon did not benefit financially from being a stool pigeon. Considering he had been part of the kidnapping plot, the Labatts justifiably concluded that he did not deserve any more of the reward money. On July 26, the day after Labatt identified McCardell, Bannon was arrested in Windsor, his hometown. Knowles could not be found, and a manhunt was launched for him.

In return for McCardell's confession and his waiving proceedings to extradite him to Canada to be tried for the kidnapping, Canadian authorities agreed to try to persuade U.S. officials to drop the robbery charges against him in the produce truck holdup. The Americans agreed, provided that McCardell be returned to the United States, after serving his sentence in Canada for the kidnapping, to stand trial for additional crimes.

On August 1, Crown Point prison authorities handed McCardell over to Inspector Gardner and Sergeant Weeks so that he could be taken to London for trial. They were accompanied by the FBI agent to make certain that McCardell had no chance to escape. They drove to nearby Chicago, where they boarded the 9:19 a.m. train for London.

They arrived in London at 6:47 p.m. Waiting for them on the station platform were Newton, an OPP sergeant, two London detectives, and a horde of newspaper reporters and photographers. Inspector Gardner got off the train first, followed by McCardell, who was shackled to Weeks. "He was wearing a dark blue suit and had a straw hat held closely to his face to keep photographers from getting a picture," the *London Free Press* reported. "Only for a second did McCardell peek around the corner of his hat just after he had stepped from the train. He looked frightened and tired."

Continuing to shield his face with his hat, McCardell was led by Weeks and Newton across the platform and through the station to a waiting police car. Photographers dashed after them, trying to get McCardell to lower his hat so that they could get a picture. When he refused, a photographer yanked his hat away. "You've broken my arm!" McCardell cried out. Nobody believed him because he continued to clutch the battered remnants before his face. When he entered the Middlesex County Jail he dropped the hat. A few minutes later, he fainted. The jail physician was fetched, and when he confirmed that the arm had indeed been broken, McCardell was taken by taxi from the jail to the Victoria Hospital for his arm to be set. He was then placed in a prisoner's cage within the hospital, where he was to spend the night, with a police guard keeping watch.

At about 10:30 the next morning, with his arm in a sling and a grey coat buttoned around him, he was brought to the county police court. "He looked thin and tired but not as flustered as when he stepped off the train the previous night," the *London Free Press* reported. Convivial by nature, McCardell chatted with police, smiling several times. He nodded in a friendly manner at reporters, smiled at them, too, and told them he harboured no ill will over the accidental breaking of his arm. "I know it wasn't intentional, so there are no hard feelings."

McCardell's court appearance was brief and dramatic. Police Magistrate C.W. Hawkshaw began reading the charge against him. "Michael McCardell, you are charged that on August 14, 1934, in the County of Lambton, and the County of Middlesex, and elsewhere you unlawfully did kidnap John Labatt with intent to cause him —"

"I plead guilty," McCardell interrupted.

Hawkshaw responded that McCardell would first have to go to trial and began to reread the charge.

"I want trial by magistrate here," McCardell interrupted once again.

"You haven't got a lawyer," Hawkshaw pointed out. "Would you like to wait and get the advice of a lawyer before you plead?"

"No."

"Would you like an adjournment to think it over?"

"No, I am prepared to plead guilty," McCardell insisted.

The magistrate then reread the kidnapping charge.

"Guilty," said McCardell, and this time the plea was officially recorded.

Hawkshaw proceeded to the second charge, of armed robbery. Once again McCardell asked for trial by magistrate, but when asked to plead, replied, "Not guilty."

"I would ask you to dismiss the charge," Norman Newton interjected. "In view of the plea of guilty in the kidnapping charge, I offer no evidence in the armed robbery charge." In other words, a quid pro quo deal had been struck between McCardell and Newton whereby, in return for McCardell's guilty plea to the kidnapping charge, Newton would overlook his robbing Labatt of the $99.

Newton then asked for sentencing to be delayed for about two weeks, expecting that, in the interim, McCardell would be testifying at Bannon's preliminary hearing. As it turned out, McCardell was not sentenced for several months.

A police escort then returned McCardell to the hospital. During his appearance, Bannon had been sitting in a corner of the room, awaiting a date to be set for his own preliminary hearing. At one point he lit a cigarette, a breach of courtroom etiquette. "Bannon, put that cigarette out," a police officer ordered. Bannon, sullenly, did not reply.

His hearing was set for August 26. Before he was returned to the Middlesex County Jail he asked George Mitchell, a London lawyer and alderman who was watching the proceedings, to represent him. Mitchell said he couldn't because he was defending "Piccolo Pete" Murray, also accused in the kidnapping. Although months had passed since his arrest, Murray had yet to be tried and was languishing in limbo in the county jail.

On March 25, 1935, Murray's wife Vera, who worked as a waitress in a Covington cafe, had written John Labatt: "We are a poor family and we do not have any money for which to fight such a case. We now have no home for I had to sell everything we had to live on while my poor husband is in jail…. I cannot bring any of the witnesses to his trial for I have not the means of getting there or myself either." She did not receive a reply.

On August 5, three days after McCardell's guilty plea, Gerald Nicholson, who had driven Labatt and his kidnappers from Muskoka to Toronto, was arrested in his hometown of Windsor and charged as an accessory. That left only Knowles and Pegram to be apprehended. One week later, Nicholson was released on $5,000 bail while awaiting trial.

While Charles Bell was by far the best known defence lawyer in the Labatt trials, Bannon's counsel, Alexander Stanley Fergusson of London, was also highly regarded by his peers. Born in 1900, Fergusson enrolled at the University of Western Ontario when he was just sixteen. Besides being a brilliant student, he was a football star. Upon reaching the age when he could enlist, he joined the Royal Air Force in 1918, the last year of World War I. Afterward, he was in the first class of veterans to enroll at Osgoode Hall in Toronto.

John Labatt was not called as a witness at Bannon's August 26 police court hearing because Crown Attorney Norman Newton believed McCardell's testimony would be more than enough to convince the magistrate that Bannon should be tried.

Newton began his questioning of McCardell by asking, "You know John Bannon?"

"Yes."

"You were a member of the band that kidnapped Mr. Labatt?"
"Yes."

McCardell named himself, Russell Knowles and Albert Pegram as the actual kidnappers and Bannon as an accomplice in planning the crime. He proceeded to give the "inside story" of the kidnapping.

Within minutes he rocked the courtroom with a bombshell: a claim that Louis McCaughey, the sales manager at John Labatt Ltd., was to have received a share of the ransom money from a 1931 kidnapping plot against John Labatt planned by McCardell, Earl Rossi (a Chicago gangster who was now dead) and Bannon. McCardell said the idea for that plan had been Rossi's and that Rossi had proposed giving McCaughey a "split" as a reward for information he had provided. McCardell said he had brought Bannon into the scheme after meeting him in 1931, but that the plan was abandoned when McCardell learned Labatt was in poor health. McCardell said he never met McCaughey, and had only heard about him from Rossi.

The Labatts had trusted McCaughey, an ex-policeman, so implicitly that Hugh had asked McCaughey to drive him, per the kidnappers' instructions, to the Royal York Hotel on August 14, 1934, because he was too upset to drive himself.

McCaughey was in court with his lawyer during McCardell's testimony. So was Hugh Labatt. During an adjournment, Hugh suspended McCaughey from his job until the accusation was confirmed or proved false.

Newton took McCardell through the June 1934 conference in Detroit to discuss kidnapping Labatt. He started by asking who attended.

"Russell Knowles, Albert Pegram, John Bannon and David 'Ted' Meisner. We met in Meisner's room." His mention of Meisner's name seemed to confirm that he had indeed been part of the kidnapping, but McCardell quickly dashed this assumption.

"Ted was asked to go in on it, but he said he didn't like the proposition and didn't want to have anything to do with it. He was to have met us again the next morning but he packed his bag and returned to Covington. I never saw him again."

"Never again?" asked Newton.

"Never!" McCardell repeated. "That's the man who stands wrongly convicted."

Newton then placed in evidence three revolvers and six tear-gas cartridges. These were the weapons the police had recovered from the golf course near the Muskoka hideout. "Whose is this?" Newton asked, putting a gun on the ledge of the witness stand before McCardell and then picking it up so that the jury could see it more clearly.

"Pegram's."

"And this?" Newton displayed the second.

"Knowles'."

"And this is yours?" inquired Newton, showing the third gun.

"It *was*," McCardell replied dryly, his emphasis of the past tense touching off laughter in the courtroom.

Turning to the question of proving Bannon's involvement, Newton asked McCardell which kidnappers had rented the Muskoka cottage.

"Around August 1, 1934, Pegram, Bannon and I went to Muskoka to rent a cottage in which we could hide Labatt. Bannon was not right there while we rented the cottage from Mr. Prowse."

McCardell then gave a detailed account of the kidnapping: the car chase; the note Labatt was forced to write his brother; the goggles; parking Labatt's car in front of St. Joseph's Hospital in London; instructing Hugh to go to the Royal York Hotel in Toronto and wait for instructions about the ransom; Knowles' dinnertime encounter at the King Edward Hotel with the unsuspecting RCMP officer; Pegram's stranding of his erstwhile partners; turning to Nicholson for help in driving Labatt to Toronto; "getting rid of" Labatt in Toronto.

"All the things that Labatt said Meisner did were what I did, but how he got us so mixed I don't know. Ted Meisner is a light-built fellow, but I weighed 190 pounds. As for this fellow [Piccolo Pete] Murray, I never heard of him."

August 26, 1935, had proved to be a memorable date in the Labatt kidnapping case, a possible turning point for David Meisner. "If McCardell's confession is true, the conviction of David Meisner will likely become famous in Canadian court history," the *London Free Press* wrote, "the first recorded major instance of wrongful identification in Canadian courts."

Based on McCardell's evidence, Bannon was committed for trial at the fall assizes in October.

Throughout McCardell's long testimony, two observers were listening particularly intently — Charles Bell, Meisner's attorney, and Alderman George Mitchell, who was Murray's. At the completion of McCardell's many hours on the stand, Bell declared, "That is the truth. I am hoping that, in the interest of fairness, what we heard today will be applied to all. I expect that the Department of Justice will be informed of what we heard today and that it will take appropriate action. If not, I will apply for a new trial."

The process of informing the Department of Justice required Crown Attorney Norman Newton to notify Attorney General Arthur Roebuck, who would forward the matter to the federal minister of justice if he felt there had been a wrongful conviction. But at this time, no official action was taken. The Crown was treating McCardell's confession with caution, weighing it against the testimony of the Muskoka witnesses who had testified Meisner was one of the kidnappers. "Powerful interests set out to block Meisner's release," Bell wrote in "Ditching David Meisner." "After repeated efforts, I desisted for the time being. I knew it was only a matter of weeks when the final showdown must come." This was a reference to Bannon's upcoming trial.

For "Piccolo Pete" Murray, the prospects were better. George Mitchell conferred with Newton immediately after Bannon's hearing ended, urging that Murray be given a non-jury trial the very next day before a county judge, rather than the jury trial for which he had opted. Newton agreed and scheduled it for the very next morning before County Judge Uriah McFadden.

Murray's trial on August 27 was over in minutes, a mere formality.

"How do you wish to be tried?" McFadden asked.

"By a county court judge without jury."

"How do you plead, guilty or not guilty?"

"Not guilty, Your Honour."

Newton then said, "In my opinion, there is not sufficient evidence for the trial to proceed. Therefore, I will offer no evidence against him." However, he added that the minister of justice had ordered Murray's deportation back to the United States that day.

"Very well," McFadden said. "The Crown has offered no evidence and the verdict is not guilty. The prisoner will be turned over to the immigration authorities."

Mitchell then attempted on Murray's behalf to get compensation for Labatt's wrongful identification. "There is no doubt he made a mistake. Whether or not there were reasonable grounds for the mistake, I am not prepared to say."

"But the verdict is not guilty," the judge interrupted.

"But this man was arrested and yanked from his country over here," Mitchell declared vehemently. "He has been held in custody for seven months and thirteen days. I believe this man is entitled to some compensation. He is destitute and penniless. I understand he is to be given a railroad ticket and dumped back into his own country."

"It has been regrettable," Newton stated, "but we moved to release him at the earliest possible moment."

"This is not the court in which to seek compensation," McFadden said, forestalling further pleas by Mitchell.

With a brief "thank you," Murray left the courtroom with Mitchell. Surrounded by reporters and photographers, he courteously thanked them for the way they had reported his case. "I feel you were my friends throughout," he said. Then he walked over and shook hands with Inspector Gardner of the Ontario Provincial Police and Sergeant Weeks of the RCMP. "Inspector Gardner and Sergeant Weeks have been good to me ever since my arrest. I believe they really believed I was innocent from the first."

"Were you worried while you were in jail?" Murray was asked.

"You bet I was. It was mighty close to fifteen years for me.

"It will be great to get back to Covington," he added. "My wife will be waiting for me. She wrote me every day."

Asked about his immediate plans, he said, "I'm going back home, and then this winter I am going to Florida and try to catch up on some of the summer I missed."

"Where are you going to get the money?"

"I don't know, but I'll get it."

Newton asked Murray what he would like to do while he waited for the immigration officials. "I'd like to see this town," he responded. "I haven't seen anything of it except from a jail window. But that's the truth. I'd like to look it over."

Newton agreed, and Murray was given a tour plus dinner. During his car ride, he asked the driver to stop at a tavern so he could try a glass of Labatt beer. "What do you think of it?" he was asked.

"I think I will reserve my judgment," he replied. Then he uttered his only complaint. It was brief and barbed: "I wanted to see if Labatt's beer was as bad as his eyesight," he said.

In the interval between Bannon's hearing and his trial, yet one more peculiar development occurred. McCardell requested a meeting with Charles Bell, Meisner's lawyer, saying he wished to ask Bell about the Canadian legal system. After they had discussed certain matters on which he sought advice and which Bell kept confidential, Bell questioned McCardell about "one or two things" he wanted to know about the Labatt case.

"McCardell," Bell said, "Labatt always insisted that he could see partly through your eye coverings, and I am sure his insistence was in good faith. What was the fact about it all?"

McCardell smiled wanly. "I will tell you," he said, "just what happened. Labatt was right about court plaster having been put on his eyes. I bought him white, pink and black, and I bought him a pair of goggles with sides on them which I am sorry to say cost me $8.50. [In court, McCardell had said they cost $8.00.] I cut out round pieces of the black court plaster and stuck them on the inside of the goggles. Once those goggles were on, no living being could see anything. They were always on while we were on the road, but I took them off when we were in the cottage. He never saw a thing on the way."

"According to his evidence given at Meisner's trial," Bell remarked, "Labatt slept a good deal in the cottage."

"Never saw anybody in my life sleep like him," McCardell said. "We could hardly wake him up." He paused, then quipped, "Must be strong beer they make."

"The newspapers had a good deal to say," Bell said, "about the running gun fight in Michigan in which you were captured."

McCardell again smiled feebly. "It was certainly some fight," he declared. "The fact is I was in Calumet, Michigan, with a friend of mine. Neither of us was armed. As we came out of a roadhouse, three automobile loads of police came along. We got to our car and stayed ahead of them for a short time, but they put two or three bullets through the back of it, so we decided to quit. We stopped the car suddenly and ran in different directions into the fields. The police had one small searchlight which they put on me, and next thing I knew they shot off my finger. The police then took our car up a side road and riddled it with bullets. They shot out all the glass there was in it, then towed the car and showed it to the newspaper reporters to prove what a desperate battle they had had. Then they took me over, first to Hammond, Indiana, and then to Crown Point."

"But I don't understand that," Bell replied. "In the United States you have to be extradited from one state to another."

"Oh, they didn't bother about that," said McCardell. "They just went ahead and kidnapped me." McCardell spoke earnestly, apparently oblivious to the irony of his remark.

"Outrageous," Bell murmured, tongue-in-cheek. "Kidnapping is the most cruel of crimes."

"Now let me ask you one more thing," said McCardell. "Is it true that in Canada there's one law for the rich and another for the poor?"

Bell replied, "Three-fingered Abe, I said before you were a simpleminded person. In Canada there is no law for the poor at all. That is, unless the poor can induce some lawyer to put up a fight for them. But there is one piece of advice I'll add to that I have already given you. When you get out after doing your time in the Kingston Penitentiary, if you can't go straight, take up something else than kidnapping. It really isn't in your line."

Jack Bannon's trial began on October 17. A few minutes before it started he was brought up to the courtroom from the cells below. The husky, two-hundred-pound Bannon was fashionably dressed in a dark grey suit with a light blue shirt, matching tie and a matching handkerchief in the jacket's breast pocket. "He seemed a little worried," the *London Free Press* reported. "He looked around the courtroom, nodded to reporters and smiled a number of times."

By coincidence, Justice McFarland, who had presided over Meisner's trial, was once again on the London circuit and was the judge in Bannon's case, too. Sitting at the prosecution table with Crown Attorney Norman Newton were Ontario Provincial Police Inspector Hamar Gardner and RCMP Detective Sergeant Ted Weeks, the two main investigators in the kidnapping. John and Hugh Labatt sat in the front row of the spectators' seats. Charles Bell was there, too.

The jurors had made an unusual request of the judge. Anticipating a long trial, the twelve jurors and one alternate were unhappy that, because they would not be allowed to read the newspapers out of concern that they might be influenced by stories about the case, they would not be able to follow their beloved comic strips in the *Free Press*. They persuaded McFarland to order that the comics be cut out of the paper daily and distributed to them so that they could keep up to date. This was done throughout the seven days of the trial.

When court opened, Bannon was arraigned on charges of kidnapping and armed robbery.

"John Basil Bannon, how do you plead?"

"Not guilty."

At this point, Newton asked to have the indictment against Bannon amended because of a typographical error that mistakenly gave the date of the kidnapping as August 14, 1935, rather than August 14, 1934. Coming from a man who had won the case against Meisner in some part because of a discrepancy in dates between what Detective Hall said in his testimony and his records, this was an embarrassing moment for Newton.

Noting that the Labatt kidnapping case had been referred to as the "most important case in Canadian criminal history," he reviewed the circumstances of the kidnapping and the ransom note. "The Crown doesn't claim that Bannon was one of the three who held up Labatt and kidnapped him," he said. Instead, it had charged Bannon under the "common purpose" section of the Criminal Code.

"As early as 1931 a plot was hatched by the accused to kidnap John Labatt. There were two previous attempts before 1934 to kidnap John Labatt. There were different gangs involved, but we allege that the man Bannon was the one who was in every attempt."

As evidence of Bannon's involvement in the actual 1934 kidnapping, Newton said Bannon had gone with McCardell and Pegram to rent the Muskoka cottage and had kept the kidnappers' revolvers at his house while they prepared for the abduction. For the first time, Newton divulged publicly that Bannon was a police stool pigeon and had squealed on both Meisner and McCardell in return for a share of the $5,000 reward being offered for information leading to the capture of the kidnappers. Newton revealed that Bannon had received $500 for what had been thought to be helpful information regarding Meisner and had attempted to reap an additional portion regarding McCardell.

Provincial Constable Ford Thurston of Windsor was the first witness called. He told of arresting Bannon in Windsor nearly three months earlier, on July 26, and then searching his home, where he found a hollow post on the verandah. "The top lifted off, leaving a hollow about three feet deep," he said. That cavity was where McCardell had said he, Pegram and Knowles had hidden their revolvers in advance of the kidnapping.

After Thurston's brief appearance, John Labatt took the stand. His demeanour was markedly different than at Meisner's trial. "He seemed a shaken man, displaying considerably more nervousness than when he appeared against David Meisner," the *London Free Press* reported. "As before he gave careful consideration, showing even hesitancy, as he answered questions."

Charles Bell also observed a big change in Labatt. "John Labatt's appearance is a positive shock," he wrote in "Ditching David Meisner." "Torn as he was by anxiety in the winter, today he looks a wreck. Wrangling detective and police officials who are keeping the stiletto ever handy for use on each other, wire pullers and grafters galore looking for personal kudos and 'sugar' have made John Labatt's life a hell on earth during all the summer and autumn down to now. Given his choice between some of the minions of the law and the jailbirds, he would plump unhesitatingly for the latter."

As Labatt recounted the now-familiar story of his kidnapping, captivity and release, he carefully substituted "my guard" for those instances when he had previously said "Meisner."

As Bell took notes, Crown Attorney Norman Newton raised the issue of whether Labatt had mistakenly identified Meisner.

"In January last year, you gave evidence at the trial of David Meisner?" Newton began.

"Yes," Labatt replied.

"You identified him as one of three men who captured you?"

"Yes."

"You said he was your guard?"

"Yes."

"On July 25, 1935, you were at the Crown Point, Indiana, prison, along with me, and had a long conversation there with Michael McCardell?"

"Yes," said Labatt.

"As a result, what conclusions did you arrive at?"

"I came to the conclusion he must have been my guard."

Justice McFarland interjected, believing Labatt's statement needed clarification: "Instead of Meisner?"

"Yes, my lord, instead of Meisner."

Following this admission, Newton turned to the issue of tying Bannon to the crime by having Labatt describe the Christmas Eve 1934 meeting at which Bannon tried to extort $5,000 of the $25,000 payment Labatt had pledged to make in exchange for his release.

"Bannon said, 'You've been a prospect for a long time,'" Labatt testified. "I understood him to remark, 'I'm not in the kidnapping this year. You were wanted last year [1933]. You remember in the summer of 1933 you were at Sarnia and you and Mrs. Labatt went to the ticket office. On the way back to the beach you passed a parked car. I was in that car. Meisner was in that car. Earl Rossi was in it and someone else, I think Russell Knowles.'"

On cross-examination, Bannon's lawyer, Alexander Fergusson, questioned Labatt about his identification of Meisner and Murray. In contrast to his certainty when he was answering Newton, Labatt now hedged.

"Is it true that you said at Meisner's trial that you would never forget the face of the man who held you up?" Fergusson asked.

"I never will. I remember clearly those features. Both Meisner and McCardell have thin features."

"Is there any doubt in your mind it was David Meisner who held you up?"

"I don't know whether it was Meisner or McCardell."

"And is there any doubt about 'Piccolo Pete' Murray?"

"Murray looks just like the man. That's all I can say," Labatt replied. "I must say," he added after a pause, "that I feel a little startled about identifications. I don't feel as sure about those things as I did."

Labatt was followed to the stand by a tall, thin man with dark hair greying slightly at the temples. The spectators craned forward in their seats to stare at this unexpected witness, a newcomer to the case. Newton asked that the man be sworn in as "Mr. X" rather than by his real identity, "because the underworld has its own way of dealing with men who talk out of turn." This statement caused a sensation in the courtroom. A buzz of puzzled, speculative comments burst out. Court officials moved swiftly to restore quiet. Newton showed a piece of paper with the man's real name printed on it to Justice McFarland and Fergusson. The lawyers had to shout at Mr. X because he was hard of hearing.

Identified as an illegal drug dealer, Mr. X testified that Bannon had proposed to him in 1932 that they kidnap a Hamilton man. "When that project fell through, Bannon suggested we kidnap Labatt and I refused," he said. "Three or four months later, Bannon brought up the idea again at a Toronto hotel during a meeting to which I brought Albert Pegram. The meeting originally was called to discuss how to get some narcotics to sell. We concluded we couldn't get any then, so Jack proposed kidnapping Labatt and Pegram seemed interested."

In a blistering cross-examination, Fergusson scathingly attacked Mr. X's credibility as a witness in view of his lengthy criminal record.

"Are you not a rum-runner and narcotics dealer, and have you not been arrested several times for armed robbery?" Fergusson demanded.

"Yes," Mr. X admitted.

"And you have been a police stool pigeon, too, haven't you?" Fergusson continued.

"Yes," Mr. X. conceded.

"And what are you being paid to inform on others in this case?" Fergusson asked sharply.

"Nothing. I am doing it because I think it is my duty."

"You mean you deal in narcotics and then get other poor suckers into trouble?"

"I do my duty," Mr. X repeated.

"Does it give you a pleasant feeling to do your duty?"

"Yes."

"So you are a stool pigeon. Well, that's enough." With a contemptuous wave, Fergusson, whose client was also a stool pigeon, indicated that he was through with Mr. X.

Most of Friday, October 18 and Monday, October 21 were occupied by McCardell's testimony. He repeated the assertion he had made at Bannon's August preliminary hearing that Bannon was involved with him and the now-dead Earl Rossi in a 1931 plot to kidnap Labatt as well as in the actual 1934 abduction.

"From 1931 to 1934, did you take part in any kidnap plans?" Newton asked. Mr. X had said Bannon had plotted to kidnap Labatt in 1932, while Labatt said Bannon told him he was planning it for 1933.

"No," McCardell answered.

"Did Bannon tell you of any plans?"

"He told me he and Rossi and another man came to kidnap Labatt in 1933. In April 1934 I went to Windsor and discussed the proposed kidnapping of Labatt with Bannon. We had a meeting, but at that time we didn't have finances enough to go ahead with it."

McCardell went on to describe the June 1934 conference, which had included Meisner, that he had convened, then proceeded to do his best to clear Meisner. "Ted Meisner tried to persuade us not to kidnap John Labatt. He said he didn't want to have anything to do with it and that he thought we shouldn't touch it, either."

As he recounted his tale of the kidnapping, some minor discrepancies arose between his version and Labatt's. Labatt had stated that the ransom note was written right after the kidnappers surrounded his car and yanked him out of it. McCardell said Labatt was driven away for a mile first. Labatt said the first words spoken to him were, "Stick 'em up quick. This is a kidnapping." McCardell stated he said nothing about it being a kidnapping when he first approached Labatt.

McCardell also claimed that, during the whole investigation of the kidnapping, Bannon had provided him with "inside" information on what the police were doing.

Under cross-examination, McCardell conceded that he had done nothing to help Meisner avoid conviction, then added: "We were making plans to do a little fixing to get Meisner out — fixing as we sometimes do it in the United States. I knew he was innocent and he was a friend of mine and I wanted to get him out."

McCardell, who had a penchant for braggadocio, did not elaborate on what he meant by "fixing." There had been only one attempt to break into the Kingston Penitentiary during its century-long history. In 1857 an inebriated former inmate used a ladder to climb to the top of the prison wall, lowered himself onto the other side with a rope, then went to the clerk's office and robbed the cash box. Unfortunately for him, the rope unfastened as he began his return trip and he fell back into the prison grounds. He took shelter under some straw in the stable, but was soon discovered. After serving a six-month sentence, he impudently returned to the prison and demanded that the warden return his coat, which he had left behind. The warden refused and sternly directed him to leave town, which he did.

Moreover, in its long history there had been very few escapes from the Big House. The most recent had occurred on September 10, 1923, when Norman "Red" Ryan, serving twenty-five years for armed robbery, and four other inmates climbed over the wall and fled in a car stolen from a nearby property. Two months passed before he was captured on December 14 in the United States.

The next witness was RCMP Sergeant Ted Weeks. It was Weeks's appearance in the courtroom along with the American G-man during Meisner's trial that had triggered the flight of Meisner's alibi witnesses, Detectives Hall and Seiter. Weeks made a startling admission: he had known all along that the contradiction between the date on which Hall testified he had seen Meisner at the Covington railway station (August 17, 1934) and the date in Hall's report (September 17, 1934) was due to a typographical error made at the Covington police department.

Charles Bell had been right in suspecting that the "just one month out" date in the report was peculiar, but he had been wrong in attributing it to a "smart trick for a rig on the part of someone in Kentucky." The discrepancy was not due to sinister tampering but to sloppiness, spotlighting the great harm that can be inflicted on a person's life by clerical errors and a failure to check for accuracy. Weeks testified that he had been asked when he left Covington for London to inform Hall and Seiter about the error, but that he had not done so.

"Why not?" Fergusson demanded.

"Because when I arrived at the courthouse, Hall was already on the stand."

"As a matter of fact, didn't you arrive three hours before he went on the stand?" Fergusson pressed.

"I believe that's so, but since the message had been given to me by a person who had no use for Hall or Seiter, I made no attempt to give Hall the message," Weeks responded. Fergusson dropped the issue.

Weeks went on to explain that he had turned to Bannon for help in tracking down the kidnappers because for a long time Bannon had been a reliable source about underworld activities. Soon after Labatt's release, Weeks had sought out Bannon at his favourite hangout, Peter's Restaurant, in his home town of Windsor. Plying him with drinks because "the more Bannon drinks, the more he talks," Weeks pumped him for information. "More than anyone else in Windsor, I believed he was able to supply information about people in rackets and people likely to do kidnapping."

"He told me that Meisner had been in on three kidnappings and might be involved in Labatt's, and also told me where I would find him in Covington," Weeks recalled.

Continuing his recollection of his conversation with Bannon, Weeks said he had told Bannon that he thought Albert Pegram was involved. "He told me, 'Pegram doesn't have enough guts.' 'Why do you say that?' I asked. Bannon replied: 'Because the last time I saw Pegram he called me a liar and socked me in the mouth.'" Like Bannon, Pegram was husky and weighed about two hundred pounds.

Bannon and Weeks — posing as "Whitey Connelly," a supposed racketeer — had gone to Nashville, Tennessee, where Pegram's mother lived, to try to persuade her to contact her son and convince him to surrender. Bannon had given her a letter that Weeks had drafted for him to sign.

"Dear Al," the letter said, "You will no doubt be surprised to hear from me. I have an important message to give to you. It will be to your advantage to try and connect with me there or later in Windsor at my home." Bannon gave his picture, along with the letter, to Pegram's mother for her to show Pegram as proof of his veracity. Whether the letter was passed on to Pegram was never determined, but he did not surrender.

Many months passed until Weeks realized that, instead of outsmarting Bannon, it was Bannon who had duped *him*. "I began to think he knew quite a bit about the kidnapping — in fact, too much," Weeks testified ruefully.

The next witness was Gerald Nicholson, who had driven McCardell, Knowles and Labatt to Toronto after Pegram had fled with the kidnappers' car. He had been convicted as an accessory and given a one-year probation term.

After Nicholson described his role as chauffeur, he was followed to the stand by a teenager named Fuller Pines who said it was his car that Nicholson had borrowed for the drive. His brief time on the witness stand produced some unexpected merriment.

"Do you own the car that Gerald Nicholson used?" Newton asked.

"Well, I don't own it. Dad bought it; it's registered in Mother's name and I drive it," Pines replied.

"An entirely modern family," Justice McFarland remarked wryly to the chuckles of the spectators.

Pines' car had been parked outside the courthouse in case further proof was needed that it was the one in question, but his testimony was regarded as sufficient.

Although an accused does not have to testify, Bannon elected to do so. His turn came on October 23, the fourth day of the trial (a weekend had intervened). "He seemed to be carried away with excitement while telling his story and had to be checked more than once by the judge. He continued to go into long explanations on minor points," the *London Free Press* wrote.

On the official records Bannon's employment was listed as being in real estate, but when he was asked in court for his occupation he said that he had been "a railway man and was later in the whisky and beer business."

Bannon admitted he had dealt in "bootleg gold" — high-grade liquor — and was aware of schemes in the past by hoodlums other than McCardell, Pegram and Knowles to kidnap Labatt. However, he denied he was the contact man in the actual 1934 snatch. He said he had first heard plans to kidnap Labatt back in 1928 or 1929 at a Windsor hotel where racketeers made their headquarters. "I had been supplying beer to the men. A man from Chicago mentioned that the Labatt boys were slated for a touch. Another of the crowd suggested they take a Labatt manager instead of one of the Labatts. That was all that was said about it at the time.

"A month or two later, when I was going through London on a liquor deal, I went to [Labatt sales manager] Louis McCaughey's home and told him somebody was planning to take a shake from the Labatts. McCaughey told me I must be wrong because they could never get away with it. He said that with Inspector Gardner [of the Ontario Provincial Police] in charge of police here, no one would try such a thing in this district."

Bannon's lawyer, Alexander Fergusson, then moved forward in time to 1934.

"Did you meet with McCardell in June 1934, as McCardell claims?"

"No, sir." That was denial number one.

"Where were you on August 14, 1934, the day John Labatt was kidnapped?"

"Around my home, around the corner, in the park."

"Did you enter into any plot or have any arrangement with anyone regarding the kidnapping of John Labatt?"

"No, sir." Denial number two.

"Was there any arrangement [whereby] you were to share any ransom?"

"No, sir." Denial number three.

"Do you know of any arrangement whereby Louis McCaughey, the sales manager at the Labatt brewery, was to get any share of the money?"

"No, sir." Denial number four. More were yet to come.

"I suppose you, like everyone, read of the kidnapping in the newspaper."

"That afternoon I read of it."

"When did you first take an active part about the kidnapping?"

"That afternoon, Alex Colvin of Labatt's Windsor office approached me while I was in a saloon to see if I could help find the kidnappers because I have a reputation around the Border Cities [Windsor and Detroit] as a kidnap expert."

Bannon did admit he had driven to Muskoka twice with Pegram prior to the kidnapping, but insisted there was no connection. "The first time, we went to collect a debt from Gerald Nicholson, who owed

Pegram money, and the second time we stopped on the way back from North Bay, where we had got some high-grade bootleg gold."

Crown Attorney Norman Newton began his cross-examination by inquiring, "Have you a good memory?"

"Not extra good."

"Then you'll agree with me that if a man is telling an untrue story and he has told it before, he needs a good memory?"

"Yes, sir."

"I suggest to you that when you previously told me of the meeting with McCaughey, you told me it was in 1931 at the Hotel London." Bannon had just testified that the meeting was held in 1928 or 1929 at McCaughey's home.

"I don't remember telling you of a meeting."

"You told me a Ted Newbury was at the meeting. Did you set back the date of the meeting because you knew Newbury was dead in 1931?"

"He was killed after 1931."

"I suggest to you the time you were in the Hotel London, you were there to decide the Labatt kidnapping."

"That is positively not true." Denial number five.

"In 1931, did you not discuss the Labatt kidnapping with Pegram and Mr. X?"

"Positively not." Denial number six.

"Did you know Mr. X went to the police the day after the Labatt kidnapping?"

"I wouldn't be surprised," Bannon laughed. "Mr. X has been very active with the police."

When asked about the December 24, 1934, and January 3, 1935, meetings with Labatt, Bannon categorically denied saying that he, Earl Rossi, Meisner and Knowles had followed Labatt in 1933 in an effort to kidnap him. Denial number seven.

"You thought with Meisner in prison, McCardell could not be extradited," Newton suggested, "and so it would be safe to name McCardell, and as he could not be brought here, you could collect the reward."

"I didn't ask for any reward." Denial number eight.

"Do you remember one day coming to my office and pushing the police out and closing the door and then saying to me, 'For God's sake, can't I cop a plea of conspiracy and take a small rap? If Ted Weeks goes on the stand and tells what I did in this case I wouldn't have a chance.' Do you remember that?"

"No, I don't." Denial number nine. "The jail governor came to my cell with a note saying you wanted to know if I would plead guilty to a conspiracy charge in the morning, and I said yes if I knew what time I would have to do it."

"The only message I ever sent you was a warrant for your arrest," Newton stated sternly.

Bannon then left the stand.

Next up was Louis McCaughey. This was his opportunity to clear himself of McCardell's claim that Bannon had told McCardell that McCaughey was aware of the plot to kidnap Labatt and was to share in the $150,000 ransom.

McCaughey said his acquaintanceship with Bannon dated back to the early 1920s when there was still Prohibition in much of Canada. McCaughey, then a policeman, had arrested him for smuggling a hundred cases of liquor.

"Have you ever been involved in any attempt to kidnap John Labatt?" Bannon's lawyer Alexander Fergusson asked.

"No," McCaughey replied firmly.

"Have you ever done anything to assist anyone in the kidnapping of John Labatt?"

"No."

"Have you ever been in any position where you might expect any share of ransom money that might be collected by the kidnappers of John Labatt?"

"No."

However, McCaughey did admit the topic had come up with Bannon in 1932. He said he was called to a room in the Hotel London by two men who had accompanied Bannon to town and had explained they "wanted to get some beer for export purposes" — Prohibition was still in effect in the United States — and that he replied that "the Labatt brewery had all the business it could do in Canada and was not interested in exporting."

During the meeting, Bannon left the room for a few minutes, according to McCaughey, and "a suggestion was made that John Labatt be kidnapped. One of them, who called himself 'Cameron,' described the idea as a clever publicity stunt that would result in free advertising for Labatt and thereby boost sales.

"I was dumbfounded," he recalled. "I said Mr. Labatt was a fine man. You can't get away with that. And I warned them not to try it, telling them to get out of London and stay out." McCaughey stated that he did not know the identities of the two men then, but subsequently learned that "Cameron" was an alias used by Russell Knowles.

Asked if he had alerted the Labatts or told the police, McCaughey acknowledged he had not done so. "I was afraid that if I talked I would be killed," he explained. On suspension by Hugh Labatt since McCardell mentioned his possible connection in August, McCaughey was fired after the Bannon trial for having withheld the information about the kidnap proposals.

As the next day, Thursday, was Thanksgiving, the trial was recessed for the day. On Friday, the closing arguments were presented.

Fergusson bluntly conceded, "My client has been a fool a good portion of his life." Then he continued, "But the only direct evidence against him is that of Michael McCardell, a self-confessed desperado. And McCardell's story is a tissue of lies with two objectives. First, McCardell is determined to free his friend David Meisner. Second, he is determined to convict Bannon as vengeance for Bannon's having informed the police of his real identity when he was captured last summer."

Crown Attorney Norman Newton's summation was brief. Seizing on Bannon's description of himself as an "expert about kidnaps," he flung the phrase back cleverly, turning Bannon's self-praise into self-incrimi-nation. "In truth, Bannon's deserved reputation is that of an expert kidnapper," Newton said. "He is the one man who was connected from the first with attempts to kidnap John Labatt."

The case went to the jury at 2:45 p.m. It took five hours and forty-five minutes to reach its verdict.

Throughout the trial, Bannon had appeared carefree, joking with his guards, laughing at the Crown witnesses and making wisecracks about Newton. But as the jury returned at 8:30 p.m., "the mask fell from his face for a minute," according to the *London Free Press*. "He turned grey and shot a worried look at the foreman of the jury. But as the twelve men walked past him, each looked the other way. Not one of them glanced at the prisoner."

Legal lore has it that if jurors look at the accused after reaching their verdict, it is good news for the accused; if they avert their gaze, the news is bad. There have been numerous exceptions, but this was not to be one of them.

"Guilty," declared foreman James Dymond on both charges, kidnapping and robbery. The jury had chosen to believe McCardell rather than Bannon. McCardell had got even with Bannon for Bannon's double-cross.

Fergusson requested mercy for Bannon on the grounds that he was forty-eight years old with a wife and three children. Justice McFarland was unsympathetic.

"I am not going to deliver a lecture to you," he said. "You have had a fair trial and have been brilliantly defended. The sentence is fifteen years' imprisonment on each charge, with the terms to run concurrently."

"The sentence ended another chapter in Canada's most famous kidnapping," the London Free Press reported after Bannon's sentencing. "Bannon was convicted largely on the evidence of Michael McCardell, confessed kidnapper. This was a strange twist of fate, for police say Bannon first tipped them off to where they could locate McCardell. Police also say Bannon led them to Meisner."

Meisner's lawyer, Charles Bell, was at his home in Hamilton when he learned from a long-distance telephone call that Bannon had been convicted. "In view of the jury believing Michael McCardell, David Meisner should be released from the Kingston Penitentiary within the next twenty-four hours," Bell insisted. "The federal minister of justice should take decisive action immediately."

One week after Bannon's conviction, McCardell received a twelve-year sentence, three years less than Bannon even though he had been the ringleader. The lesser sentence was a reward for pleading guilty and for testifying against Bannon.

McCardell and Bannon had received their comeuppance, but Knowles and Pegram were still at large.

The time seemed propitious for the injustice against Meisner to redressed. As Charles Bell wrote in the final paragraphs of "Ditching David Meisner" in his book Who Said Murder?:

And now the big question arises. Twelve men having found upon their oath that McCardell's story is true, the story in which he has again and again reiterated the innocence of Meisner, what is the Department of Justice going to do about it? If the answer is to be "nothing," then the administration of justice in this country will have received a blow from which it will not recover for many generations.

As the Toronto *Globe* well said, "A thing of greater importance than any one man's guilt or innocence is involved now in the Meisner case. That thing is public belief in the honest and disinterested administration of criminal justice in this Province and Country."

It is undeniably true that the Meisner case has almost from the start proved a battleground for warring police factions. Are they or any of them now going to be able to keep this man in the Penitentiary in order to satisfy their private grudges against each other?

That question demands an answer and it will not be kept down.

Chapter 10
CHANGE OF FORTUNE

With Michael McCardell (convict #4006) and Jack Bannon (convict #3996) imprisoned in the Kingston Penitentiary where David Meisner was already incarcerated, the search intensified for Russell Knowles and Albert Pegram. But it was not until nearly two months after Bannon's trial that RCMP Sergeant Ted Weeks received a "hot tip" about Knowles from an undercover FBI agent in Detroit. According to the tip, Knowles was with a former Detroit bar operator named Herman Kierdoff in Ottawa, Illinois, a small community ninety miles west of Chicago. Weeks and four FBI agents tracked down the hotel where the men were staying, and on December 10 took rooms on either side of them. The conventional next step would have been to burst into their rooms and arrest them, but Weeks and the others waited until December 11 to take action.

There were conflicting accounts as to how Knowles was captured. One version was that Weeks and the FBI agents met their quarries by chance in the hotel lobby and Knowles and Kierdoff dashed away. The other version was that the confrontation occurred on a side street on the outskirts of Ottawa. Both versions held that the two men surrendered after a brief foot chase.

"You got me just in time," Knowles told Weeks. "In a few hours we would have been away from here." In Knowles' room Weeks found two guns, a road map covering 638 miles of state highways that had been marked in very thorough detail regarding speed limits, curves, intersections and right- and left-turn lanes, a large bag of burglar tools, and a long list of prominent Chicagoans enumerating their business and social connections, incomes and wealth.

Denying that he had anything to do with Labatt's kidnapping, Knowles said that Meisner, "my friend of seventeen years," also had nothing to do with it. Of course, he could have cleared Meisner in September 1934 when he accompanied his "friend" as Meisner surrendered to the Detroit police. But at that time, and right up until his capture, he had put himself first. Now he accused Weeks of sending Meisner to the Kingston Penitentiary "when you knew he was innocent."

"I was quite frank with him," Weeks told reporters. "I admitted to him there was a doubt in many minds and among police officers as to Meisner's guilt. I told Knowles, 'There is honour even among crooks, and the only way this matter can be cleared up is for you to return to London and stand trial.'" Knowles then signed a voluntary waiver of extradition proceedings, agreeing to go back to London even though he said with a shudder, "I would rather serve life in an American prison and rot there than serve five years at Portsmouth [the Kingston Penitentiary]." That was the awful fate, to which Knowles had, up to now, callously subjected his "friend" Meisner — and for a fifteen-year term.

Knowles' trial began on January 29, 1936, a day after mayors across the country had declared a holiday so that everyone could attend special memorial services in honour of King George V. The beginning of the trial coincided with the violent end of Richard Loeb, who, twelve years earlier with his friend Nathan Leopold, had cold-bloodedly killed Loeb's young cousin in the belief that they were so brilliant they could get away with murder. It was one of the most heinous American crimes of the twentieth century. Loeb was killed in prison by another inmate.

Like Meisner, Bannon and McCardell, Knowles was charged with kidnapping and armed robbery. However, unlike the others, he was also charged with extortion attempts against Hugh and then John Labatt. These new charges read, "On August 14, 1934, did send or cause to be sent to Hugh Labatt a letter demanding money with menace. [This charge applied to the $150,000 ransom note.] Between August 14 and December 31, 1934, unlawfully did send to John S. Labatt letters demanding money with menace. [This charge referred to the $25,000 payoff the kidnappers had sought from John in return for his release.]"

Presiding at Knowles' trial was forty-five-year-old Ontario Supreme Court Justice Charles McTague, making his first-time appearance at the

Assizes Court in London. Like Charles Bell, McTague was a man of
many diverse parts. He was a professional baseball player, teacher, soldier,
lawyer, judge, politician and community worker. Born in Guelph in
1890, McTague was the oldest of seven children. When the piano and
organ company for which his father worked went bankrupt, the young
McTague decided it was his responsibility to earn a living. He left high
school, where he had been a star football player despite weighing only
133 pounds, and took teachers' training courses. Upon receiving his
teaching degree he answered a newspaper ad for a mathematics teacher
at Assumption College in Windsor (a predecessor of the University of
Windsor) but was hired to teach English and history. To supplement his
salary, he played professional baseball, usually at second base, for two
teams across the border in Michigan. From Assumption, McTague went
to St. Michael's College in Toronto, where, in addition to teaching
English and history, he coached the hockey team.

After serving in World War I, McTague took an accelerated postwar
course in law, articled with a Toronto firm and then moved back to
Windsor, where he started his own practice, McTague and Springsteen,
which became the city's most prominent law firm. During the Great
Depression, as president of the Windsor Chamber of Commerce, he
organized a massive effort to feed and clothe the needy.

McTague served on the Supreme Court of Ontario from 1934 to
1938. "He had been a very able lawyer with a broad range of clients, and
he brought this solid experience, plus a large measure of common sense,
to the bench," says the retired Ontario Court of Appeal justice who
spoke to the author about the legal figures in the Labatt trials.

Crown Counsel Norman Newton was unable to participate in the
Knowles trial because he was then serving as counsel for an Ontario government Royal Commission investigating whether members of Toronto's
police force had tipped off gambling houses about planned raids and the
question of why a fired police constable had been reinstated. Although the
Toronto *Telegram* accused Newton of overstepping his authority in
conducting an undercover investigation of the police department, the
heads of the commission supported him, praising his integrity.

Taking over for Newton in Knowles' trial was a rising star, thirty-seven-year-old Joseph Sedgwick, a solicitor in the Ontario Department of the Attorney General for six years, representing it as counsel in assizes and appeal cases. His title in the Knowles case was Special Crown Counsel.

Sedgwick was a larger-than-life character known as much for his peerless skill as a raconteur, enjoyment of horse racing, poker games and good food and drink, and his vast literary knowledge as for his legal talent. Much in demand as an after-dinner speaker and a toastmaster, he could always be counted on to be entertaining and graceful in his remarks. "He was one of the best-read men I ever met," says the retired justice. "He could quote Shakespeare by the yard."

"Joe Sedgwick is the spice of the legal profession," *Canadian Lawyer* said in an April 1978 retrospective of Sedgwick's career, "Essentially Joe."

> He is the kind of man other lawyers quote in their speeches. He has probably entertained more judges — in and out of the courtroom — than any other lawyer you could name.... A few steal his stories for themselves but most are happy to give the author his due. Sedgwick could care less either way — unless you happen to be one of those witless, unfortunate fellows who can't carry it off with flair. Philip Isbister, Sedgwick's junior and later his associate for 21 years, recalls with some amusement, "Nothing I can think of irritated him more than to see someone else who had a good story kill it by not telling it well. He'd be furious when someone would blow the last line. 'He shouldn't be trusted with that story,' he'd say to me afterwards."
>
> Respect is too cold a word to describe the feelings other lawyers have for Joe Sedgwick. How can you respect a man who loves the Queen and the horse races with equal fervor? A man who plays poker with as much cunning and zeal as he would to argue a case before the highest court in the land. "He loved matching his wits with his contemporaries," Isbister recalls. "He'd

plan his schedule not to let anything interfere with his game." Respect? Hardly. Delight seems more appropriate. Others remember with glee his fierce debates with the most Reverend J.R. Mutchmor, a United Church leader of eloquent persuasion, a staunch advocate of prohibition and the limitation of liquor outlets. They were great friends but fought like cats and dogs in public.

Sedgwick traced his lineage back to English nobility via an out-of-wedlock connection on the paternal side. As he explained:

> The name Sedgwick which I and my family bear is only ours by adoption. Because the story will probably die with me unless I set it down, I do so for the benefit of my own progeny and those of my relations to whom it will be of interest.
>
> My grandfather, Harry Sedgwick, died about 1900, and as I was born in 1898, I do not remember him. What follows was told me in part by my father's sister, Sally, who lived in Toronto for a year or so just before the 1914–1918 War; confirmed in part by my father and mother, and in much more detail by my father's youngest sister, my Aunt Maggie, who died in Leicester, England, in 1959, the last of my father's family.
>
> The Harry Sedgwick whose grandson I am was born at Winmarleigh, Lancashire, in 1838, the natural son of John Wilson-Patten, who later [1874] became the first [and last] Baron Winmarleigh. He was for a time [briefly] Chief Secretary for Ireland, also Chancellor of the Duchy of Lancaster, and a member of Disraeli's Government. He is mentioned in Blake's *Disraeli*.
>
> My paternal great-grandmother's name was Sawerbutts, and she was when her son was born a servant in the old Wilson-Patten home Winmarleigh. Her father was a tenant farmer on the Patten estates and the boy was brought up by his maternal grandparents until he

reached school age, when he was sent to Preston grammar school. There he remained until he was seventeen. He was then apprenticed to a cabinet maker, and on the completion of his apprenticeship his natural father [Wilson-Patten] bought him a complete and very good set of cabinet maker's tools, lathes, etc. and started him up in his trade.

Though never openly acknowledged as Wilson-Patten's son, the father was at no pains to conceal the relationship. While the boy was at school his father's valet visited him regularly to bring him money and to get reports on his progress. His apprenticeship was arranged by Wilson-Patten, and after the boy was twenty-one the father continued to take an interest in him. He was however, proud, and resentful of his illegitimacy, and once he started work as a journeyman he refused further help from his father. The breach was of his making — not of the father's.

As to the name Sedgwick, not very long after her lapse, Miss Sawerbutts married a man of that name who owned the George Inn in Preston, and her illegitimate son assumed it in order to avoid comment. My paternal grandfather married a Catherine Stancliffe, who was born at Caton, near Lancaster. She was of Border descent and her mother was a Charteris of the well-known family of that name in Carlisle. Her brothers established the famous London hatter's firm of Charteris in the early 1800s.

As for his mother's side of the family, Sedgwick explained:

My mother, Amy Charlotte Gedge, was of a family originally from Suffolk. She was born in London, the daughter of William Blanchflower Gedge and Jemina (Turner). His father, born early in the nineteenth century was Horatio Nelson Gedge.

My grandfather Gedge was in the jewellery business and moved to Manchester to manage a shop there, where he died quite young. That accounts for my mother's presence in the North. Hers was an old, armigerous though undistinguished family.

In 1963, when he was sixty-five, Joseph Sedgwick applied for and received permission from the Court of Heralds in London for a grant of arms to himself based on his heritage: sable and ermine lozenges (diamond-shapes) from the Wilson-Patten arms and a gold field with six cinquefoils gules (five-leafed clovers of red hue) from his maternal grandfather's arms.

Sedgwick was born in Leeds in the Yorkshire district of England and came to Canada with his family when he was six years old. His father William was poor, described as "an artisan" by Sedgwick in a May 1966 story about him in *Canada Month*. "He was in the piano business. He reminded me somewhat of Mr. Micawber in Dickens' *David Copperfield*. He was not much educated but he was a great reader and a great lawn bowler." William encouraged Joe and his older (by four years) brother Harry to read voraciously: the Bible plus Shakespeare, Dickens and other English classics. For the rest of his life, Joe was able to quote lengthy passages from them by memory, an essential reference for a lawyer, he believed. "I think the well-rounded lawyer should have in his mind something more than a knowledge of the law itself," he once told a gathering of Osgoode Hall students. "Unless one flatters oneself by thinking that out of your own head you can do better, it is well to have in your legal memory some old and tried quotations. And I think it is no bad thing to know where they come from."

Joe adored his brother Harry, who became president of the Toronto radio station CFRB. As an adult, Harry recalled that as boys he and Joe "worried the police by playing ball on the street," and that they swiped apples from a "convenient" tree and got into fist fights with rivals for the choicest newspaper pitch. But their chief preoccupation was "to nail down a job before or after school," Harry said. "There were newspapers to deliver, errands to run, all sorts of odd jobs. Work like that does not mix with juvenile delinquency."

Harry articled with a law firm until World War I, and went into business after it. Joe enlisted in the army in 1916. Shortly afterwards, in May 1916, H.M.S. *Hampshire* struck a German mine and sank with all aboard, including Earl Horatio Herbert Kitchener, the British secretary of state for war. On the same day, Sedgwick was promoted from a private in the Canadian army to a lance corporal. He wrote his mother, "General Kitchener went down with the ship and we all moved up one!"

After the war, Joe decided to pursue his boyhood resolve to become a lawyer. In those days, undergraduate study at a university was not a prerequisite to enrolling in law school; it was sufficient to have graduated from high school and articled for two years. Two Ontario chief justices took the same route. The University of Toronto had an accelerated course for veterans, and Joe completed it and law courses at Osgoode Hall in record time. By May 1923 he had been called to the bar of Ontario.

He then started his own firm with only a secretary and one law student — Morley Callaghan, who went on to become a famous writer. As Callaghan recalled those days: "I was articled to a plump and amiable young lawyer named Joseph Sedgwick who was just getting established. I used to go to morning law classes and often doze in my chair — the law came easily to me — and then I would go to the law office. If Joe Sedgwick wanted a title searched I did it, then wrote what were my first stories. In those days Sedgwick's secretary always had time to retype my manuscripts. I had a very jovial relationship with him."

In 1924, then twenty-six years old, Sedgwick became junior partner in the law firm of Forsyth, Martin and Sedgwick. Forsyth later became a provincial judge. Also in 1924, Sedgwick married Torontonian Emma Irene McLaughlin. "She hated the name Emma, so I called her Mac," he told the *Toronto Star* in a 1981 interview. "Ours was a good marriage. Like all marriages, it had its bad moments, but it endured. She never understood my work but she admired me; she was a good mother and a good housekeeper." They had a son, who became a lawyer, and a daughter.

Sedgwick, like Charles Bell, was a Conservative, but unlike Bell he never ran for office. Sedgwick preferred backroom organizing, a preference inherited from his father, also a Conservative, who had knocked on doors to get out the vote.

Sedgwick first ventured into politics in 1925. The Tories were campaigning to end Prohibition in Ontario and Sedgwick, who enjoyed after-hours drinks, was "interested in getting a civilized drink," as he recalled forty years later to *Canada Month*. His favourite drink was Scotch. "I once drank milk, but it made me ill," he enjoyed saying. "My doctor said, 'Give up the milk and go back to whiskey and you'll be all right.' I did and I was."

Sedgwick estimated that he wrote "hundreds" of speeches over the following decades in Tory politics. He also raised party funds, helped formulate policy and worked out internal party problems.

In 1929, at the age of thirty-one, he was hired by Conservative Premier George Ferguson for the Ontario attorney general's department, where he spent eight years, the last six as solicitor general. "I wanted to do litigation and it was very difficult to do it on your own," Sedgwick told *Canadian Lawyer* in a 1978 story. The magazine described his courtroom style this way:

> High oratory was in vogue, especially among such leading advocates of the day as Charles W. Bell, Arthur Slaght, and T. Herbert Lennox. Sedgwick's peers will tell you that he is one of Canada's best read men and an eloquent speaker. But he did depart somewhat from the grand tradition of his predecessors. Although something of a virtuoso in his ability to recite passages by memory from Shakespeare, Byron, Shelley, Keats, Chesterton, Churchill, and several other great men of letters, Sedgwick knew well that the courts — and juries in particular — are less impressed with a great show of learned quotations than with their judicious application to the facts of a case. Sedgwick's was more the folksy style than the dramatic actor's style. One of the reasons he was so successful as a jury lawyer was because he listened to people. He very quickly found a rapport with them.

Two years after joining the attorney general's department, Sedgwick was thrust into the national limelight as junior counsel in the sedition case against Canadian Communist Party leader Tim Buck, a trial that landed Buck in the Kingston Penitentiary. Following the birth of the Dionne quintuplets in 1935, Sedgwick was assigned by the Ontario government to protect their interests. He helped draw up the 1935 *Dionne Quintuplets Act* under which the province negotiated all contracts for the girls.

Like Charles Bell, Sedgwick preferred male witnesses to female. "Black is to women blacker and white whiter than to most men," he believed. "Never cross-examine female witnesses except when absolutely desperate." He favoured farmers as jurors and was wary of barbers. "They talk too much," he claimed. "Juries will often believe the most improbable stories," he added. "The lawyer's duty is to go into court and make the best case he can with the facts at his disposal. It's up to the jury to decide if the truth is being told.… I have heard it said that juries, whose duty it is to try the accused, not infrequently try his lawyer."

Stocky, of average height, with a square face, Sedgwick had a reputation for liking "good food and good drink." A pipe smoker, he had a collection of about ten pipes in his office and more at home.

Sedgwick deplored the seemingly unlimited appointment of lawyers as King's (Queen's) Counsel, although he himself was named a KC in 1933. Most of the other lawyers in the Labatt trial were also KCs. "There are far too many of them," he said. "They're meaningless. When everyone has a nose, noses aren't distinct."

Although a brilliant improviser and good cross-examiner in the courtroom, Sedgwick did have his faults. Foremost, according to the retired justice who knew most of the lawyers in the Labatt trials, Sedgwick "disliked the hard work involved in preparation."

Knowles' trial gave Sedgwick's oratorical skills as a lawyer an opportunity to shine.

Knowles was defended by James Donahue, then forty-seven, who was one of western Ontario's best-known criminal lawyers. In becoming a lawyer, Donahue had followed in the footsteps of his father Dennis, also a prominent lawyer who had become senior judge of Ontario's Renfrew County from 1904 until his death in 1912. While studying law at Queen's University in Kingston, James Donahue managed the university hockey team. Whereas his father had specialized in civil law, James preferred criminal cases, similar to the contrasting preferences of Charles Bell and his father. After serving a short time as a Crown prosecutor in Welland County, he went into private practice.

He had successfully defended several murder suspects in Middlesex County before the Knowles trial. A shrewd cross-examiner and also a powerful summation speaker, Donahue often conducted cases both in the County and Supreme courts without resorting to legal texts or notes. In 1920 he entered politics, running as an independent candidate for the Ontario Legislature from London. He was defeated by the much better known Sir Adam Beck, who had been the first head of the Hydro-Electric Power Commission of Ontario which had been established in 1906.

Knowles' trial got off to a brisk start. Despite eight challenges to potential jurors by Donahue and seven by Crown Counsel Joseph Sedgwick, for a total of fifteen set aside, the jury panel was completed in just twenty-two minutes. John Labatt and Hugh Labatt and his wife sat behind the prisoner's dock, in which Knowles was flanked by Ontario Provincial Police officer Eric McMillen — formerly Labatt's bodyguard — and William Gray, the chief turnkey of the Middlesex County Jail. Louis McCaughey, the former sales manager of Labatt's and before that a policeman, sat on a bench usually reserved for police. Knowles' pretty blonde wife sat in a front row, "quietly dressed in a black gown and black hat," according to the *Toronto Daily Star.*

In his opening statement, Sedgwick began by noting that "to some extent the plans of the kidnappers miscarried. They had hoped the ransom note would not be made public and they would collect from the Labatts and safely make their way out of the country. But there was a great deal of publicity. One of the kidnappers [Pegram] took flight and left the others with Labatt on their hands."

Sedgwick then moved on to portray Knowles as a major player in the kidnapping even though McCardell was the acknowledged head of the gang. "Knowles was one of the men who kidnapped Labatt and took him to the lonely hideout in Muskoka. It may not have been the hand of Knowles that wrote the ransom and extortion notes but it was the brain of Knowles that dictated them. Knowles plotted the crime, was in it from the time the conspiracy was hatched and he was at all times a plotter, if not the chief plotter of the crime."

The first witness for the Crown was RCMP Sergeant Ted Weeks, who reviewed the details of Knowles' arrest. Then John Labatt, who had previously sworn that David Meisner, "Piccolo Pete" Murray and Albert Pegram were his abductors, took the stand. He recited the by-now-familiar story of his abduction.

"One man got out and ran to my car. Almost immediately behind this person, two other men came up. One pointed a revolver at me and opened the door. The third man was also pointing a gun at me. The first man said nothing at all, but stood aside."

"Do you know the man who pulled you out?" Sedgwick asked.

"In the first trial I identified that man as David Meisner. I am not so sure now."

"You have since learned otherwise? Is that correct?"

"Yes — this man had a straw hat, thin face and very prominent ears. At the first trial I thought David Meisner was that man."

At this point Justice McTague interjected. "Mr. Sedgwick, I do not know that this is relevant."

"I do not want to pursue it," Sedgwick answered.

Labatt resumed his testimony, telling of signing the ransom note. To support the armed robbery charge against Knowles, he described how he was ordered while in the kidnappers' car to hand over his money — $99.

The prosecution had arranged for McCardell to be brought from the Kingston Penitentiary to testify against Knowles. Neither the prosecution nor the defence had elected to call Bannon as a witness. As he had at Bannon's trial, McCardell said that Knowles and Pegram were with him when Labatt was kidnapped.

Turning to the charge that Knowles had written "letters demanding money with menace," Sedgwick asked the confessed kidnapper about the letters written to Labatt demanding the $25,000 he had promised to pay them.

"We wrote those at the Marquette Gardens in Detroit," McCardell testified. "I did the writing myself but we all composed it, Bannon, Knowles and myself."

At this point McCardell was turned over for questioning to James Donahue, Knowles' lawyer, who asked him about the preparations for the kidnapping.

"I didn't have much to do with it. They were largely handled by Knowles and Bannon," McCardell replied. Donahue then asked about Louis McCaughey's alleged connection to the kidnapping, an issue that had first arisen during Bannon's preliminary hearing. This was in preparation for Knowles' intended defence that the snatch had been a publicity stunt devised by the Labatts, with McCaughey as the intermediary between Labatt and the kidnap team of himself, McCardell, Bannon and Pegram.

McCardell reiterated what he had said at Bannon's trial, that he had no firsthand knowledge of any involvement on McCaughey's part. "Knowles said he had contacted McCaughey. He said the company would be glad to pay for the publicity they would get out of it."

"Do you mean McCaughey and Labatt were in on it?" Donahue asked.

"Well, I never agreed with the proposition. I said it was like having a bank president in on the robbery of his own bank. I wanted to take Labatt on the square. I asked to meet McCaughey, but the others would never let me."

"But you were told this was strictly an inside job?"

"Yes. That is why Knowles had no pistols when he went to Toronto to make the contact."

In his cross-examination, Sedgwick concentrated on Knowles' claim that the kidnapping was an "inside job."

"McCaughey was the inside man, is that it? Do you suggest that John and Hugh Labatt knew anything about it?"

"No," McCardell replied, "I don't suggest that. I was told by Knowles that they would be glad to pay the money for the advertising they would get out of it. That was what McCaughey was supposed to have said. I never agreed. I wanted to carry it out as a real kidnapping."

At this comment, Sedgwick could not resist the opportunity to display a flash of his renowned humour. "Might we say you wanted it to be an honest kidnapping?"

"Yes," replied McCardell. He was then dismissed as a witness.

Gerald Nicholson, the man who had driven Labatt and two of the kidnappers to Toronto, identified them as McCardell and Knowles.

Next, McCaughey repeated the assertion he had made at Bannon's trial — that he had had no connection with the kidnapping. He described how Knowles had told him of his plans to kidnap Labatt as far back as 1930 or 1931 and then again in 1931 or 1932. "Both times I said they couldn't get away with it." But on neither occasion had he alerted the Labatts or the police because "I knew if I talked, they would blast me off the earth."

On Friday, January 31, the second and final day of the trial, Knowles took the witness stand on his own behalf.

Speaking in what the *London Free Press* described as a "deep, strong voice," Knowles claimed that he had discussed kidnapping John Labatt with McCaughey on numerous occasions. "I first met McCaughey in 1930 at the Hotel London in London through a mutual acquaintance named Butler, but known to McCaughey as 'the little man.' From the conversation between McCaughey and Butler, I gathered that they had discussed the idea of kidnapping Labatt on previous occasions but were not in a position to approach anyone about the idea at that time."

Subsequently, Knowles said, he met with Butler, Bannon, McCardell and Earl Rossi at the Prince Edward Hotel in Windsor and discussed the Labatt brothers. "We then went to London and stopped at the Hotel London. McCaughey was called again and came to the room. We again discussed kidnapping John Labatt. McCaughey said he was sick, but we might be able to take Hugh Labatt. McCaughey told us to let him know before anything was done so he would be at the brewery to keep Mr. Burke, the brewery manager, from notifying the police." McCaughey said he was in a position to do anything he wanted with the police.

"Early in 1932 I met McCaughey once more at the Prince Edward Hotel in Windsor. He said it was too bad that nothing had been done on the proposition. He said the boys — meaning Hugh and John Labatt — had $50,000 that could be had at any time. He said they would be glad to pay it if they could get some advertising.

"In the summer of 1933, Earl Rossi and I and two others [unnamed] came to London again and spoke again to McCaughey about kidnapping John Labatt. McCaughey told us Labatt was at home. When we went there, we saw Labatt and two women come out of the house and get in their car. We followed them as they drove to Sarnia. One of the women got out at Sarnia and Mr. Labatt and his wife went to their summer home. We went back to Sarnia and did nothing further."

Early in 1934, Knowles said he and Bannon had met together with McCaughey. "He explained that he had gone to John Labatt and told him that some Chicago rum-runners had come to him and wanted to know why the Labatts had never paid off. Lou said Mr. Labatt told him they wouldn't pay it and he had replied that the refusal to pay off might be serious for him and he would try to contact the rum-runners again. He said Mr. Labatt asked him if he thought the boys were entitled to any consideration. McCaughey said he thought they were. He explained that other brewers had donated large sums of money to the rum-runners.

"Mr. Labatt told McCaughey that it would be impossible to get the company to pay $25,000 without any action, without something happening. He said he would not mind spending the night with the boys some place if they treated him all right. The money could be paid that way. My understanding with McCaughey was that if we could get a cottage or a house or even an apartment in town for keeping Mr. Labatt, he wouldn't mind going with us."

Then Knowles told of trying to get David Meisner to join in the "proposition" but that Meisner refused.

Knowles said he discussed with McCaughey that McCaughey would hand over the money to him on Labatt's behalf in front of the Windsor church across from Bannon's home. It would be split in five equal amounts among McCaughey, himself, McCardell, Bannon and Pegram, who was brought in later to be the driver of the getaway car.

Continuing his story, Knowles said that when he was alone with Labatt at the Muskoka cottage, he told Labatt that "our demand for $150,000 had no foundation and that $25,000 was the amount to be paid. I said that we were former rum-runners who had handled his merchandise and we thought we were entitled to this."

"Was that true?" asked Donahue.

"No. That was the story McCaughey told me he had told Labatt."

Donahue then asked Knowles how Labatt was treated in captivity. In line with his tale that it was "a friendly kidnapping," Knowles maintained that "I said to Mr. Labatt it was not necessary for him to be blindfolded and chained. He said his other guard — that was McCardell — had done this and that he was satisfied."

At this point, Donahue turned Knowles over to Sedgwick for questioning. Sedgwick started by asking Knowles about his "past experiences." Knowles said he had been in advertising, in the liquor business, and had a financial interest in two taverns. He said his only trouble with police before was on a shoplifting charge.

"So this was your first experience in kidnapping?" Sedgwick inquired.

Knowles did not fall into this trap. "I did not consider this a kidnapping," he answered.

Sedgwick then got Knowles to admit that Labatt had asked McCardell if there was any danger of the kidnappers' killing him while he was asleep.

"So Mr. Labatt didn't know that it was a friendly kidnapping?" Sedgwick asked.

"We assured him he was in no danger."

"Nice of you," Sedgwick remarked sarcastically.

Sedgwick then asked Knowles who the man he called Butler was. "Is it his real name?"

"No, just a name I have used here in court to protect him"

"Is his name not Bert Wilton?"

"Yes," Knowles admitted reluctantly.

"Is he the man now serving fifteen years in the United States for safe-breaking?"

"I believe he is," Knowles replied.

Sedgwick then turned to the extortion letters sent to Labatt after his release, demanding the $25,000.

Describing the threats in the letter to the jury, Sedgwick snapped at Knowles, "These do not look like the letters of a friendly kidnapper."

Sedgwick then recalled Labatt to give evidence in reply to Knowles' testimony.

"Did you know of any arrangement between McCaughey and these men?" he asked Labatt.

"Nothing whatever."

"Did McCaughey say anything to you about paying money to rum-runners?

"No. He never said anything of the kind."

Sedgwick then asked about Knowles' claim that Labatt's brewery had benefited from the publicity of the kidnapping.

"It was doing all the business it could handle," Labatt responded.

On re-examination, Donahue inquired if it was not "more accurate to say that the Labatt brewery business had doubled" since the kidnapping.

"The increase in business has not been that great," Labatt declared.

In his summation to the jury Sedgwick drew attention to Bannon's absence. "If there was one iota of truth in Knowles' story, why wasn't John Bannon called as a defence witness?" Sedgwick demanded. He also scoffed at the concept of a "friendly kidnapping," reminding the jurors about the revolvers loaded with tear gas, the tape blindfold, and the dog chain used to fasten Labatt to the bed.

After four hours' deliberation, the jury returned with a verdict of guilty on all counts. Knowles showed no reaction. Justice McTague then took the opportunity to address Knowles' charges about Labatt.

"If I may step out of character as a judge for a few minutes, I would like to say a few words to you," he told the jurors. "On account of the nature of the defence, this was really a trial within a trial. In a degree, John Labatt was standing trial also — not actually, but in effect. In my opinion, your verdict is a clear and clean vindication of Mr. Labatt. As a result, the rumours that have surfaced from time to time of more or less sinister character have been dispelled, I hope, for good and all time."

At his sentencing on February 14, Knowles was dapper as always. He wore a smartly cut dark grey suit and chatted amiably with his guard while waiting for McTague to deal with his case. His wife, dressed in what the press described as a "becoming" black fur coat and small matching hat, sat in the spectators' gallery. It was not the way she had anticipated spending Valentine's Day.

Although the maximum prison term for kidnapping was twenty-five years, Sedgwick did not ask for Knowles to be treated differently than Meisner and Bannon, both of whom had received a fifteen-year sentence. McTague sentenced Knowles to an additional fifteen years for the robbery charge and seven years each for the two extortion charges. If consecutive, the sentences would have totalled forty-four years, but McTague granted some leniency in declaring that they be concurrent.

Knowles paled a little when his sentence was pronounced. His wife burst into tears and continued to weep for some minutes as he was led away to the jail. No charges were laid against McCaughey because there was no substantiation that he was involved in the snatch. Knowles (convict #4141) was transported to the Kingston Penitentiary, the prison he so dreaded and in which his co-conspirators McCardell and Bannon were as well as Meisner.

The case had dealt a drastic change to the fortunes of Knowles, Bannon and McCardell. Soon, Meisner hoped, his luck would change for the better.

Chapter 11
VINDICATION

Now that Russell Knowles and Michael McCardell had both testified that David Meisner had not been involved in Labatt's kidnapping, and now that Charles Bell, Meisner's loyal attorney, had spotlighted his plight in the recently published *Who Said Murder?*, there was considerable hope that Meisner might finally be freed.

The machinery was finally set in motion immediately after Knowles' sentencing. Bell was in the courtroom, waiting for a jury to return its verdict for another client he was defending. As soon as the judge had uttered the final word of Knowles' sentence, Bell leaped to his feet and made an eloquent plea that Meisner be granted a retrial. "May I very respectfully ask that Your Lordship make a separate report to the federal minister of justice as to what this trial has shown concerning David Meisner? Recognizing the fact that Your Lordship has long been known for your humanitarian view and knowing also that you will be motivated by a strong sense of justice, I have no hesitation in making this request. From the first I have believed this man to be innocent, and what has since developed has but confirmed that belief."

McTague's response was encouraging. "No doubt I will be called upon to make the usual report. I believe it is true that there has been more evidence as to what actually happened in the kidnapping developed during this trial than at the others. I will give your request my serious consideration."

Immediately after Knowles' trial concluded, Crown Counsel Joseph Sedgwick telegraphed the verdict to Ernest Lapointe, the federal minister of justice. "The minister didn't request a wire, but I thought Ottawa would like official word as soon as possible in case any new move is being contemplated in the Meisner case," he told reporters.

Ernest Lapointe, in whose hands Meisner's fate now lay, was that rarity among politicians, a man respected and admired — even loved — by his opponents as well as by his supporters. He came from humble beginnings. Born in 1876 on a Quebec farm, he studied law at Laval University in Quebec City, then practised law in Rivière du Loup from 1898 to 1919. In 1904, when he was twenty-eight, he was acclaimed in a federal by-election to represent the riding of Kamouraska. He succeeded H.G. Carroll, the solicitor general, who had been appointed to the bench. He was re-elected in the general elections of 1904, 1908, 1911 and 1917. In 1919, upon the death of Liberal leader Sir Wilfrid Laurier (who was prime minister between 1896 and 1911), Lapointe was chosen to fill his seat in Quebec East. This was considered a great honour. He retained the seat until his death in 1941.

For two decades, first in opposition and then in government, Lapointe was the closest friend, adviser and political associate of William Lyon Mackenzie King. They sat side by side in the House of Commons. Lapointe became King's Quebec lieutenant. Prior to 1936, he had been minister of marine and fisheries (appointed 1921), minister of justice (1924), a delegate in 1922 to the League of Nations formed two years earlier, and had negotiated treaties with France and the United States. A treaty with the United States that he negotiated and signed on behalf of Canada was the first pact to be signed by a Canadian with full powers from the British Crown. He became minister of justice again in 1935.

Born and raised in a French-Canadian environment, Lapointe did not learn English until he was in his twenties, and he waited for twelve years to give a speech in English in the House of Commons. By that time, he was more eloquent in English than many native speakers. Largely self-taught, he carried an English dictionary from room to room at home, at his office, and whenever he travelled on a train, to learn new words.

The legal community regarded Lapointe as a first-rate minister of justice who conscientiously applied himself to all legal matters over and above the scrutiny of his staff. "This fearless champion of worthy causes," as King would eulogize him on his death in 1941, was the man who held Meisner's future in his hands. The outlook for Meisner was promising.

Lapointe moved extremely quickly. Knowles' conviction had taken place late in the day on a Friday. Nobody would have blamed Lapointe if he had waited until the following Monday to render his decision; but this was not an ordinary case and Lapointe was not an ordinary man. He decided not to wait over the weekend to take action. On Saturday, February 15, the day after Knowles was convicted, he ordered that Meisner be granted a new trial. In his letter to Ontario Attorney General Arthur Roebuck, which was released to the press, Lapointe indicated that the statements of McCardell and Knowles absolving Meisner of the crime had influenced him to some extent. It was an historic moment in Canadian jurisprudence, the first time a retrial had been granted because of the possibility of mistaken identity in a major case. It was another historic first for the Labatt snatch. Lapointe's statement read:

The King v. David Meisner.

Whereas the said David Meisner was convicted of (1) kidnapping, (2) forcible confinement, (3) robbery while armed, at sittings of the Supreme Court of Ontario held at the city of London, in the Province of Ontario, before the Honourable Mr. Justice McFarland during January and February, 1935, and was thereupon sentenced to imprisonment for fifteen years;

And whereas an application for the mercy of the Crown on behalf of the said David Meisner has been presented;

And whereas, upon the said application for mercy, I, the undersigned, Minister of Justice of Canada, have considered the same, and the developments upon the trials of Michael McCardell and Russell Knowles, alleged accomplices;

Now, therefore, I do hereby in my capacity as Minister of Justice as aforesaid, under the authority vested in me by Section 1022 of the Criminal Code of

Canada, order and direct that a new trial of the said
David Meisner, for the aforesaid crimes, be had at the
next sitting of a court of competent jurisdiction for the
trial of criminal causes at the City of London, or at any
special sitting of the court which may be ordered by
competent authority for the trial at the City of London,
or elsewhere of the said David Meisner.

Dated at Ottawa this 15th day of February 1936.
(Sgd.) Ernest Lapointe,
Minister of Justice

Section 1022 of the Criminal Code dealt with the justice minister's
prerogative of mercy. He could take three courses of action: grant a new
trial, refer the case to a court of appeal or ask the court of appeal for its
opinion on any point arising from the case as a guideline for how he
should rule on a petition made under Section 1022.

Meisner's trial was granted under subsection 2(a) of Section 1022 —
that for new trials. It read:

2. Upon any application for the mercy of the Crown on
   behalf of any person convicted on an indictment, the
   Minister of Justice,
   (a) If he entertains a doubt whether such person
       ought to have been convicted, may, after such
       inquiry as he thinks proper, instead of advising
       His Majesty to remit or commute the sentence,
       direct by an order in writing a new trial at such
       time and before such court as the Minister of
       Justice thinks proper.

Meisner was in the Middlesex County Jail in London when Lapointe's
statement was issued. He had been transferred there from the Kingston
Penitentiary in the possible event of his being called as a witness in
Knowles' trial. He reacted joyfully. "It's the best news I've received in a

long time," he said after being awakened Monday night, February 17, by jail officials to be informed of Lapointe's decision.

"If I ever get out of jail, I'm going to build myself a cabin in the woods where I'll have only the birds and beasts of the forest for companions," he added. "That will suit me fine. I am so tired of hearing the word 'kidnapper' that I just want to be alone."

Meisner's second trial was scheduled to start a month later, on March 16. In the meantime, he was sent back to the Kingston Penitentiary, where he resumed his duties as one of three prisoners placed in charge of a storeroom in which sheets were kept.

Why hadn't Meisner been granted a retrial after McCardell's August 1935 confession that he had not been involved? Or after Bannon's trial in October 1935, when McCardell exonerated him again? Actually, it was not an unusual delay for that era. Sittings of the Ontario Supreme Court of Ontario were not continuous; rather, they took place only four times per year, with gaps between the end of one session and the start of the next. Also, federal and provincial justice authorities felt that Knowles' trial should be held first, according to a letter written by Arthur Roebuck on January 24, 1936, five days before Knowles' trial began. Attending a meeting in Ottawa with Deputy Attorney General I.A. Humphries, Roebuck took the time to write Joseph Sedgwick, in longhand on Château Laurier Hotel stationery, expressing his views on the case and what the department's strategy should be if Lapointe ordered a new trial. It is clear from the letter that Sedgwick was convinced of Meisner's innocence but that Roebuck had some doubts. Although he had known Sedgwick for years and it was a private letter, his salutation was "Dear Mr. Sedgwick."

Dear Mr. Sedgwick

I was glad to have your report on the latest developments in the Labatt case, together with your reaction in the Misner [sic] case. It is not to be forgotten.

(1) I reported the facts to Mr. Lapointe and asked him to make an investigation emphasizing those who had no

previous touch with the case, and he has actually done something in this connection. It is not to be expected that he will act until the present cases are completed. When he does do so I would be very glad to have your view before his department.

(2) Should he order a new trial, it must not be a sham fight. You say we could offer no evidence and let Misner go home. We can decide this when the time comes, but off-hand this does not seem to me to be what we should do. If it is a trial at all it should be a real trial & all the former evidence should be presented together with what his former associates may say as to his innocence. The jury might then make the decision.

Yes, I have read Bell's book, and in particular his chapter on Misner. It is a fine piece of special pleading. He says Misner is innocent. I am not prepared to go with him in this unreserved way. He may be innocent, notwithstanding his conviction. Innocent men have been convicted. The question for me to consider is whether I have done my duty in the matter. I am not permitted to make that decision, & I have made a report to the person who is charged with the duty and asked him to investigate, and I have offered every assistance by the Provincial staff. The department of Justice will be informed as to the prospective trial. Have I not done enough?

Sedgwick probably had in mind a quick, uncontested trial like "Piccolo Pete" Murray's.

Soon after Lapointe's announcement, it became apparent that Roebuck had prevailed and the Attorney General's department was going to put up a "real," and not a "sham" fight against Meisner being acquitted in the retrial. On March 5, the *London Free Press* wrote:

The criminal investigation branch of the Ontario Provincial Police is to open an entirely new investigation into all angles of the now famous international crime.... The reported intention of the Crown in preparing for the Meisner trial is to treat the kidnapping as if it had not occurred and to commence the investigation all over again.

All former witnesses, it is said, will be re-interviewed and new statements taken from them. The cottage hide-out in Muskoka, where Labatt was chained up, is to be revisited. The actual scene of the snatch will also, it is understood, be checked up again.

All the previous witnesses have been subpoenaed, it is understood. One witness, Mrs. Mary Lythe, whose positive identification of Meisner as a man she saw in the Muskoka district while Labatt was held as a prisoner contributed to Meisner's conviction, subsequently died.

The paper also reported that "Attorney General Arthur Roebuck has taken over complete direction of the case and that Crown Attorney Norman Newton, who personally participated in the hunt for the subsequently convicted McCardell and Knowles, is no longer associated with it." The intriguing question of why Newton was sidelined would hang in the air, unanswered, for some time.

As the trial date approached, Meisner and McCardell — who was to testify on Meisner's behalf — were transferred from the Kingston Penitentiary back to the Middlesex County Jail, where they had been only a month earlier. In advance of the trial, the Muskoka witnesses who had insisted that Meisner was the kidnappers' ringleader were taken to the jail to see if they could identify McCardell. Most of the witnesses maintained they had never see him before, but as they walked up to take a look at him, McCardell called a number of them by name and greeted them like old friends.

Overseeing Meisner's retrial was Ontario Supreme Court Justice Arthur Courtney Kingstone, who went by his middle name. He had been on the court since 1932. Born in Toronto, he attended two of Canada's most exclusive private boys' schools — Upper Canada College in Toronto and Ridley College in St. Catharines. Before being appointed to the Ontario Supreme Court, he was senior partner in the best-known law firm in St. Catharines — Ingersoll, Kingstone and Seymour — specializing in general and commercial law. Kingstone also did some trial work. He became vice-president and a member of the board of governors of Ridley College, as well as vice-president of the Niagara Falls Suspension Bridge Company.

Because Kingstone had done relatively little litigation, some members of the bar looked askance at his appointment as a trial judge. But he turned out to be a good choice. "He was very able and a hard worker and gained an excellent reputation," says the retired Ontario Court of Appeal justice who knew most of the legal figures in the Labatt trials. "He was somewhat reserved and serious-minded and a no-nonsense judge in the best sense of that term." Kingstone was fairly tall, about five feet nine inches, and beanpole thin, weighing only 150 pounds.

The specially appointed Crown counsel for Meisner's retrial was sixty-five-year-old D'Alton Lally McCarthy, a very experienced trial lawyer with a distinguished pedigree. Called by his middle name — which was also his mother's surname — by friends, McCarthy was the grandson and son of lawyers also named D'Alton. His father cofounded the law firm of McCarthy, Osler, Hoskin & Creelman and was a member of Parliament for twenty-two years.

Lally McCarthy, like John and Hugh Labatt, attended Trinity College boys' school in Port Hope, Ontario. Subsequently, Lally studied at Marchiston Castle School in Edinburgh and Trinity College [affiliated with the University of Toronto]. After graduating, he joined McCarthy, Osler. His cousins, Leighton and Frank, joined soon afterward; all three were to leave in 1916, after a dispute between Leighton and other partners at the firm over the sharing of fees, and establish the firm of McCarthy & McCarthy.

Lally stayed with McCarthy & McCarthy until 1931, leaving at the age of sixty-one, to practise with his son-in-law Ian Sinclair at the Toronto firm of Armstrong and Sinclair. The firm cofounded by his father is now Osler, Hoskin & Harcourt. McCarthy & McCarthy is now McCarthy Tétrault. Both are among Canada's largest law firms.

SUSAN GOLDENBERG

Even though his father had been killed in a dogcart accident, Lally drove to the office in a high-wheeled dogcart. He had a compelling appearance and magnetic personality. "He was a magnificent figure of a man — over six feet tall, sturdily built and still had a full head of hair in his later years, although it had turned white," recalls the retired justice. "He had an excellent speaking voice and a great gift of language, including the ability to speak impromptu. During his prime he was probably one of the five top trial and appellant lawyers in Ontario."

McCarthy honed his skills as a trial lawyer in the late 1910s and early 1920s by representing the Toronto Street Railway in the court cases that arose with great frequency from accidents involving its streetcars. "This experience made him very quick on his feet and a great master of the English language, important skills for a trial lawyer," comments the retired justice.

McCarthy became Ontario counsel and Toronto agent for the Grand Trunk Railway until it was taken over by Canadian National Railways. Over the years he gained a reputation for his ability to paint such a vivid picture of evidence that, as the *Globe and Mail* commented in its 1963 obituary on him, "Judges were induced to forget the dull briefs of the morning and to smile kindly on his case."

McCarthy had a large practice even though his fees were high. He successfully charged the Ontario government $100 a day despite its rule against paying outside counsel more than $60. When the attorney general's office hired him for a five-day period for a total of $300, he worked only three days so that he made his usual daily rate. When this became known, the attorney general's office rationalized that he had been "thinking the other two days." Of course, compared to today's legal fees of $400 or more per *hour*, McCarthy's $100 does not seem steep — until inflation is factored in.

McCarthy's one weakness as a lawyer, and it was a very serious one, was his distaste for the often-tedious task of preparing for litigation. Such homework is regarded as the secret of success in most trials. "He was renowned more for his style than for depth of thought," according to Christopher Moore's *The Law Society of Upper Canada and Ontario's Lawyers, 1797–1997*. A popular anecdote recounted in the legal world about his legendary laziness concerned an incident that occurred while

McCarthy was counsel at Armstrong and Sinclair. One of its members, Kenneth Morden, who later became a justice of the Ontario Court of Appeal, acted as McCarthy's junior in many cases. One Monday morning, McCarthy strolled into Morden's office and tossed a brief onto his desk with the comment, "Ken, that's a very interesting case." (A brief is a memorandum of the facts, points of law and precedents, prepared for the guidance of counsel when arguing a case in court.) When Morden turned over the cover of the brief, he found that McCarthy had written on the first page, "This case is going to be adjourned." The notation made it obvious to Morden that McCarthy had not even opened the brief.

It was said that McCarthy once began arguing the wrong side of a case, and when a junior alerted him to his mistake he continued imperturbably, saying that it would be his opponent's argument and laying out the reasons to reject it. "He liked his women and his liquor and society and he liked his law — maybe I have given that in the wrong order," a "young lawyer who admired McCarthy" is quoted as saying in the *Law Society of Upper Canada and Ontario's Lawyers 1797–1997*. "He had a flair for appearance."

McCarthy did not hesitate to give credit to his junior lawyers, earning their affection despite their disapproval of his neglect of preparation. Some became legal stars, such as Justice Morden and Barry Pepper, who established the litigation department at Fraser and Beatty, now Fraser, Milner, Casgrain. The former Ontario Court of Appeal Justice recalls appreciatively an incident from his days as a young lawyer, when, at a conference of lawyers from several firms regarding a major case, McCarthy insisted that the senior partner at a major Toronto law firm listen to a point he was trying to make. When the veteran lawyer unkindly remarked that a youngster could not have anything constructive to contribute, McCarthy intervened: "This young man has something worthwhile to say." It turned out to be an observation that the other lawyer had to admit was valuable and furthered the then junior lawyer's career.

In his younger days, McCarthy served as a cavalry officer in the Governor General's Body Guard, a volunteer militia cavalry regiment that dated back to 1855, and then in the Toronto Light Horse.

Twelve years before he was appointed Crown counsel in the Meisner retrial, McCarthy was in the national spotlight as the Ontario government's prosecutor in the trials arising from one of Canada's worst financial scandals, the 1923 collapse of the Home Bank, which had sixty thousand depositors across the country. The chief reason for its collapse was that its principal client, Sir Henry Pellatt, owner of the ninety-eight-room Casa Loma in Toronto, was unable to repay huge loans when a real estate venture of his failed.

The bank's failure plunged thousands of Canadians into financial ruin. Many lost their life savings. At least one person committed suicide. The treasuries of several communities were depleted.

The bank's general manager died shortly before the bank collapsed, and the president passed away before the trial. McCarthy obtained convictions for conspiracy and filing false returns for the vice-president, chief accountant, auditor and five of the directors, but they never served their sentences; they successfully appealed on the grounds that they had had to rely on reports from the bank's president.

McCarthy's victory seemed to be for nought. But it was not the end of the matter. Public outrage led to a major overhaul of Canada's banking system, including the establishment of the Bank of Canada and the office of Inspector General, a federal agency empowered to inspect the books kept at the banks' head offices so as to provide depositors and shareholders with some protection. Another repercussion was a further consolidation of Canada's banks because of public concern about the soundness of other "small" banks.

Although McCarthy's political affiliation as a Conservative was well known, the Liberal government of Premier Mitchell Hepburn would not have held this against him in selecting him as the special counsel in the Meisner retrial because he was not active in the Conservative Party, nor did he do any work for it. It might have been a different matter if the assignment had been an ongoing contract. It is not unusual for politically connected lawyers to complain about their nonpartisan brethren getting a contract from the government of the day. The retired justice, in his days as a prominent lawyer, was once briefly cut off by the Liberals in Ottawa and the Conservatives in Ontario because of such complaints.

McCarthy's main concern was not that he might lose in Meisner's retrial, but rather whether he would receive the high fee he usually commanded, since both the federal and provincial governments had reputations for being miserly in their payments to outside counsel.

With McCarthy acting for the Crown and Charles Bell once again defending Meisner, the retrial was shaping up to be a battle of legal titans. McCarthy was assisted by Joseph Sedgwick, who had successfully prosecuted Russell Knowles. Aiding Bell was Howard Cluff of London, his associate in Meisner's first trial.

As Meisner made his way to the prisoner's dock in the main courtroom of the Middlesex County Courthouse on Monday, March 16, it was obvious that his physical condition had changed significantly during the thirteen months since his conviction. Prison life had made the already frail Meisner even thinner. Surprisingly — and contrary to the gloomy prediction that Bell had made at the first trial that Meisner would likely go blind while in jail due to the cataract obscuring his vision — it had not harmed his bad eye. Indeed, quite unexpectedly, the growth had shrunken considerably. "A year ago Meisner's eye was so noticeable that it was the one thing about his appearance that attracted attention. It had a large white spot on it that seemed to stand out like a beacon," the *London Free Press* wrote. "Now, however, the white spot seems to have diminished in size. It is no longer as noticeable as it was at the first trial. So while prison life has made Meisner paler and thinner, it seems to have improved the outward appearance of the blind eye." The eye had not been operated on; the growth had shrunken on its own.

In his opening statement, McCarthy requested the jurors to wipe from their minds the fact that Meisner had been tried before. "After talking with McCardell, Mr. Labatt had a serious doubt in his mind about Meisner," McCarthy stated. "The Crown does not want a man convicted if there can be a reasonable doubt. It was to his credit that Mr. Labatt at once notified authorities of his doubt. So the minister of justice has said Meisner must be tried again. That is how he comes to be in front of you."

McCarthy then proceeded to outline the Crown's case, emphasizing that in most abductions, "There is a mastermind who organizes the gang and directs it in the actual snatch.

"The prosecution," he went on, "still believes Meisner was involved in the snatch. The Crown charges that David Meisner was implicated in the kidnapping. What his participation in it was, you gentlemen of the jury will have to judge.

"We hope to bring evidence to show that he was one of the men who rented the cottage hideout. I expect to provide reputable witnesses who were called upon by the men who rented this cottage. I believe they will identify one as the prisoner, David Meisner."

These remarks made it clear that the new investigation instigated by Roebuck — at the expense of taxpayers — had turned up no new evidence whatsoever and that McCarthy was going to rely on the Muskoka witnesses who had testified a year earlier.

Labatt was the first Crown witness. It was the fourth trial at which he told about his kidnapping and captivity. By now, the rest of Canada was probably as familiar with the main points of his testimony as he was. But there were some significant changes. Elaborating on the night of August 16, 1934, Labatt said, "Two men came to the cottage and talked to my guard. I heard them say 'The papers are full of it.'"

"You said two men came to the cottage?" McCarthy asked.

"I believe there were two," Labatt replied. Not once before had he referred to two men.

"One of the men came in to talk to me," he continued. "He said they couldn't make contact with my brother because the police and newspapers had learned of the kidnapping. He then said, 'What we should do with you is tie a stone to your feet, rip you up and throw you in the lake.'" Under this duress, Labatt said he had agreed to pay $25,000 for his release. "The money was to be paid in five portions of equal amounts, three portions in American money and two in Canadian."

Continuing, Labatt said his kidnappers had asked him to name a payoff man, and he had suggested Louis McCaughey, then sales manager of Labatt's, and Alex Colvin, the brewery's Windsor representative. "The kidnappers were satisfied with these men," he said, and again referred to there being three members of the kidnapping gang in the cottage — his guard and two others. This recollection conflicted with Labatt's testimony in the earlier trials, when he placed only "his guard" and one other man in the cottage; it also ran counter to the accounts of McCardell and Knowles, both of whom had said they were the only men in the cottage with Labatt. As well, Knowles had said he was the one who talked with Labatt about the $25,000, although in his version he had not threatened Labatt with death.

McCarthy then turned to Labatt's initial identification of Meisner as one of his kidnappers. Labatt explained that he had made his identification based on sorting through mug shots supplied by the police and by visiting Meisner at the Middlesex County Jail after he was extradited to Canada. "I couldn't positively identify his voice, but I thought he was the man who guarded me," Labatt said. As both Meisner and McCardell had been born in southwestern Ontario, their accents could very well have been similar, even though both had lived in the United States for years. "I could not recognize McCardell's voice nor recognize his features when I looked through a peephole at him," Labatt said.

Subsequently, in the presence of Norman Newton, the Crown attorney in the first trial, Labatt had met face to face with McCardell. "I was not allowed to question him, but McCardell recalled the most minute instances about the trip to Muskoka and the kidnapping," Labatt recounted. "He talked to me in a low voice and I recognized it as the voice of my guard."

"Have you formed an opinion about who this man was?" McCarthy asked.

"My belief now is that McCardell was really my guard," Labatt responded. "Furthermore, I believe he is the man who held me up."

This ended McCarthy's questioning of Labatt.

Charles Bell began his cross-examination by producing a picture of Albert Pegram clipped from a newspaper and asking Labatt if he could identify him as one of his captors. Labatt said he could. Next, Bell sought to clear up the confusion caused by Labatt's new claim that there were three men at the cottage. Bell had Labatt review at some length the activities of himself and his guard during the time they were at the cottage. Under Bell's questioning, Labatt said that from the time Pegram left to go to Toronto on Tuesday night, August 14, 1934, until Thursday,

August 16, there was no one in the cottage but him and his guard. This testimony served to bring Labatt's story back into line with what he had said at the earlier trials.

Bell then turned to the significant differences in appearance between Meisner and McCardell. "In your first description of the kidnappers, given shortly after your release, did you not describe your guard as 170 pounds in weight; thin, dark face; straight nose; and of an athletic type? Now, look at my client. He has a delicate frame and weighs only 118 pounds. He looks like a man whose only athletics was marbles. Instead, your description fits Michael McCardell."

Hugh Labatt followed his brother to the stand. Under questioning from McCarthy, he reviewed how he had responded to Three-fingered Abe's phone call and ransom note. "I received two telephone calls from a man calling himself Three-fingered Abe. That was my only contact with the kidnappers," he said. In his cross-examination, Bell introduced a letter that he said, according to the postmark, was sent to Hugh (and intended for him and John) after Meisner's arrest and before his first trial. The letter was signed "Three-fingered Abe" and told John he had made a mistake in identifying Meisner as one of the kidnappers.

Next, the parade of Muskoka witnesses began, starting with Horace Prowse, owner of the cottage where Labatt had been held captive. He set the tone for the rest.

"Have you changed your mind that Meisner was one of the three men who rented your cottage?" McCarthy asked.

"I have not," Prowse declared firmly.

"Since you have seen McCardell, have you had any reason to change your opinion about Meisner being the man you saw at Muskoka?"

"Not the least."

Under cross-examination by Bell, Prowse conceded that he had had to look at Meisner a number of times in the police lineup before he said he detected a resemblance between him and the man in Muskoka.

Matthias Harrison, the Prowse campground workman who had claimed at the first trial only to have seen Meisner, now said he had seen both Meisner and McCardell.

"On the fifteenth of August, I saw the prisoner," Harrison said, pointing to Meisner. "He was walking toward the Prowse cottage. He walked past me within almost eight or nine feet. I saw McCardell on August 16. I was working around the Crews cottage near the Prowse cabin and saw him carrying a pail of water from the Crews' spring to the Prowse cottage. He had a worried look on his face. I said 'Good morning' to him and he replied, 'Good morning.'"

"Have you seen this man you say was McCardell since then?" McCarthy asked.

"Yes," replied Harrison. "I saw him in the jail yesterday."

Bell made little attempt to shake Harrison in his story.

Albert Crews, the kidnappers' next-door neighbour in Muskoka, also insisted he had correctly identified Meisner.

"Have you had an opportunity to see Michael McCardell?" McCarthy asked.

"Yes, this morning. This is the first time I've seen him. I never saw him before in my life."

"Do you see any resemblance between the accused here and McCardell?" interjected Justice Kingstone.

"Not the least," replied Crews.

"Is there any doubt in your mind that Meisner is the man you saw?" Kingstone continued.

"Not the slightest. I never saw McCardell before in my life."

An argument broke out between McCarthy and Bell when McCarthy wanted to read the deceased Mary Lythe's testimony from the first trial into the record. "I have no opportunity to cross-examine her on McCardell's statement that it was he, rather than Meisner, whom she met," Bell objected. McCarthy withdrew his request.

The next day of the trial began with the rest of the Muskoka witnesses also sticking to their stories, including Gordon Bannister, the Port Carling hardware store clerk who had said he had sold three men a dog chain for "a savage dog."

"I never saw McCardell before," he stated emphatically. In his cross-examination, Bell got Bannister to admit he had seen Meisner's photo in newspapers before identifying him as one of the men in the store.

McCarthy then called McCardell to the stand as a Crown witness. After recounting his version of the kidnapping, McCardell contradicted Bannister, insisting the chain was purchased at Brownlee's hardware store in London. He said London was also where he had shopped for sheets and blankets for the Muskoka cottage, but he couldn't remember the name of the store.

Asked about Meisner's attendance at the June 1934 meeting to plan the kidnapping that he, McCardell, had convened, McCardell said he had invited Meisner "because he was a gambler and we thought he might be interested in a little stealing. But he didn't like the proposition. He didn't think it would work as smoothly as we planned. He said he would have nothing to do with it and we shouldn't, either. I told him we would abandon it."

"You didn't abandon it, though," McCarthy observed.

"No, we didn't abandon it. If we had, I wouldn't be here now. We just told Meisner we were abandoning it. We didn't want too many to know about it."

For the first time, McCardell divulged what he had done after releasing Labatt. Instead of hiding out in some remote locale, as would be expected of a criminal being hunted by the police forces of two countries, he had stayed for a month at the Hotel Ambassador in Detroit, in effect in plain view. "I never felt any danger," he explained. "I didn't think I was under suspicion." He was right.

Under questioning by McCarthy about his background, McCardell insisted he had never before served a prison sentence.

"Have you not been imprisoned for manslaughter?" McCarthy demanded.

"I was arrested once in Alabama for running a car into a horse and another time in Texas for a Hallowe'en celebration," McCardell replied.

At this point, McCardell's testimony was abruptly interrupted to make way for a defence witness — and what an absolutely astonishing surprise he was!

The man coming to the witness stand was none other than Norman Newton, the Crown attorney who had obtained Meisner's conviction in his first trial. His appearance as a defence witness caused a sensation, and it represented one more peculiar twist in a case filled with the highly unusual. Here was the answer to the month-old puzzle as to why he had been removed from the case by Attorney General Arthur Roebuck.

Newton explained that he had decided to testify on Meisner's behalf because he had become convinced of Meisner's innocence when he and John Labatt met McCardell at the Crown Point, Indiana, jail in July 1935. "When we walked in, McCardell said 'Hello, John' to Mr. Labatt," Newton recalled. "I asked Mr. Labatt to address no conversation to McCardell but to let him do all the talking. I was convinced that what McCardell said was true and that there had been a case of mistaken identity in Meisner's case."

Immediately after the interview with McCardell, Newton had telephoned the Windsor police authorities and ordered that John Bannon be arrested. Newton also enlisted the willing help of RCMP Sergeant Ted Weeks in an effort to dig up new evidence to help Meisner. "I am thoroughly convinced there was a case of mistaken identity in Meisner's case," Newton declared once more. "I am convinced of the truth of Michael McCardell's story."

Newton was criticized by some lawyers for "not giving evidence but merely placing the weight of his opinion on the scales," but he felt he was repairing a wrong. The ultimate responsibility for allowing him to testify lay with Justice Kingstone, who permitted it.

After Newton's brief but highly sensational appearance, McCardell returned to the stand. McCarthy asked why he confessed to the kidnapping following his arrest and not before.

"It seemed logical to me that if they convict an innocent man, they wouldn't have much trouble convicting a guilty one," McCardell replied, characteristically wisecracking. He rejected McCarthy's inference that he had confessed in return for a promise that it would be arranged for charges against him in the United States to be dropped. "No promise was made," he insisted.

"You think that without your confession Meisner would have been released?"

"I think they were convinced he was innocent and that I was the man."

Louis McCaughey was called as the next Crown witness. Once again he denied any involvement in the kidnapping. His testimony ended the Crown's case.

On Friday, March 20, the fifth and what would turn out to be the last day of the retrial, Bell called only one witness, Governor Charles Mitchell of the Middlesex County Jail. His stay on the witness stand was extremely brief. Bell had him describe how Meisner stood out in the identification lineup arranged by Mitchell before the first trial. "Meisner was the only one in neatly pressed clothing. The other eight — five convicted prisoners and three awaiting trial — were in wrinkled clothing that had just been taken out of a canvas bag," Mitchell said.

Bell then announced that the defence rested its case. It is customary for the defence to call very few witnesses when it wants to signal to the jury that it believes the prosecution has no case. Moreover, McCardell, although a Crown witness, had proved helpful to the defence. McCarthy said he would present no reply evidence.

Justice Kingstone then startled the spectators by recalling John Labatt to the witness stand. Realizing that Labatt's memory as to who really had been his guard was pivotal to Meisner's fate, Kingstone asked Labatt to go over the issue yet again.

"At first I was convinced Meisner was one of the kidnappers and my guard, but after meeting with McCardell at Crown Point I became convinced Meisner was not the kidnapper or guard," Labatt declared. "I became convinced McCardell was."

"Are you able to say whether or not Meisner was near or about the cottage where you were held?" the judge asked, in reference to the Muskoka witnesses' assertions.

"Not that I know of," Labatt declared.

This answer concluded the presentation of evidence in the retrial. It was 11:30 a.m.

Howard Cluff, Bell's associate, then sought to have Kingstone dismiss the case, arguing that the prosecution — and not only the defence — had presented evidence pointing to Meisner's innocence.

Kingstone refused. "I believe this is a proper case to be decided by the jury. The motion is dismissed."

In Bell's closing statement, summoning all the skill and eloquence that had won him his reputation as the best criminal defence lawyer in Canada, he delivered an impassioned plea to the jury to acquit Meisner. "It is true that David Meisner has been a racetrack follower and small-time gambler, but his rights so far as these charges are concerned are as strong as the rights of any man who might come before you. It may be true that he had some friends who were not the best. But when the

King's Plate is run at Toronto or horse races held in London, you and I are the people who are affording support for the David Meisners of the racetrack.

"But because Meisner associated with racetrack followers is no evidence against him in this case. It is obvious that there were four kidnappers and that those men were McCardell, Bannon, Knowles and Pegram."

Dealing with the certainty of the Muskoka witnesses in identifying Meisner as one of the kidnappers, Bell said they had made an "honest mistake" and that their testimony was outweighed by Newton's. "There have been many miscarriages of justice in the history of jurisprudence and many innocent men sent to prison as a result," he said.

Bell moved on to stress an issue that had been ignored in this trial, one that had been foremost in the first. "Not a single witness who identified Meisner mentioned his eye, in which there is a cataract."

Turning to the jury, Bell resoundingly wound up his summation. "I am not begging for mercy for David Meisner. If you believe Meisner is guilty, then send him back to the Kingston Penitentiary. But if you feel he is not guilty, do that which will give you the satisfaction of having righted a hideous wrong. I say to you this man is not guilty."

It was now the noon hour. Kingstone adjourned the trial until after lunch.

At the opening of the afternoon session, McCarthy proceeded to sum up for the Crown, saying the issue was whether the Muskoka witnesses who had placed Meisner near the kidnappers' hideout were mistaken. "They are unprejudiced witnesses compared to McCardell, who may have been trying to get himself out of a mighty hot spot — the prison term he was facing in the United States — by saying he is the man for whom Meisner was mistaken. It is conceivable that in some way McCardell received information which enabled him to recognize the Muskoka witnesses."

In an effort to downplay the potential impact of Newton's testimony on behalf of Meisner, McCarthy said, "I was somewhat surprised at a Crown officer going before a jury and expressing an opinion. Moreover, Newton, be he the Crown attorney or not, has no right to ask you to substitute his opinion for yours. Mr. Newton is not the person who was kidnapped."

But McCarthy's concluding sentence indicated that he would not be unhappy if Meisner were acquitted. "If right is done, the Crown will be satisfied," he declared, epitomizing what the role of Crown counsel is supposed to be — the Crown should neither be glad nor sorry at the result of a trial.

Justice Kingstone took an hour to review the evidence for the jurors and outline the law for them. "If Meisner assisted in renting the hideout cottage and helped lay plans for the abduction, he would be as guilty in the eyes of the law as the men who took Mr. Labatt from his automobile," he said. He concluded on a sympathetic note to the jurors, "You have a difficult task. I don't envy you." When he sent them off to the jury room, it was 4:30 p.m.

Kingstone's prediction turned out to be true. It was a difficult task for the jurors. After five hours, they returned to the courtroom. There was a flurry of excitement that a decision must have been reached, until foreman C.O. Shoebotham requested that the testimony of Albert and Ida Crews, the next-door neighbours to the hideaway cottage, be repeated to the jury. The court reporter read the transcript, and the jurors went back to their deliberations. It took them two more hours, for a total of seven, and a dozen votes before they reached a consensus.

Shortly before midnight, they returned with their verdict. The tension in the courtroom was palpable as jury foreman Shoebotham was asked the jury's decision.

"Not guilty," he announced.

The spectators burst into cheers and applause. The courtroom guards sharply rebuked them and demanded silence.

"Well, Mr. Foreman and gentlemen of the jury, I am sure, judging by the length of time you took in your deliberations, that you have given the very best consideration you are capable of to this case," Kingstone said. "It is not my province to comment on what you have done. I am satisfied that you have done what is right as you have seen it."

Dismissing the jury, Kingstone turned to Meisner and addressed him.

"I suppose you feel that you are a very fortunate and happy man," he said. "I congratulate you on having such able counsel, prepared at great sacrifice to himself to devote his talents to your defence." In a rebuke of

Meisner's lifestyle, Kingstone added, "The way of transgression is very hard and doesn't pay in the long run." With that, he discharged Meisner.

The courtroom erupted again into pandemonium. Meisner was surrounded by a milling crowd of men and women showering their congratulations on him. He broke away from them to solemnly and emotionally thank the devoted Charles Bell, who had defended him twice, virtually for free. Once again Bell was the "man who gets all of them off"; vindication at last for Meisner's protestations of innocence and Bell's unswerving loyalty to him. After eighteen nightmarish months, Meisner's ordeal was finally over.

As Meisner was hustled out of the courtroom to obtain his belongings en route to his freedom, he encountered jury foreman C.O. Shoebotham and two other jurors, Cliff Sanborn and W.J. Paynter.

"I hope you profit by this," Sanborn said as he shook Meisner's hand.

"I want to assure you gentlemen now that it is all over with, that I never had anything to do with the kidnapping of John Labatt," said Meisner, nodding his head to add further confirmation to his low and solemn tone of voice.

Wearing a light brown overcoat and peaked cap, Meisner was then rushed from the courthouse by Bell's London associate, Howard Cluff. Meanwhile, down in his cell, McCardell celebrated Meisner's release almost as enthusiastically as if he himself had been freed. John Labatt, who had sat in court throughout the trial, told reporters he was pleased with the verdict but declined to comment further.

The first thing Meisner did was to telegraph his common-law wife in Covington to inform her of the verdict. He expressed some bitterness to reporters that his elderly mother had died during his imprisonment and therefore would never know he had been cleared, although she always believed in his innocence.

"Imprisonment has taken a lot out of me," he told reporters before heading off to a celebration with friends. "I feel I aged fifteen years while I was in the Penitentiary. I lived always in the hope that a change of luck would come and that some development would occur to prove I had been wrongfully convicted."

His mood then changed from melancholy reflection to one of jubilation. "You boys can't imagine how I feel. Here I am, a free man enjoying a good cigarette for the first time in nearly two years. Believe it or not, I'm dancing on air," he rejoiced.

"What of your relations with John Labatt?" he was asked.

"No comment," Meisner replied, using the response recommended by Bell and Cluff.

Later, he ran into Alex Colvin, Labatt's Windsor agent who had aided the police in their investigation. Bygones were bygones as they slapped each other on the back in celebration.

"My boss is the squarest shooter in the world and did the manly thing," Colvin said proudly of Labatt, referring to the brewer's willingness to admit he had mistakenly identified Meisner as one of his kidnappers.

That prompted Meisner to break his silence about Labatt. "I'll say this for him — he must be a square shooter and a dandy fellow to go into the box to help me just as readily as he had gone against me. When he found he was wrong, he set it right and I want him to know that I appreciate it."

"What about Jack Bannon?" a reporter asked.

"No comment," Meisner quoted his lawyers again.

"And McCardell?"

"You can say I appreciate very much the testimony he gave. He told the truth about my relations with him. It is true that I was asked to go into the proposition, but as he said, I refused and I know nothing whatsoever about what happened later."

Meisner left the prison with only seventeen cents in his pocket. "I haven't a cent in the world but I'm happier than I've ever been in my life," he said. When asked his plans, he said he would settle in Windsor, where several of his brothers and sisters lived and where his mother had died. "The first thing I intend to do is visit my mother's grave," he said.

Justice at last had been done. An editorial the next day in the *Toronto Daily Star* summed up the national reaction:

MEISNER IS ACQUITTED

It is greatly to the credit of justice in this province that David Meisner was given a second trial and acquitted of the crime of kidnapping John Labatt after having been convicted and sentenced to fifteen years in the penitentiary.

It is not much in the practice of justice here, or anywhere else, to confess a major miscarriage as in this case. The courts do not like to admit that they err. Nor do the Crown attorneys, the detectives and the police. They do not like to admit that a whole string of witnesses as to identity were wholly mistaken. The acquittal of Meisner on his retrial will do much to discredit the too glib evidence as to identity which is so readily produced.

AFTERWORD

Today, wrongfully convicted persons can demand financial restitution from the government. But in 1936 there was no law in Canada that provided for reparations by the federal or provincial governments and there had been no prior instance in Canadian history of voluntary restitution by a government. Despite public clamour that David Meisner be recompensed, neither the federal nor Ontario government did so.

Although John Labatt came to Meisner's rescue at his retrial and Meisner graciously acknowledged his assistance, the fact remained that Labatt's mistaken identification was largely responsible for Meisner's conviction at his first trial. In 1937, Meisner sued Labatt for "malicious prosecution and for negligence in the identification of the plaintiff." A settlement was reached whereby Labatt paid Meisner $5,500, equivalent to $70,775 today.

Meisner used some of the money for a cataract operation. He heeded the advice of Justice Kingstone and juror Cliff Sanborn and honoured his pledge to Charles Bell "to repay my obligation" by reforming his lifestyle. He opened the Yo-Kum-In restaurant in Windsor at 2343 Pillette Road, not far from Tecumseh Road, a major thoroughfare, and operated it for twenty years, until he was in his late seventies. The restaurant's name was taken from the surname of the main character in the *Li'l Abner* comic strip, which had debuted in August 1935 while Meisner was in prison. Meisner decorated the Yo-Kum-In with characters from the comic strip. He lived at 271 Pillette, listing himself in the Windsor telephone book as "D. Meisner."

"Piccolo Pete" Murray received a financial settlement from an unknown source for the seven months he spent in prison. He opened a tavern in a suburb of Covington, Kentucky, and invested successfully in real estate.

The Labatt case was never fully closed because Albert Pegram, the kidnapper who had snatched the kidnappers' car, thereby stranding his accomplices, eluded the police for the rest of his life. From time to time the police heard through their contacts in the underworld that Pegram was in one place or another, but each time they were poised to swoop down on him, he skipped out just before they arrived. In August 1935, shortly after McCardell and Bannon were identified as two of the kidnappers, police along both sides of the Canada–United States border were tipped off that Pegram had died close to the border. But since the police could not find his body, they concluded that they had been deliberately misled, perhaps by Pegram himself.

In October 1935, the police thought they might finally be able to track Pegram down when his wife abruptly left their home in Detroit. They speculated that she was setting off to join him near Nashville, where his mother lived, but neither Pegram nor his wife showed up in Tennessee. Instead, they disappeared without a trace. There was speculation they were victims of gangland violence, but a definitive answer to his whereabouts was never found.

Bannon and Knowles did not serve their full sentences of fifteen years. They were given early release in 1943, about halfway through their terms. Bannon settled in Windsor and became a labourer at the Canadian Bridge Company. He maintained his innocence, and retained Windsor lawyer William MacLeod to appeal his conviction or seek a new trial. Knowles went to the Boston area. Soon after the two convicts were released, John Labatt received a number of threats and mysterious long-distance calls from the vicinity of Boston. A November 17, 1943, memorandum written by Cecil Snyder, then the deputy attorney general of Ontario, to Attorney General L. E. Blackwell, described the situation:

> R. G. Ivey, K.C., of London, accompanied by Mr. Hugh Labatt of London, attended in my office recently to discuss this matter as they were much concerned over the state of health and nervous apprehension that John Labatt is now in as a result of the calls and messages

which he has received in the past few months. He is fearful that some personal injury may be done to himself or members of his family, and it was indicated in one of the telephone calls he received that a substantial sum of money should be forthcoming from him without delay.

It is not definitely known if Bannon is really desirous of a new trial or if he is attempting to get information which may assist him in making a demand for money from John Labatt. Therefore, relying on grounds of public policy as set out in my letters to Mr. MacLeod of Windsor, this department has, so far, declined to make public any documents, many of which are secret police reports, in connection with the Labatt case. For all we know, there may be some truth in Bannon's allegations, but the propriety of opening up our files to his solicitor is questionable. Bannon can make a motion before the Chief Justice for leave to appeal, or the Minister of Justice may refer the whole case to the Court of Appeal. This has not been done although the Department of Justice has a very complete picture of this trial.

In the past few years I have on several occasions reviewed the Labatt file. It presents a confusing picture. The manner in which the Crown acted before and during the trial may be open to severe criticism. The proceedings were, in my opinion, far below the level which we seek to maintain in the administration of justice in Ontario. No person now connected with this department, nor with the Ontario Provincial Police nor with the Crown Attorney's office at London, took any major part at these proceedings in 1934 and later.

John Labatt resumed his business and civic activities after the kidnapping. During World War II, he was an executive member of the National War Finance Committee. His wife, Bessie, who shared his commitment to public service, joined the national directorate of the United Emergency

Fund for Britain, an organization that raised money to feed the needy in wartime England. In 1940, she accepted the position of London District Superintendent of the Western Ontario sub-district of the St. John Ambulance Association, a post she held for seven years. Her husband made her job easier by providing her with a chauffeur-driven limousine and daycare staff for their three children. The Labatt company provided uniforms for two ambulance divisions, plus a fully equipped ambulance. The brewery also made it a policy that all company drivers were required to become members of the Association and train in first aid.

In 1945, Labatt converted John Labatt Ltd. from a privately held company to a public corporation, thereby setting the stage for it to eventually pass out of family hands. But while the family no longer controls or runs the business, it still bears the name of the three generations of John Labatts who headed it.

In 1948, John and Hugh Labatt were among a number of prominent business leaders who proposed the creation of a business school at London's University of Western Ontario, which had been providing business administration courses since 1922. As a result of this initiative, Western became the first Canadian university to offer a Master of Business Administration (MBA) degree. In 1996, the school was named the Richard Ivey School of Business in honour of Richard Macaulay Ivey, the son of Richard Green Ivey, John Labatt's lawyer. The designation recognized the Ivey family's contributions of more than $37 million over fifty years, including a gift of $11 million from Richard Macaulay Ivey in the fall of 1995 — the largest single donation in the school's history.

John Labatt remained president of Labatt's until 1950, when his brother Hugh succeeded him. That same year, Michael McCardell, the leader of the gang that snatched Labatt, died of cancer while working as a janitor in a Windsor pool hall. He was given a pauper's funeral.

John Labatt remained a director and senior brewing consultant of Labatt Ltd. He continued to participate in many civic and charitable causes in London. A park he donated to the city was named Labatt Park in his honour; he was a trustee of the London Public Library; honorary chairman of the London-Middlesex advisory board of the Canadian National Institute for the Blind; and an honorary member of the Ontario Provincial Command of the Canadian Legion.

Throughout the kidnapping there had been fears that the shock might cause Labatt, who had a weak heart, to suffer a fatal heart attack. When he died on July 8, 1952, at the age of seventy-two — a month shy of eighteen years after the kidnapping — it was due to a heart attack. He was stricken at his summer home at Port Stanley on Lake Erie, twenty-five miles from London. London and provincial police sent a motorcycle escort with oxygen tanks, which his doctors used in a vain attempt to save him. Despite all he had gone through and his poor health, he had lived to a good age.

Bessie continued to live in their home at 256 Central Avenue. She remained involved in a wide variety of causes. She helped found the Family Service Bureau in London, became a life member of the National Council of Women in Canada, a member of the National Board of Women in the United States and honorary vice-president of the Girl Guides of Ontario. In 1962, when she learned that the United Nations Children's Fund was unable to provide direct aid to developmentally handicapped schoolchildren in Jakarta, Indonesia, because the government there refused to acknowledge the existence of such children, she took action on her own. She purchased a bus that UNICEF said the children needed and flew to Indonesia to present it as a gift from the Labatt family and to meet the children.

In London, she continued to pay personal attention to the needy. Father Jim Williams, the rector of St. Peter's Basilica, which was across the street from Bessie's home, recalled after her death how she had conscripted him into action, taking him in her chauffeured limousine to a low-rental home to help an ailing woman and her family. She assigned him the task of cleaning the bathroom while she herself scrubbed the floors. She died in 1975 in her mid eighties.

Hugh Labatt died in 1956, at the age of seventy-three, while on a business trip in Portugal. As his brother had four years earlier, he died of a heart attack. Their uncle, Major General Sidney Chilton Mewburn, was ninety-three when he died in 1956, four months after Hugh.

Arthur Labatt, a baby when his father was kidnapped, cofounded Trimark Financial Corporation, which became one of Canada's largest mutual fund companies. In 2000 it was sold to AIM Funds Management, which renamed it AIM Trimark Investments; Arthur is chairman. He inherited his parents' commitment to philanthropy, giving $1 million to King's College at the University of Western Ontario, the largest single donation in the college's history, for an academic centre named after his mother. He and his wife Sonia contributed $5 million for the establishment of a brain tumour research centre, the first of its kind in Canada, at Toronto's Hospital for Sick Children. In 2004, Arthur Labatt was named chancellor of the University of Western Ontario.

Charles Bell died in 1938, at the age of sixty-two, two years after Meisner's acquittal. "A Legal and Literary Genius," the *Globe and Mail* headlined its tribute:

> It is doubtful that this country has produced a man of so many talents and who made fuller use of them. Mr. Bell's legal business was so extensive that it seemed sufficient to absorb all his time and attention and still he found time for other pursuits. As a Parliamentarian in the Federal House, his duties received careful attention and in the legislative chamber he was as much at home as in the courts.
>
> But that was not all. From law and legislation he turned readily to literature and had to his credit many interesting books. Perhaps by way of relaxation Mr. Bell interested himself in the stage and his contributions enjoyed prolonged success, even in critical New York. The average individual, with the so-called "single-track mind," perhaps doing one thing well, is bewildered by the versatility and energy of men such as Mr. Bell. How do they stand the strain? Each of Mr. Bell's pursuits called for exactness as well as colour.

Ernest Lapointe remained federal minister of justice until his death in 1941. In the 1937 coronation honours list he was made a privy councillor, entitling him to the designation "right honourable," the only Canadian mentioned. But he remained a man of the people and was equally delighted with a dinner given in his honour in Quebec City in 1939 to mark his thirty-fifth year in Parliament, one that was attended by Quebecers in country garb as well as evening clothes.

Lapointe strongly supported Canada's participation in World War II, even though many Quebecers advocated "benevolent neutrality." When the Union Nationale government of Premier Maurice Duplessis called an election, hoping to capitalize on public sentiment against participation in the war, Lapointe, who was the chairman of the federal government's war committee, coordinated a declaration by his French-Canadian colleagues in Cabinet that they would resign if Duplessis won. This led to Duplessis being defeated.

Although doctors had warned him he was in danger of losing his life if he did not slow down, Lapointe believed it was his responsibility to remain at Prime Minister William Lyon Mackenzie King's side during the war as the foremost representative of French Canada. He felt it essential to underscore the unity between English and French Canada at this critical time in the country's history.

There was a huge outpouring of grief at Lapointe's death in November 1941. People from all walks of life came from every part of Quebec, and from outside the province, to file past his coffin, which lay in state in a chamber of Quebec's Legislative Council. Newspapers calculated that two thousand people per hour paid their respects.

Mackenzie King bestowed the highest of praise on Lapointe, saying, "Every unity cause had in him a fearless champion. His support was with the people in their struggle for economic and social freedom. He was very solicitous of the rights of minorities and the welfare of those in humble circumstances."

The *Christian Science Monitor* declared in its obituary:

> Ernest Lapointe was for more than thirty-five years an outstanding spokesman of French-speaking Canada. He was a true man of the soil of Canada, a patriot loyal to his people, the descendants of the pioneers of New France, to his country, to the British Commonwealth and to the cause of democracy.

The *Toronto Daily Star*'s obituary commented:

> It is not easy to see now who can replace in Canada public service this lovable French Canadian whose flashing brilliance of mind, broad humanity, and large unwavering loyalty to high national ideals have exerted a strong influence in Dominion affairs. Few there are who would dispute the statement that Ernest Lapointe was the greatest French Canadian of his generation; he had been frequently called Sir Wilfrid Laurier's political heir, French Canada's outstanding spokesman, Mackenzie King's right-hand man.
>
> He was all these and more. Ernest Lapointe will be missed, both personally and as a tower of strength in the government of the country. Mr. Lapointe was as great a Canadian as he was a French Canadian, although he himself would probably have protested the making of a distinction between the two terms.

Ontario Attorney General Arthur Roebuck became known as "No Ransom Roebuck." He was credited with coordinating federal, provincial and municipal police in the Labatt snatch, as well as with Labatt being released unharmed with no ransom being paid. Roebuck remained attorney general until 1937, when his career in the Ontario cabinet came to an abrupt end due to a clash with Ontario Premier Mitchell Hepburn. Roebuck returned from a holiday to find that Hepburn had called police from all over the province to control strikers at the General Motors plant in Oshawa. At issue was whether the U.S.–based CIO (Congress of Industrial Organizations) would be allowed to represent the workers. Hepburn was opposed to a "foreign" union; Roebuck believed the workers had the right to choose the union they wanted and didn't think it was legal to have called in the police. Hepburn fired Roebuck.

In 1940, Roebuck was elected to the House of Commons as the member for the Toronto riding of Trinity. In 1943, at the age of sixty-five, he ran for the leadership of the Ontario Liberal party, thinking he had the backing of federal leaders, but this was not so. "They got me out on a limb and sawed it off," he said. the *Globe and Mail*, however, put the blame on him.

MR. ROEBUCK'S SWAN SONG

> The ballots have been counted in the Ontario election, but otherwise there is one aspect worthy of notice. That is the complete repudiation of Mr. Arthur Roebuck and his tactics. Adept at mud-slinging, a past master of the kidney punch and the lifted knee in campaigns, the complete and humiliating defeat of those candidates for whom he did most of his work should be Mr. Roebuck's swan song.

But it was not his swan song. In 1945, Roebuck was appointed to the federal senate, where he chaired the committee that reformed Canada's divorce laws, introducing legislation that permitted divorce on grounds other than adultery. He spoke out for portable pensions and against insurance companies cancelling accident and sickness policies when an insured turned seventy years old. "I myself am not too old to be a good risk," Roebuck, then seventy-seven years old, said. He described 1965 legislation that called for senators to retire at age seventy-five as a "brutal thing." He was then eighty-seven and refused to retire.

He died in 1971 at age ninety-three. A *Toronto Star* editorial said:

> Though he never won the big prizes, Roebuck was a creative politician. His old crusades left an enduring legacy. The cheap hydro that helped Ontario grow, the strength of our trade unions, the application of decent industrial standards in factories, the federal law against racist propaganda and the modern divorce system all owe something to the fastidious conscience of that energetic man in the wing collar.

Justice George Frank McFarland, the judge in the first Meisner trial and in Bannon's, died in 1950 after a long illness, during which he had insisted on carrying out his judicial duties. In its obituary, the *Globe and Mail* said: "He was a man of congenial personality who enjoyed a wide circle of friendship. He brought to his office a well-stocked mind and temperament suited to the judicial function. Of his standing as a lawyer and judge, his colleagues speak in unstinting praise."

Norman Newton's unconventional decision to testify on behalf of David Meisner in his second trial after obtaining a conviction in the first did not hurt his career. He remained Crown attorney until 1942, when he resigned in protest over a controversial political manoeuvre by Mitchell Hepburn. When, after a number of (mostly self-inflicted) setbacks, Hepburn decided to resign as Ontario premier, he arbitrarily picked his successor rather than follow the proper procedure of consulting his party caucus and the lieutenant governor. The successor would normally have been the deputy premier, but the abrasive Hepburn had quarrelled with him, as with many others, and instead chose a more junior member of the Cabinet: Attorney General Gordon Conant.

Newton insisted that he still held "warm affection" for Hepburn, noting, "I was the first man to suggest that he should be the Liberal leader of Ontario and was a delegate at the convention at which he was chosen." He also maintained that his resignation was not a reflection on Conant, but "against the manner in which the whole thing was done. I think the Liberal Party was sold down the river." Newton was not alone in his criticism: two Ontario Cabinet ministers had already resigned, including Deputy Premier Harry Nixon, and there was strong condemnation in the press.

Conant, who had clashed in the past with Newton and had tried to force him to resign, responded by publicly issuing a statement saying he was "glad" to accept Newton's resignation. To say "glad" is extraordinary, even when there is intense animosity between politicians. Usually, a pretence of regret is expressed or the resignation is received without comment.

After quitting as Crown attorney, Newton concentrated full time on his private practice in London, which he had continued to operate while serving as Crown attorney. He fell ill six years later, in 1948, and remained in poor health until his death in 1964 at the age of seventy. His wife had predeceased him. One of his sons followed him into public service, becoming treasurer of Middlesex County. The other son became an executive at the Chrysler Corporation.

John Claude Manley German, the Crown counsel in Meisner's first trial, continued to practise law in Toronto until 1942, when he was appointed a judge in the Northumberland and Durham Counties Court, based in Cobourg, Ontario. According to the retired Ontario Court of Appeal justice who spoke to the author about the legal figures and issues in the Labatt trials, German was charged with drunk driving during the time he was a judge. He did not resign from his position, but the incident did harm his reputation. He returned to private practice in 1946 after four years on the bench. That year he was elected president of the Federation of Law Associations of Ontario. He became a member of Cobourg's park and hospital boards and continued to be active in the Ontario Liberal Party. In October 1963, while German was hospitalized, he was made a life member of his district law association and its honorary president. He died one month later, at age seventy-two.

Alexander Stanley Fergusson, Jack Bannon's lawyer in the second trial arising from the Labatt snatch, later acted on behalf of the Crown in a number of cases. Prior to World War II he joined the Middlesex and Huron Regiment as a lieutenant. He served in the regiment until 1941, when he was sent to the Army School of Administration at Esterel, Quebec, to take a course given for a special panel of court martial officers. On completion of this course he returned to London and served on the staff military headquarters there. In 1945, while he was on a leave of absence from the Army, he ran in London as the Liberal candidate for the Ontario Legislature but was defeated. At the end of the war he returned to private practice, then joined the law firm of Jeffrey & Jeffrey as counsel in 1951. He died in 1956 at age fifty-five.

Charles McTague, the judge in Russell Knowles' trial, was appointed to the Ontario Court of Appeal in 1938. Shortly afterward he was involved in an unparalleled situation in the history of Canadian jurisprudence. One afternoon, as a lengthy trial neared its end, a witness — J.M. Godfrey, head of the Ontario Securities Commission — asked McTague to persuade the plaintiff's lawyer to finish questioning him that afternoon because his appointment as a justice on the court of appeal was scheduled to be made after that day's session. McTague refused, and Godfrey had to return to the witness stand the next day, the only instance in Canada in which someone was appointed a judge while in the witness box.

During World War II, while still serving on the bench, McTague was appointed chairman of the War Contracts Depreciation Board (1940–43) and chairman of the National War Labour Board (1943–44) by Prime Minister William Lyon Mackenzie King. McTague was a Conservative, but talent was given precedence over party affiliation during the war.

In 1944, McTague resigned from the Ontario Court of Appeal to become chairman of the Progressive Conservative Party and was a candidate in the1945 general election. "When I left a judgeship to enter the field of politics in an active way, it was a decision taken with the most careful consideration," he explained. "That step would never have been taken had I not deemed it an imperative duty to do my share toward bringing about national unity in the place of disunity, sectionalism and racial prejudice which have been sweeping across the country as the price necessary to be paid for expediency in party politics."

Defeated, McTague was appointed chairman of the Ontario Securities Commission by the province's Conservative premier, George Drew. He held the position for three years and then returned to private practice. He also became a director of many companies, including John Labatt Ltd., and was active in community affairs.

In 1963, he was sitting in the stands behind the Boston Bruins bench during a game in Toronto between the Maple Leafs and Bruins when a long shot by Maple Leafs centre Leonard "Red" Kelly, who was also a Liberal member of Parliament at the time, bounced over the boards and struck McTague. He suffered a compound fracture of the nose and was taken to the Toronto Western Hospital, of which he was a member of the board of governors, for treatment. "Puck Deflected: Shot By Liberal

Breaks PC's Nose," read the headline in the *Globe and Mail*. McTague died in 1966 at the age of seventy-six.

Joseph Sedgwick, special Crown counsel in Knowles' trial and assistant to D'Alton Lally McCarthy in Meisner's retrial, remained in the Ontario attorney general's department until 1937. In interviews over the years, Sedgwick maintained that he was fired that year as the result of a disagreement with Mitchell Hepburn. "Mitch thought I had been advising David Croll against him and he fired David and myself," Sedgwick told *Canadian Lawyer* in 1978. Hepburn had fired Croll, who was then Ontario's minister of labour, at the same time he fired Arthur Roebuck over the dispute regarding union representation at General Motors' Oshawa plant.

However, the retired justice who spoke to the author about the legal figures in the Labatt trials and a longtime friend and admirer of Sedgwick's, says Sedgwick was not fired. According to him, Sedgwick left of his own accord as the result of clashes with Cecil Snyder, a Hepburn crony who had become deputy attorney general. "Sedgwick did not have a lot of respect for Snyder," says the retired justice. "They parted by mutual consent, and on bad terms." This animosity could have been the reason for Snyder's criticism of the Crown in the Labatt trials, contained in his November 17, 1943, memorandum to Attorney General L.E. Blackwell about the threats to John Labatt.

Sedgwick came to regard the rupture as "a great favour" because it led him to return to private practice. One of his most publicized cases was his successful 1945 defence of federal civil servant Eric Adams against charges of spying that had been levelled by Igor Gouzenko. Gouzenko was the Soviet Embassy cipher clerk and double agent who exposed the names of alleged members of a spying ring, which he said was operating in Canada and passing classified information to the Soviet Government. Adams denied he was a spy, saying that his interest in the Soviet Union was related purely to keeping tabs on developments there on behalf of the Canadian government. Sedgwick believed Adams was a victim of the anti-Communist "witch hunt" that gripped much of the West after World War II.

Sedgwick dressed elegantly, always wearing a bow tie and a rose or carnation boutonniere. The antique walnut desk in his office was given to him in lieu of fees by a client he had represented in a divorce case.

Sedgwick continued to be active in backroom politics in the Conservative Party and was regarded as the leader of Toronto's Tory establishment. He was co-chairman of the platform committee at the convention that chose John Diefenbaker as Conservative federal party leader. He later split with Diefenbaker on the grounds that "the party faces ruin through the obstinacy of one man."

In later years, Sedgwick served on a Royal Commission that reviewed and simplified Canada's Criminal Code. Despite his lifelong allegiance to the Conservative Party, Liberal Prime Minister Lester Pearson asked him to undertake a study on immigration issues. When the work was completed, a pleased Pearson said, "Joe, if knighthoods were still in fashion, I could probably get you a KCMG [Knight Commander of the Order of St. Michael and St. George]."

Sedgwick died in 1981 at age eighty-three. "He earned the respect of his peers by the artistry of his defences, the depth and range of his knowledge and the richness of his oratory," the *Toronto Star*'s obituary said.

James Donahue, Knowles' lawyer, remained in practice for twenty more years after Knowles' trial. He died in 1956 at the age of sixty-seven, one month after the death of his only child, a daughter who was the mother of three children.

Justice Arthur Courtney Kingstone, the judge in Meisner's retrial, died in 1938, the same year as Charles Bell, of a heart attack suffered while visiting a son in Vancouver. Just the day before, he had told the Vancouver *Daily Province* how much he was enjoying his trip. "The western provinces have a charm all their own," Kingstone said. "They are so different in some respects from the East that it is difficult to believe they belong to the same continent."

D'Alton Lally McCarthy, the Crown counsel in Meisner's retrial, remained in practice until the age of seventy-five in 1945. He played polo until the age of seventy and, as Master of the Foxhounds, rode to hounds until he was seventy-five. He died in 1963.

The kidnapping of John Labatt is notable for its many firsts, now a part of Canadian history. Labatt was the first important Canadian to be kidnapped. He was the first to be kidnapped for a high ransom. It was the first Canadian kidnapping to receive widespread international news coverage. It was the first kidnapping in Canada to come to trial. It was the first recorded major instance of mistaken identity in Canadian courts.

Some of the most colourful judges and lawyers of the day, including the most famous criminal defence lawyer of the era, participated in the trials. The trials spotlighted the important issue of the great harm that faulty testimony by "eyewitnesses" can cause. They also highlighted how a case can abruptly take unexpected twists and turns.

Kidnapping is an extremely serious, nasty crime. Yet there is a considerable amount of quirky humour associated with the Labatt snatch — the unusual choice of location of the hideaway cottage; the selection of a busy hotel as the site of ransom negotiations; the unconventionally courteous treatment of Labatt as a captive, including overfeeding him to the extent that he got indigestion; the bizarre dinner that kidnapper Russell Knowles shared with the RCMP officer who was unaware of his identity; the kidnappers' decision to provide Labatt with cab fare upon releasing him; kidnap ringleader Michael McCardell's complaint that *he* had been "kidnapped" by police officials when they took him from one state to another.

The Labatt snatch was indeed a peculiar kidnapping.

ACKNOWLEDGMENTS

I wish to express my deep appreciation of the considerable time and help given me by a retired Justice of the Ontario Court of Appeal who wishes to remain anonymous.

Thanks also to Marc Garson, Director of Crown Operations, West Region Directorate, Ministry of the Attorney General, Province of Ontario and to the following libraries for their assistance: the Bora Laskin Law Library at the University of Toronto; the Cobourg Public Library; the Governor General Historical Research and Documentation Centre; the Law Society of Upper Canada Archives; the London (Ontario) Public Library; the Toronto law firm of McCarthy Tétrault; the Middlesex Law Association in London, Ontario; the John P. Robarts Research Library at the University of Toronto; the Strathroy Public Library (branch of the Middlesex County Library); the Toronto Reference Library and the North York Central branch of the Toronto Public Library (especially Mr. Philip Singer); and the Toronto law firm of WeirFoulds.

BIBLIOGRAPHY

BOOKS

Armstrong, Frederick Henry. *The Forest City: An Illustrated History of London.* Burlington, Ont.: Windsor Publications, 1986.

Bell, Charles William. *Who Said Murder?* Toronto: Macmillan, 1935.

Brown, George W. *Building the Canadian Nation.* Toronto: Dent, 1942.

Canada. Department of National Defence. *The Regiments and Corps of the Canadian Army.* Ottawa: Queen's Printer, 1964.

Canada. Parliament. *Canadian Parliamentary Guide.*

Canadian Who's Who. 1936 through 1938 ed.

Carty, Edmund J. *London, Canada Coronation Souvenir.* London, Ont.: Carty Service, 1937.

Casucci, Piero. *Classic Cars.* Trans. by James Ramsay and Neil Stratton. Chicago: Rand McNally, 1981.

Corfield, William E. *Towers of Justice.* London, Ont.: London and St. Thomas Real Estate Board, 1974.

Cole, Curtis. *Osler, Hoskin & Harcourt: Portrait of a Partnership.* Toronto: McGraw-Hill Ryerson, 1995.

Crankshaw, John E. *Crankshaw's Criminal Code of Canada.* 6th ed. Toronto: Carswell, 1935.

Curtis, Dennis, et. al. *Kingston Penitentiary: The First Hundred and Fifty Years, 1835-1985*. Ottawa: Correctional Service of Canada, 1985.

Dictionary of Canadian Biography.

Drackett, Phil, ed. *Encyclopedia of the Motor Car*. London, England: Octopus Books, 1979.

Flint, David. *Henry Pellatt*. Don Mills, Ont.: Fitzhenry & Whiteside, 1979.

Hennessy, Peter H. *Canada's Big House: The Dark History of the Kingston Penitentiary*. Toronto: Dundurn, 1999.

Hose, Reginald E. *Prohibition or Control?: Canada's Experience with the Liquor Problem, 1921–1927*. Toronto: Longmans, 1928.

Jablonski, Edward. *Gershwin*. New York: Doubleday, 1987.

MacIntosh, Robert. *Different Drummers: Banking and Politics in Canada*. Toronto: Macmillan Canada, 1981.

McClement, Fred. *The Strange Case of Ambrose Small*. Toronto: McClelland & Stewart, 1974.

McKendry, Jennifer. *Historic Portsmouth Village, Kingston*. Kingston: J. McKendry, 1996.

Moore, Christopher. *The Law Society of Upper Canada and Ontario's Lawyers, 1797–1997*. Toronto: University of Toronto Press, 1997.

Nevins, Allan, and Henry Steele Commager. *A Pocket History of the United States*. New York: Washington Square Press, 1960.

Tausky, Nancy Z. *Historical Sketches of London: From Site to City*. Peterborough, Ont.: Broadview Press, 1993.

Who's Who in America. 1988 and 1989 eds.

ARCHIVES
Archives of Ontario
RG 4-32 Attorney General Central Registry. Criminal and Civil Files, File 2432, A.G.O. [Attorney General's Department]. Re: the Investigation in the Kidnapping of one John Labatt [1934].

RG-23-26-103 Ontario Provincial Police Criminal Investigations Records, Container #E-103, Box 1. File RG 23-26-103-1.1

Law Society of Upper Canada Archives
Joseph Sedgwick Papers

Record/Information Dissemination Center, Federal Bureau of Investigation

DOCUMENTS
The Criminal Code Of Canada, Revised Statutes of Canada, 1927, Vol. I
Telephone directories for London, Ontario (1934), and Windsor, Ontario (1937–1959).

NEWSPAPERS
The Globe and *The Globe and Mail* (Toronto)
London Free Press
The New York Times
Ottawa Citizen
Strathroy (Ontario) *Age Dispatch*
The Telegram (Toronto)
The Times (London, England)
Toronto Star

PERIODICALS
Canada Month, May 1966
Canadian Business, July 1996
Canadian Lawyer, April 1978
Canadian Magazine, October 1927
London and Middlesex Historian, Vol. 17, 1990
Saturday Night, July 28, 1934, and November 9, 1935
Star Weekly